A SHEARWATER BOOK

The Rose's Kiss

THE ROSE'S KISS

A Natural History of Flowers

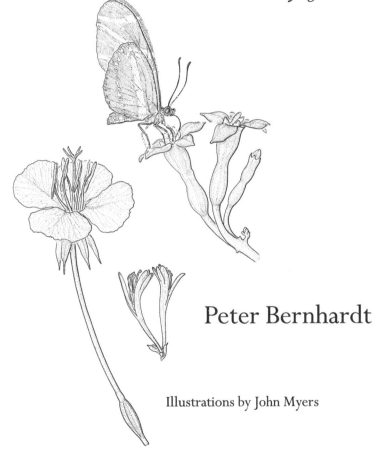

Peter Bernhardt

Illustrations by John Myers

ISLAND PRESS / Shearwater Books

Washington, D.C. • *Covelo, California*

A Shearwater Book
published by Island Press

Copyright © 1999 Peter Bernhardt

Shearwater Books is a trademark of
The Center for Resource Economics.

Caption for title page illustration can be found on page 154.

Library of Congress Cataloging-in-Publication Data
Bernhardt, Peter, 1952–
A natural history of flowers / Peter Bernhardt.
p.   cm.
Includes bibliographical references.
ISBN 1-55963-564-9 (alk. paper)
1. Flowers. 2. Plant ecology.   I. Title.
QK653.B45   1999
582.13—dc21   99-21386
                        CIP

Printed on recycled, acid-free paper

Manufactured in the United States of America

10 9 8 7 6 5 4 3 2 1

For my wife, Linda.
You were always a rose.

"The rose," I sang, "is either red or pale,
Like maidens whom the flame of passion burns,
And love or jealousy controls, by turns.
Its buds are lips preparing for a kiss;
Its open flowers are like the blush of bliss
On lovers' cheeks"

    Bayard Taylor, "Hassan Ben Khaled"

Beyond the Florist's Shop

Fresh flowers accompany us through some of the most emotional moments of our lives. High school students give and receive corsages before the prom. Courtships, weddings, and anniversaries must have their bouquets. Mourners hope that floral tributes and wreaths will lend grace to a funeral and help ease the immediate burden of grief.

As we grow more affluent, flowers often help define the quality of our lives. The more land we own around our house, the more likely we will be to garden with an eye for the most opulent colors and a nose for the richest scents. Inside the home, vases and ceramic pots contain revolving displays of blossoms independent of climate, season, or the plants' natural geography.

In his provocative book *The Culture of Flowers*, Jack Goody, a professor of anthropology at the University of Cambridge, discusses the complex relationship between fresh flowers and old religions. Some

houses of worship will never admit a bouquet because its priests regard flowers as metaphors for frivolity, sensuality, and luxury. They
may even associate flowers with the sinful practices of infidels and
foreign cults.

Conversely, there are sects that embrace flowers as symbols of joy,
renewal, and generosity and the purest evidence that there is a
benevolent Creator. Holy days and worship services are incomplete
without flowers. Public and private acts of devotion often include
the decoration of a beloved shrine or altar with flowers and the replacement of blooms as soon as they droop or show signs of decay.

In most societies, food starts with a flower. There is the immediate evidence of cauliflower, broccoli, and the many fruit and nut
crops, but then the role of flowers grows more subtle. The contents
of our toasters, pasta platters, and cereal bowls have all been manufactured by the flowers that belong to a limited number of species in
the grass family (Poaceae). Few of us notice the activity of the tiny,
short-lived flowers on corn tassels and wheat stalks, but there would
be no edible grains without them. Almost all animals raised for food,
including farm-raised catfish, are now fattened on a diet of such
grains mixed with soybeans, and all soy products start with clusters
of nodding, creamy flowers fluttering in the spring breeze.

If flowers feed the population of the United States and inspire its
culture, why do Americans seem so intent on driving them out of
science classrooms as the twentieth century comes to a close? As a
university professor, I am in an ideal position to see the lack of attention given to the science of plants. Biology teachers at high
schools in New York have told me they have eased botany out of the
syllabus because it bores their students. Teachers at primary schools
in St. Louis say they've covered botany for the year with a day's field
trip to the Missouri Botanical Garden. When teachers do perform
their jobs, parents may try to spare their children a botanical ordeal.
Mothers look up my name in the university directory and ask me to

design their kids' projects or provide them with literature. "If you don't send my son any information, he may have to go to a library," said one concerned mom.

Do not assume that botanical education improves when a young scholar enters college. At most urban campuses, many students registering as biology majors believe that a bachelor's degree in biology is merely the first step toward medical school. They tend to approach plant science with resentment, convinced that their time would be better spent on subjects that will appear on the Medical College Admission Test. Unfortunately, some universities cater to this phobia. For example, a recent educational report trumpeted the modernization of a general biology course at a prominent university in Ohio. The major improvement seemed to be an afternoon laboratory class that no longer forced students to learn the life cycle of the liverwort. At Saint Louis University, the number of courses in plant science required for a bachelor's degree in biology was recently halved (my fellow professors "revised" the curriculum while I was out of the country).

Need a college student aiming at a career in law, the arts, business, or the media ever take a course in plant life? Universities in the United States insist that all students working toward any degree in the liberal arts take one or two science courses. The problem is that larger campuses tend to offer a self-serve buffet of well-diluted subjects. Yes, there is often a "Plants for Poets" course, but it must compete with such other flimsy constructs as "Animals for Accountants," "Weather for the Weary," "Molecules for the Masses," and the ever popular "Rocks for Jocks."

Some critics insist that public disinterest in plant science is a consequence of botanists' turning the discipline into a fortress of jargon. Botanists have made the field inaccessible to bright minds, they say, by complicating it with a ponderous terminology based on the reinvention of dead languages. That's possible, but then how can the public's love of medicine be explained? The terminology of medical science is much more complex, but the obvious success of the publishing and entertainment industries shows that people are enthralled with the most technical aspects of the human body.

Ironically, botany and medicine enjoy a common origin, and both disciplines still share bits of Greek and Latin. Of course, the two fields may use the same word in very different ways. The ancient Greeks thought that the bulblike underground organs of wild orchids *(Orchis)* resembled paired testicles. Therefore, when a modern surgeon recommends an orchiectomy, the patient receives a surgical castration, not a corsage.

We seem more willing to learn unfamiliar words if they pertain to our personal health. Most educated people could probably manage a brief definition of such words as *diabetes, insulin,* and *pancreas.* The days when a family doctor could hide the seriousness of an illness from family members by lapsing into medical terminology are over, and that's a good thing. Why, then, do people recognize the medical word *pancreas* (Greek, three syllables) more readily than the botanical word *corolla* (Latin, three syllables)? Clearly, both human and plant organs ultimately influence some aspects of our lives.

The opposite condition prevailed at the beginning of the twentieth century. If old schoolbooks are any indication, most educated people at the turn of the century probably knew more about flowers than about their own insides. When I look at these old texts, I'm startled at how relevant they remain, yet in their day they were considered suitable for children before they entered high school. Had a twelve-year-old read one of these books (and studied the detailed pictures) back in 1910, he or she might have picked up more than 50 percent of what I teach my college students every autumn. There are the same life cycles of mosses, the anatomy of seeds and of the tissues in a tree trunk that conduct food to the roots and water to the leaves.

The great anthropologist Margaret Mead came from the same tradition, since her childhood spanned the early years of the twentieth century. In her autobiography, *Blackberry Winter,* she describes how her grandmother educated her at home. Grandmother sent Margaret outdoors to complete such projects as making a collection of plants in the mint family. My college students would be unable to complete such an assignment, finding it too complicated.

During the first thirty years of the twentieth century, people had the opportunity to expand their interest in flowers if they enjoyed what their schoolmarms had taught them. There were amateur societies for natural historians and plenty of popular books about plant life. Such books were relatively inexpensive and easy to obtain in North America, Great Britain, and Australia. In the United States alone, Mabel Osgood Wright, Maud Going, Thomas Lovell, Neltje Blanchan, James Berthold Berry, and Harriet Keeler all wrote about local plant life. Wright used the march of the seasons to introduce her readers to the wildflowers of New England in *Flowers and Ferns in Their Haunts* (1901). Berry showed how easy it is to identify trees that produce useful timber in his *Southern Woodland Trees* (1924).

Could an interest in plant life be rekindled and a greater understanding of flowers be fostered if the twenty-first century were to begin with reprints of these classics? There is one major problem with this plan. Botany is an expanding, changing discipline. Discoveries in plant growth, chemistry, fossils, and ecology since the late 1920s have altered the principles of the field forever. Those well-written books on natural history were published before some of the most exciting discoveries were made.

After 1930, new authors attempted to introduce the public to the broader nature of the plant kingdom. In my opinion, Harold Rickett's *Botany for Gardeners* (1957), E. J. H. Corner's *The Life of Plants* (1964), and Anthony Huxley's *Plant and Planet* (1974) were the finest examples. With the soul of a natural architect, Rickett began his book with individual cells and then worked up to tissues and how they form plant organs. Corner and Huxley presented great visions of plant evolution, taking their audience through time and diversity. They began their books with the life cycles of the tiniest algae. The reader then rises from the water to glimpse the spores flung by those humble liverworts and ferns. Finally, we graduate to the seed plants and enjoy the majesty of temperate and tropical forests.

I see great merit in this sort of approach. However, we now have superior college textbooks that explain the functions of plant cells and compare the life of a cup fungus with that of a lily bulb. The publishers of these texts have huge budgets to lavish on the finest photographs and diagrams, which fill almost every expensive page. What I propose to do here is offer a book that entertains the special interests of the early nature writers while incorporating the re-search-friendly concerns of a later generation of science writers.

Let me introduce you to my own field, floral biology. I think it has the greatest potential to encourage readers to learn even more about the lives of plants. Flowers have a far greater hold over our imaginations and affections than do bark, leaves, and roots. An added attraction is that flowers are unusually dynamic. Even the smallest buds are living factories, manufacturing organs and various chemical compounds. An open rose makes so many different things that part of the game of studying roses is finding out how such different structures and chemicals relate to one another and then telling the story in a comprehensible way.

That's why most of the chapters in this book open with quotes about roses and why I've encouraged rosebushes to bloom throughout the text. "Roses," as author Katharine Mansfield once wrote, "are the only flowers at garden-parties; the only flowers that everybody is certain of knowing." Members of the genus *Rosa,* which contains about 100 wild species, are a good place to begin when a model is needed to illustrate the life of a flower. Authors and artists have found roses a source of inspiration and delight since Greco-Roman poets made them sacred to the goddess of love. This may explain why so many passages describe affectionate flowers that kiss one another, their owners, and even their insect visitors.

In this book, the rose symbolizes my promise not to strand readers in prickly thickets of terminology and statistics. Science loses a lot of its elitism as soon as its words are defined. I don't believe for a second that botanists who lived hundreds of years ago were trying to make their subject harder for amateurs and students to understand. When the study of plants was a young discipline, *all* botanists were amateurs and students. I believe that these early scientists were trying to invent terms so sharp and clever that everyone would remember them. How could they have known that students and educators would tire of classical languages?

Here, when botanical terms become too technical, I switch to familiar words that compare activities in the flower to human versions of the same event. I know that plants are not people, but there are times when every scientist must modify the "mother tongue" to make his or her discipline easier for readers to understand.

In recent years, I have become a great admirer of Ferdinand von Mueller (1825–1896). Born in Germany to Danish parents, he spent most of his professional life as a government botanist in Australia, describing new species, establishing Melbourne's botanical garden, and convincing an empire that Australian plants had great potential as sources of medicine, timber, and beauty.

It's Mueller's public philosophy that really attracts me. He belonged to a generation of civil servants who were taught to believe that knowledge was power *and* wealth. Granted, very few botanists have built private fortunes on the basis of their knowledge of plants. This book won't increase readers' bank accounts, but my hero, Mueller, understood that wealth comes in various forms.

There is wealth in understanding the value of a kitchen stocked

THE ROSE'S KISS

A Natural History of Flowers

with different foods derived from plants. There must be wealth in both farmers' fields and suburban gardens. There is also wealth in a family legacy based on flowering plants, in the form of heirloom seeds or a cherished woodlot or orchard. Finally, there is the wealth we all share in our museums, our botanical gardens, and our government-run parks and forest reserves.

Decisions made about private wealth alter our future, and we are asked to vote on issues of public wealth, with similar consequences. Knowledge of natural diversity gives us both a wider and a better range of choices. It is my hope that the chapters that follow will help make an important part of your life a little easier to understand.

CHAPTER 1

On a summer's day, in sultry weather,
Five brethren were born together.
Two had beards and two had none,
And the other had but half a one.
　　"The Five Brethren," trans. Edward A. Bowles

Brotherhoods and
Sisters' Rooms

Many versions of this riddle are found in Latin, English, and German. It's older than Europe's first printing press. It may have been written by Albertus Magnus (ca. 1200–1280), a Dominican friar and plant hunter who became bishop of Regensburg and an early authority on soil fertility. It's hard to associate this brainteaser with such a serious man. After all, this is the same Albertus Magnus who convinced the Poles to stop killing their crippled children.

Can you guess the answer to the bishop's riddle? It would help if you could go out into the garden and pick a dog rose *(Rosa canina)*. If you don't have a dog rose, any of the fancy breeds based on hybrids with dog rose "parents," such as Abbotswood, Cheshire, Blanche Superbe, Maiden's Blush, or the White Rose of York, will do. You won't need a microscope, but one of those big, cheap plastic magnifying lenses sold in most coin and stamp shops will give you the fine detail you'll need in order to see the five brothers.

Above: The "five brother" sepals that make up the calyx of a dog rose *(Rosa canina). Below:* Floral rings and organs in a garden rose. Illustrations by J. Myers.

petals (corolla)

carpels (gynoecium)

stamens (androecium)

sepals (calyx)

First, turn your rose upside-down and find the narrow, flat, green triangular organs that make up the lowest and outermost ring on your flower. Each of these triangles is known as a sepal. The word *sepal* comes from the Latin word for "separate." Your rose should have five sepals. In a fully open flower, each sepal has a separate, pointed tip.

Now examine the margins of each sepal. Two sepals will have edges that break up into tiny, flattened "whiskers." They are the bearded brothers. Two will have smooth edges, so they can be counted as the beardless brothers. The brother with only half a beard has one smooth edge and one whiskery edge.

Sepals are usually the most leaflike parts of a flower, regardless of species. They tend to contain the same number and arrangement of veins found in the foliage, the true leaves growing on the branches below the flowers. Sepals are often as green as true leaves because they, too, store the pigment chlorophyll. This is the same chlorophyll that makes it possible for true leaves to capture energy from sunlight and then store it in sugar molecules. The skin cells of both sepals and leaves are transparent. That's why we can see the green chlorophyll, which is packed into a horizontal layer of cells arranged directly underneath the colorless skin.

Like leaves, most sepals have functional breathing pores on their skins. These breathing pores are flanked by guard cells that shut the pores when conditions become too arid. On dry days, closed pores help keep leaves from losing too much moisture in the form of vapor. Sepals may help keep other parts of the flower moist while they grow inside the bud.

Together, the five sepals form a ring called the calyx. *Calyx* is derived from a Greek word referring to a husk or envelope. The calyx is so named because it usually forms the bud of a young flower, sheathing and protecting the internal organs. The calyx does not divide into sepals until all the inner organs of the flower are ready to emerge and unfold.

The buds of some flowers wear an outer coat of sharp prickles or gluey glands. These ornaments may offer even greater protection to the young flower by discouraging insect attacks. In a few flowers, sepals are discarded as the flower opens. The sepals of poppies *(Papaver)*, bleeding hearts *(Dicentra)*, and fumitories *(Fumaria)* are little more than thin wrappers that fall to the ground once the inner organs are mature and the sepals' job is done.

In later chapters, you will see how the sepals of some other flowers do far more than act as mere protectors. These sepals may be retained for the full life of the flower and even become a part of the ripened fruit.

As important as sepals are, no one loves a rose for its calyx. Poets and artists would rather praise the petals, which are anchored above the calyx. The word *petal* comes from the Late Latin *petalum,* meaning "metal plate or blade." Together, a ring of petals makes a corolla. In Latin, *corolla* (diminutive of *corona*) means "little crown." This makes sense, since crowns are often made of a simple hoop of united metal plates or points.

The anatomy of a rose petal gives it its light, silky, and gaudy quality, which is so absent in sepals. The petals of most flowers usually contain only one or three veins. Petals house their bright pigments in cells that make up the outer layers of skin. The interior of a petal contains spongy tissue, but the individual cells are packed so loosely that lots of air pockets form. Although the petals of many flowers bear pores and unusual sculpting, these structures serve a different purpose from that of the sepals, as you will see in later chapters. It appears that such features are more likely to attract, reward, and recruit visiting animals.

To be honest, though, the difference between petals and sepals is often obscure. In some species, no obvious difference between petals and sepals can be seen, either with the naked eye or with the help of a microscope. Such flowers contain one to several rings of flat structures that have the same color and shape and the same number of veins. Sometimes these organs aren't even arranged in discrete rings. Instead, they are arrayed in a continuous spiral, like steps in a grand staircase.

When botanists can't find either an internal or an external difference between sepals and petals, they call the organs tepals. Plants as different as star anises *(Illicium),* magnolias *(Magnolia),* rushes *(Juncus),* water hyacinths *(Eichhornia crassipes),* and irises *(Iris)* have flowers with tepals arranged in rings or spirals.

The corolla of a wild rose usually contains just five petals in one distinct ring. However, your garden flower may tell a completely different story. Sometimes a single bloom will contain dozens of petals crammed into a dense, confusing package. Outside the garden, these "sports," or mutations, are usually eliminated by natural forces, since the flowers are not always hardy. It's possible that having too many petals also wastes limited construction materials, lowering seed set.

However, shrubs with mutated blossoms have been carefully protected and propagated by the human hand, giving us gardens filled with "double" flowers and hundred-petal roses. These plants have been prized for thousands of years. The Greek philosopher Theophrastus (ca. 372–ca. 287 B.C.), a pupil of Plato and Aristotle, commented on the protection and cultivation of such pretty errors in heredity. He wrote that most were grown near Philippi and were purchased from people who dug up mutant shrubs on Mount Pangaeus. Although extra petals represent developmental errors in rosebuds, in the next chapter you will see how they can help us understand the course of floral evolution.

Sepals and petals are always sterile organs in a flower, since both structures lack the cells needed to make either pollen grains or seeds. That all changes, though, when you leave the corolla and find the rings of stamens in your rose. *Stamen* is Latin for "warp thread" because stamens often resemble loose threads or pieces of yarn. Furthermore, stamens tend to be arranged lengthwise in a flower, like the warp threads on a loom.

There are some unusual exceptions to this rule. You won't find "stringy" stamens in the large flowers of some trees and shrubs, such as magnolias, star anises, Carolina allspice *(Calycanthus floridus)*, and custard apples *(Annona)*. Nor will you find them on the blossoms of some tender water plants, such as hornworts *(Ceratophyllum)*, arrow-

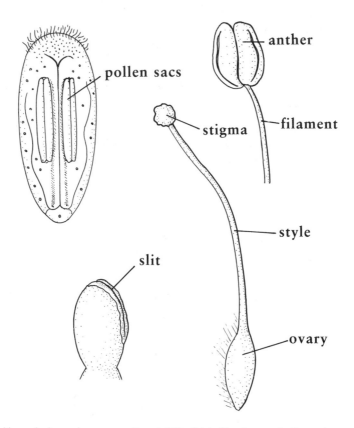

Primitive and advanced sex organs. *Above left:* The flat, leaflike stamen of a *Degeneria. Above right:* "Lollipop" stamen of a rose. *Below right:* Bottle-shaped carpel of a rose. *Below left:* Rounded carpel of a *Degeneria.* Illustrations by J. Myers.

heads *(Sagittaria),* and many members of the waterlily family (Nymphaeaceae). All these flowers have stamens that are peglike or paddle shaped. Chunky or flat stamens should contain three major veins, and there should be two or four sacs embedded in the flesh of each peg or paddle. Pollen is made inside each of these sacs.

Fossil evidence suggests that the stubby peg or paddle shape represents the oldest form of stamen. Over a period of 110 million years, plants that made flowers with skinny, stringy stamens topped with "lollipop" heads began to replace plants that made blossoms offering only chunky or flat stamens. The lollipop design triumphed, and it now dominates most of the flowering species on this planet, including the dog rose. Each stringy stamen is subdivided into two interconnecting parts, the filament and the anther.

The filament is just the long, cylindrical stalk that makes up most of the narrow length of the stamen (the word *filament* comes from the Latin word *filum,* "thread"). The filament is usually so narrow that it contains only one long vein. Close inspection of the swollen "lollipop" head of a stamen reveals that it is really made of paired sacs. This knobby head is called the anther.

Although the names of most of a flower's organs relate to their special shapes, the word *anther* derives from an odd bit of medical Latin. *Anther* once referred to a special kind of medicine made by extracting the juices and oils of flowers. Earlier generations of botanists seem to have had a good reason for calling the knobby tip of a stamen the anther. The sacs of each anther contain a most important "extract" essential to plant reproduction.

The anthers of most flowers release pollen as fine, dry grains. The Latin word *pollen* means "a fine powder or flour." Consequently, the botanical term *pollen* shares the same linguistic root as *polvo,* the Spanish word for dust, and *polenta,* the Italian word for a savory dish made of cornmeal.

By the late seventeenth century, some naturalists were comparing the pollen grains in an anther sac to sperm in an animal testicle. Stamens were seen as the "male majority" inside a flower. That's why the ring of stamens in a flower was named the androecium, a Greek word that alludes to domestic arrangements commonly attributed to homes in ancient Athens. In the days of Socrates and Aristophanes, men were entitled to occupy apartments in their houses separate from their wives and daughters.

In most flowers, the androecium is composed of one or more rings in which individual stamens are arranged in an orderly single file. Exceptions to this rule are interesting to examine with a hand lens. For example, the stamens of most St. John's worts *(Hypericum),* peonies *(Paeonia),* and some guinea flowers *(Hibbertia)* form discrete clumps or bundles, with each clump made up of two to eleven stamens. Sometimes all the stamens in these bundles interconnect at their base and share a common trunk and vein, so the stamen cluster resembles a hand of pointing fingers or a miniature candelabra.

A wild rose often contains several rings of male "apartments." Has any room been left in the blossom to accommodate females? The answer is yes. The same naturalists who saw stamens as male organs believed that the separate structures containing young seeds were womblike and unquestionably feminine. The gynoecium (from the Greek *gynaeceum,* meaning "women's apartments") lies in the center of the rose, encircled by the rings of stamens. Since the little organs that make up the gynoecium form both the final and the central part of the flower, they are organized in a clumped, continuous mass.

The gynoecium of the rose is made of greenish yellow, bottle-shaped organs known as carpels. *Carpel* is derived from the Latin *carpellum* and the Greek *karpos,* both of which mean "fruit." Cut open the base of the rounded bottom of any flower's carpel and you should find one to thousands of round or egg-shaped bodies inside. These structures, called ovules (from the Latin *ovulum,* diminutive of *ovum,* "egg"), are immature seeds waiting for sperm. That's why the swollen base of each carpel is properly called an ovary and why botanists named the centralized mass of carpels after a dormitory for women. Fertilize a carpel's ovules with sperm from pollen grains and it will almost certainly mature into a seed-filled fruit.

Every flower, then, is really a tightly compressed branch specialized for producing seeds. Within every flower, rings or spirals made of differently modified leaves play different roles in seed production. Botanists currently recognize five different living divisions of seed-making plants. However, members of only one division, the Anthophyta, make seeds inside *real* flowers. What distinguishes a rose flower from "nonflowers" such as the rigid pine cone *(Pinus)*, the squashy, fragrant cone of a juniper bush *(Juniperus)*, the red seed cup (aril) of a yew *(Taxus)*, or even the spur-shoot of lumpy seeds dangling from the twig of a maidenhair tree *(Ginkgo biloba)*?

Pines, junipers, yews, and ginkgos are some of the seed plants that always allow their ovules to grow on a thin scale exposed directly to the air. These trees and shrubs are called gymnosperms, from the Greek words *gymnos,* "naked," and *sperma,* "seed." The ovules hang naked in the breeze, waiting for pollen grains provided by puffy male cones. A gymnosperm ovule always has a single, wet pore on its outer surface to catch pollen blown by the wind or carried by a beetle or moth. Some gymnosperms give their ovules extra protection in the form of hard, flattened leaves that form tough "shingles" and attach themselves to each scale and its ovules. These shingles arrange themselves in a continuous spiral, forming the familiar female cones of pines, firs, cedars, cycads (a distinctive division of palmlike gymnosperms that survived the Age of Dinosaurs), and their kin.

If you could look into even the youngest flower bud of a rosebush, you would see a burst of development that makes all true flowers unique. The carpel starts to grow as would any flat leaf or the thin, flat scale of a gymnosperm. Eventually, one to many ovules may form as bumps on the upper surface of this carpel "leaf." However,

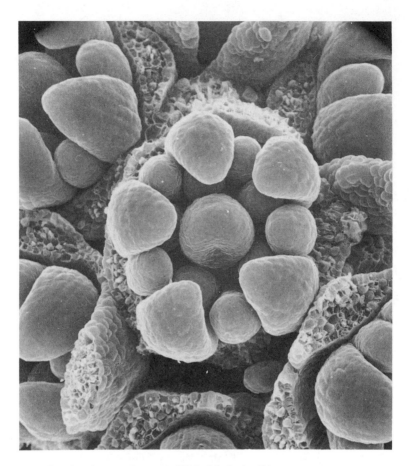

Scanning electron micrograph (SEM) of the buds of *Neptunia* flowers. The sepals of these perfect flowers were removed to reveal the early development of five fanglike petals and the sex organs. The "lollipop" anthers are so young that they are still a ring of bumps. Look at the carpel in the center. It is so young that it has not yet grown its style neck. You can see the crease on one side, showing how the flat carpel folded up to form the closed ovary. SEM by S. Tucker.

before the ovules can mature, the carpel closes up, locking the ovules inside a chamber. A carpel may simply fold over on itself, enclosing the ovules as if they were pearls inside the two valves of an oyster's shell. Or the process may occur more smoothly, with the carpel curving along its own margins until the edges meet to form a cylinder, a living bottle in which to store the ovules.

The closed carpel is the only thing that makes a flower a flower. That is why all flowering plants are called angiosperms, from the Greek words for seeds *(sperma)* inside a vessel *(angeion)*. The sperm inside a pollen grain can reach the ovule only by moving along a prescribed, specialized route, but that route is found in every carpel.

To maintain its unique shape and function, a carpel usually contains more veins than does any other organ in the flower. Ovaries have a base number of three veins, but five are common, and even more are found in some species. Each ovary has one or two structures attached on top. As is the case in most flowers, each rose carpel has a stalky or pin-shaped "neck" called the style. Indeed, the word *style* is from *stilus,* a Latin word for the ancient pin-shaped tool used to engrave words onto wax tablets. In turn, each style is tipped by a glandular head called the stigma. Stigmas are usually swollen and may be ornamented with weeping scabs, pimples, or fleshy warts. It is no surprise that in Latin, *stigma* refers to a stab wound or a scar left by a branding iron.

To reach an ovule inside the ovary of a true flower, a pollen grain must first adhere to a stigma. The sperm must then leave the interior of the pollen grain and travel down the style to the ovary. I will save the travelogue of the adventurous sperm for a later chapter.

Meanwhile, it can be said that although each true carpel has a stigma, some carpels lack styles. The carpels in flowers of magnolias, star anises, custard apples, Australian spice bushes *(Eupomatia laurina),* and Winter's bark trees *(Drimys)* never grow styles. In these flowers, the stigma is a slit, cap, or crest directly ornamenting the surface of the ovary. According to the fossil record, the absence of a style seems to be a relic of older, "unsophisticated" times in flower evolution. Not surprisingly, carpels lacking styles are often found within the same flowers that have retained peglike or paddle-shaped stamens. Some scientists have compared fossils with living plants and concluded that short, squat floral organs evolved before most pollinating insects developed either longer mouthparts or forelegs that could push, clutch, or otherwise manipulate floral organs. The descendants of some of these less specialized insects survive to this day. In later chapters, you will see how they feed within the interiors of these same flowers, rather like snuffling pigs.

The success of the closed carpel can be seen, in part, in the sheer diversity of flowering plants. Angiosperms dominate the vegetation of most continents and islands. There are at least a quarter of a million species of flowering plants, and new ones are found, described, and named every month. In contrast, there are fewer than 800 species of living gymnosperms wearing their seeds in exposed cones and cups. These days, a new species of gymnosperm is rarely found and described more than once every couple of decades. As you will see, there may be benefits to a closed carpel that are not enjoyed by plants that expose their ovules.

Of course, there are important exceptions to the observation that flowering plants always conquer and rule. For example, trees with naked seeds are more likely to fill forests in the northern interiors of the northern continents. There, soils never quite thaw out and evaporation is minimal because winter temperatures may fall as low as −50 degrees centigrade. In these snow forests, cone-bearing spruces *(Picea)*, larches *(Larix)*, and firs *(Abies)* are likely to form a canopy over the smaller flowering alders *(Alnus)* and birches *(Betula)*. Most of the densest and broadest gymnosperm forests on this planet are in Canada, Scandinavia, Russia, and Siberia. In most other parts of the world, gymnosperms must compete with flowering plants for their fair share of deserts, savannas, and rain forests.

Flowering plants make up such a huge group that scientists who classify plants have split them into two classes sharing a common evolutionary origin. Angiosperms are classified according to a broad but dependable suite of characteristics shared by the vast majority of species in each class. These include such anatomical features as the construction of the embryo in the seed and the way veins run through stems and then spread out inside leaves. Flowers also play a most important role in this suite of characteristics, as the number of organs in each ring is usually so consistent that botanists can assign each species to one of the two classes.

In some flowers, either there are no more than three organs in each ring (three sepals, three petals, three stamens, three carpels) or the organs in each ring come in multiples of three (six, nine, or twelve carpels). A flower containing organs arranged in threes is most likely to belong to a plant in the class Monocotyledonae. There are more than 65,000 species of monocotyledons, including all grasses, sedges, orchids, pineapples, and true lilies, to name but a few. The word *monocotyledon* refers to the fact that if you dissect a mature seed, you will find only one large "seed leaf" sheathing the embryo. Popcorn provides a good example. The hard brown spot in the center of a fluffy bit of popped corn is all that remains of the seedling leaf after heat made it explode out of its husk.

The second class of flowering plants, the Dicotyledonae, comprises more than 170,000 species, including almost all flowering trees and thousands of wildflowers. The word *dicotyledon* refers to an embryo with two seed leaves. These first leaves are familiar to most people as the plump "mittens" on a mung bean sprout or the green "bow tie" tipping an alfalfa seedling. Dicotyledons have the most variable number of organs in a floral circle, alternating between series of fours and fives.

The five brothers in the rose blossom are evidence that rosebushes pledge their loyalty to the Dicotyledonae. Despite mutation and hybridization, we can expect five sepals and five petals in each wild rose. The stamens and carpels in the flower may be too daunt-ing to count, but it is safe to predict that they will occur in incre-ments of five, ten, fifteen, twenty, and so on.

Fascinating as these counting games may be, they are only one of the tricks botanists use to help identify plants. Flowers have many more design secrets that contribute to their distinctiveness and their reproductive success. Prepare yourself for these details and gather another fresh rose.

CHAPTER 2

Queen rose of the rosebud garden of girls,
Come hither! the dances are done;
In gloss of satin and glimmer of pearls,
Queen lily and rose in one
  Alfred, Lord Tennyson, "Come into the Garden, Maud"

Limits to Perfection

If each flower is a reduced branch, then each floral organ must be a special leaf modified to aid in some part of reproduction. Sepals are often so similar in structure to foliage leaves that in many cases, they've changed only enough to sheath and protect. You've seen how the stamens of the most primitive flowers are little more than flat leaves filled with pollen sacs. Carpels hide their leafy origins from view by folding up to make "seed bottles." How, then, can we account for petals?

One of those fancy double roses or a specimen of an old breed with a hundred petals would be useful right now. You'll need a rose stuffed with dozens of petals that hide the stamens and carpels from view. Plant breeders have learned different ways to increase the number of petals in a flower. These tricks are based on preserving the genetic "mistakes" that are usually rejected by natural selection. What makes these mistakes important is that they can teach us something about real trends in the history of flower evolution.

The extra petals in your double rose are actually transformed sta-

mens. This is where a hand lens would be most useful. Start picking
the petals out of your flower. Begin with the petals closest to the
green sepals, and follow the circular corolla. As you run out of petals
and get closer to the obscured stamens, you will see how the remaining petals change in size and shape. They become smaller and
irregular, and some have a tiny empty "box" along the rim. That box
is all that is left of the original anther.

Developmental differences among stamens, from
fertile "lollipop" to sterile petaloid, in a cultivated
hundred-petal rose. Illustration by J. Myers.

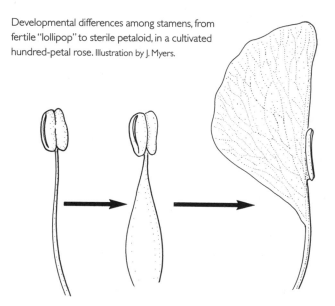

The gene (or genes) controlling the number of organs in your
cultivated flower has mutated. This mutated gene now sends out a
partially scrambled message to the circles of organ bumps developing inside the rosebud. Some bumps are waiting for a message telling
them to grow into stamens. In breeds of double flowers, this message
is never fully received. Instead, some of the bumps, once destined to
become fertile, pollen-filled "lollipops," change into sterile, painted
"sheets."

It's not much of a stretch to turn a stamen into a petal. Remember, stamens and petals within the same flower almost always begin life with the same number of veins. Since the internal plumbing is identical, all that remains is to make the mutated stamen's filament grow flatter, wider, and more colorful. Meanwhile, the development of the anther is either stopped completely or suppressed to the point that pollen grains never form.

Over the past few thousand years, European and Chinese horticulturists have prided themselves on their efforts to add extra petals to flowers. Roses, peaches *(Prunus persica),* cherry hybrids (P. x yedoensis), and peonies *(Paeonia)* are a few of their oldest and most visible successes. However, evidence suggests that the natural process of flower evolution has played a similar game. The main difference is that the organs in flowers have undergone modification for more than 100 million years. There appears to have been at least two natural solutions to the evolution of petals, both of them based on the developmental principle of "fiddling with spare parts."

First, in some flowers, such as wild roses, it's suspected that all petals were probably derived from the extra stamens that grew closest to the ring of sepals. Over time, these stamens became longer, broader, sterile, and more colorful. The idea that a petal is just a transformed stamen is an old one and was first proposed by poet, playwright, and botanist Johann Wolfgang von Goethe (1749–1832) as early as 1790. When evolution turns a stamen into a petal, there is only a minimal effect on the plant's ability to make pollen. After all, five stamens will never be missed, since each flower on a wild rose contains more than a hundred fertile stamens.

Second, in other plants, both the petals' outer form and internal "skeleton" suggest that they represent an extra inner ring of transformed sepals. The glorious petals of waterlilies *(Nymphaea),* for example, appear to be little more than sepals that have grown longer and wider and lost their protective leathery texture. The flowers of the sacred lotus *(Nelumbo nucifera)* and those of many true cacti (Cactaceae) show such a smooth transition between sepals and petals that organs intermediate in thickness, size, shape, and color are found on the same flower. The outermost rings of these flowers are made up of short, tough, drab sepals, but follow the repeating rings and you will see how the sepals grade into longer, more delicate and colorful petals.

Gather as many different wildflowers as you can find and you will see that their natural diversity seems to reflect the differences between "haves" and "have-nots." The flowers produced by waterlilies, lotuses, and cacti seem to belong to the haves, as each flower owns more than one ring of petals and more than one ring of stamens. In contrast, the buckwheat *(Fagopyrum)* is a have-not, as its flower contains only a single ring of five sepal-like organs. A separate ring of true petals never forms, and there is only one solitary ring of five stamens.

Sometimes you can find haves and have-nots within the same group of closely related plants. Within the buttercup family (Ranunculaceae), each flower of the buttercup *(Ranunculus),* the columbine *(Aquilegia),* and the larkspur *(Delphinium)* contains an outer ring of five sepals and an inner ring of five petals. In direct contrast, windflowers *(Anemone),* virgin's bowers *(Clematis),* and liverleafs *(Hepatica)* have large sepals but always lack petals.

Without petals, the sepals of windflowers and liverleafs may do more than one job in the lives of their respective flowers. As usual, the sepals form an outer, protective bud case. Once the bud opens, though, the sepals are often as large and colorful as true petals. These gaudy sepals often spend the rest of their lives attracting insects to the flower to encourage cross-pollination.

The flowers of some plants show signs that a developmental "decision" might have been made gradually over a period of time. If you examine them carefully, you will see organs that have been reduced to remnants. All that remains, for example, of the sepals and petals of the bulrush *(Scirpus)* are six wispy bristles. If you're lucky, you might even be able to find the four little scales that are the closest things a mulberry *(Morus)* flower has for sepals.

Scientists of the eighteenth and nineteenth centuries tried to make sense out of all this floral variety. Flower construction seemed both unique and self-consistent, promising to become a beautiful tool for identifying and classifying plants. This required the invention of a new vocabulary for the science of botany. We continue to use parts of this vocabulary to the present day.

This earlier generation of scientists realized that a flower could contain a maximum of four different kinds of organs. If a flower consisted of at least one sepal, one petal, one stamen, and one carpel, it was properly known as a complete flower. Conversely, if a flower contained fewer than four different kinds of organs, it was incomplete.

Your wild rose is complete, and so are buttercups, columbines, and delphiniums. The anemone, clematis, and hellebore are incomplete because they always lack petals. The flowers of the bulrush and the mulberry must also be regarded as incomplete because their sepals have been reduced to minute, almost invisible, wisps or stubs.

If plants can alter the number of sepals and petals in their flowers or even eliminate them, can they do the same thing with their sex organs? They can, and they do. In fact, that older generation of botanists invented new words to point out sexual differences. A bisexual flower (containing both stamens and carpels) was perfect. A unisexual flower (containing either stamens or carpels) was imperfect. Therefore, the rose is a perfect flower, while the flowers of willows *(Salix),* marijuana plants *(Cannabis),* melon vines *(Cucumis),* and moonseed vines *(Menispermum)* are among nature's imperfect blossoms.

In the eighteenth century, the science of botany was dominated by gentlemen of rank and privilege. They did not question their status in society or their right to dominate the study of nature. Why, then, would this earlier generation of smug heterosexual males insist that a bisexual flower was a perfect flower? The simplest explanation is that they believed it was most normal and natural for a stamen to deliver its pollen to a carpel found in the *same* flower. Bisexuality, then, represented both the dominant state in nature and the perfect condition for the manufacture of seeds.

The idea that a stamen always "marries" a carpel in the same flower would not be blown to bits until the second half of the nineteenth century. Later, I will show you how many perfect flowers manage to avoid "marrying themselves." Even so, the logic of the old language of botany remains to the present day. That logic states that every imperfect flower is incomplete, but not every incomplete flower is imperfect.

Meanwhile, there is so much variety among the imperfect flowers on different plants that botanists celebrate these forms of sexual variation with a second vocabulary. First, some lily-like plants, such as death camas *(Zigadenus),* early Nancy *(Wurmbea),* and the relatives of asparagus, actually cluster both perfect and imperfect flowers on the same stem. Botanists say that such plants are polygamous. I suppose the odd ratio of bisexual flowers to male and female flowers on the same plant could suggest the old stereotype of a sultan's palace. Separate "dormitories" appear to be devoted to the harem (female flowers), the bachelor princes (male flowers), and the sultan's boudoir, in which male rulers consort with their favorite concubines (bisexual flowers).

In contrast, melon vines lack bisexual flowers, bearing male and female blooms together on the same stem. Botanists say that these plants are monoecious. This is a Greek term that means "one house." For example, the stamens and carpels of a watermelon appear to live in separate "bedrooms" (flowers) but share the same mansion (the whole vine).

In contrast, the male and female flowers of willows seem to have undergone a "divorce." A willow tree produces either male *or* female blooms but never both together on the same plant. Willow trees appear to have two genders, as with men and women or cocks and hens. Botanists say that these trees are dioecious. Their stamens and carpels live in two separate houses. That means that every willow tree is either male or female.

Why do some plants always make imperfect flowers? The standard explanation is that it encourages cross-pollination while lowering the chances of making unhealthy, puny offspring, which often result from the "accidents" of self-pollination. Charles Darwin was among the first to argue that imperfect flowers allow some plants to become sexual specialists and that this increases their efficiency as mothers or fathers. For example, under certain circumstances, a male willow can father more offspring than can a rosebush with its bisexual flowers.

However, imperfect flowers can't always prevent self-pollination. Self-pollination will occur, for example, if a bee visits male and female flowers on the same melon vine. In later chapters, you will see that most plants employ a combination of tricks to avoid "selfing."

I believe we are missing something very subtle and special about the nature of imperfect flowers. Botanists forget to mention that imperfect flowers can also show a terrific range in size. Both the smallest and the largest flowers on this planet are imperfect, and I don't think that's a coincidence. There seems to be something about stopping the development of a ring of stamens or a ring of carpels that makes the length and width of a flower unusually plastic.

Plants bearing the tiniest flowers float on the surface of water, seeming equally at home in fish tanks and slow tropical rivers. They are the seven known species of watermeal *(Wolffia),* which belong to the duckweed family (Lemnaceae). A watermeal plant rarely consists of more than one dangling root attached to a reduced greenish, flat-

Size differences in plants with imperfect flowers. *Above:* An entire duckweed plant *(Lemna),* with two male flowers and one female. *Below:* Solitary male flower of a queen-of-the-parasites *(Rafflesia arnoldii).* Illustrations by J. Myers.

tened body that resembles a floating leaf scrap. The adult plant is very small. One South American species "migrates" to new pools on the feathers of waterfowl. When a watermeal "blooms," both male and female flowers are confined to pockets on the same tiny plant. Watermeal flowers have no petals or sepals. A male flower consists of nothing more than a single stamen less than a millimeter in length. A female flower consists of a single reduced carpel.

At the opposite end of the scale is the aptly named queen-of-the-parasites *(Rafflesia arnoldii)*. This monarch is now confined to a few remaining undisturbed forests on the Indonesian island of Sumatra. The plant spends most of its life underground, attacking the roots of woody vines belonging to tropical members of the grape family (Vitaceae). An observer can't tell that the queen-of-the-parasites is present until it is ready to flower. Then, it pushes its massive buds up above the leaf litter on the forest floor, though some buds may wait as long as nine months to bloom. When a bud finally opens, the male or female flower may be as large as two and a half feet in diameter and weigh more than twelve pounds! These blossoms are so broad and fleshy that most botanists have given up trying to collect them by pressing them between alternating layers of newsprint, blotting paper, and cardboard. To preserve the flower's shape, it's better to "pickle" it in a preservative solution, as if it were a frog or snake specimen.

However, most plants with imperfect flowers seem to opt for reduced size. The smaller the flowers, the more likely they are to be bundled together on stalks or stems according to sex. This is particularly common in the trees and bushes of Europe and North America. From late winter until mid-spring, clusters of male and female flowers can be found on oak *(Quercus)*, birch *(Betula)*, beech *(Fagus)*, chestnut *(Castanea)*, and walnut *(Juglans)* trees.

Flowering stalks consisting exclusively of male flowers often appear on dangling stalks wearing protective layers of hair. The old nature books called them catkins because of their resemblance to caterpillars or fuzzy kittens. After catkins release their pollen, the entire stalk snaps off, pelting our windows and sticking to our cars on wet days.

Some trees make the stalks that bear male flowers much longer than the stalks that hold female flowers. Stalks of female flowers are often rounded or chunky and contain fewer blossoms than do male-bearing stalks. This difference in size, shape, and number seems tied directly to the form and future of female flowers. A female flower needs a little extra space and a stronger stalk because it contains at least one plump ovary. The ovaries of female flowers are not expected to dry up and drop off the tree. They should expand and mature into bulky acorns, nuts, seed-packed capsules, or even those menacing "balls" found on sweet gum trees *(Liquidambar)*. A male catkin on a shagbark hickory tree *(Carya ovata)* is packed with dozens of flowers, while the female catkin rarely contains more than five blossoms.

The bush or tree is on a budget. Female flowers live longer than males, and they drain the plant of water, food, and building materials, investing these resources in healthy seeds and thickened, protective fruit walls. In contrast, male flowers are disposed of immediately after they release their more cheaply produced grains of pollen. That's why male flowers usually outnumber females on the same tree.

Under certain conditions, though, some plants are flexible about the ratio of male to female flowers produced each season. Sometimes the budget relates directly to the age of the plant. Many members of the jack-in-the-pulpit or philodendron family (Araceae) crowd male and female flowers on the same fleshy stalk, usually hiding the bulkier female flowers toward the bottom. The younger the jack-in-the-pulpit, the smaller the plant, and the smaller the plant, the fewer resources it has to invest in female flowers. Therefore, the first season a jack-in-the-pulpit blooms, its flowering stalk may consist only of male flowers. Female flowers will be added sparingly in future seasons as the plant grows larger and stores up more starch and minerals to be spent on reproduction.

The ratio of male to female flowers may also be influenced by the environment, a fact that can have a profound effect on the amount of food we harvest. Vines of melons, gourds, squash, and cucumbers (Cucurbitaceae) rarely live more than a single season. If the climate is mild enough that these vines can be set out early in spring, they are likely to grow more fruit than they would if planted in early summer. Why?

One important reason is that the number of female flowers made by these vines depends directly on the number of hours of daylight they receive when young. Vines enjoying a cycle of short periods of daylight and cool days in early spring produce a hormone that encourages the formation of female flowers. Plants that don't start active growth until summer are exposed to a cycle of longer, hotter days. This combination of more light and higher temperatures cues the vine to produce a second hormone that favors the manufacture of male flowers.

I suspect that this is an adaptation our garden vines inherited from wild ancestors that originated in dry zones. A wild vine that is able to start growing early in the wet season has a longer life span, giving it more time to assemble the water and sugars needed to make such large fruits by late summer. That's probably why the hormone for female flowers is activated during the shorter, cooler days of spring. If female flowers bloom too late in the hot, dry season, it's unlikely that their fruit will have time to develop seeds or ripen flesh.

That's why delaying the planting of gourds, squash, or pumpkins *(Cucurbita)* until early summer may turn a young vine into a bachelor party. The longer hours of sunlight encourage the late vine to shift its limited resources to making cheap pollen. It won't make fruit, but it can still produce offspring by cross-pollinating with any females blooming on vines started weeks earlier.

Of course, male flowers can still be a source of food for people. If

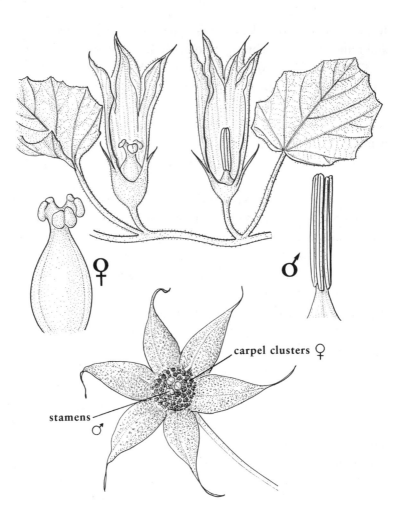

stamens ♂

carpel clusters ♀

Above: Male and female squash blossoms grow on the same vine. *Below: Lacandonia* is the only plant in which the carpels have exchanged places with the stamens. Illustrations by J. Myers.

you don't like squash blossom fritters, there is always the Mexican alternative. In central Mexico, male squash and pumpkin flowers are sold in produce markets. Cooks chop them up and add the scented morsels to cream soups and vegetable broths.

Is the expression of sex more stable in species in which a single plant makes either male or female flowers? Under the microscope, we can see that gender in a marijuana plant is controlled by X and Y sex chromosomes, just as in human beings. When X and Y meet in a human embryo, the baby should be born with a penis and testicles. When X and Y meet in a marijuana seed, the plantlet should grow up to produce only male flowers.

Some plants keep sex chromosomes under far greater control than do many animals because plant chromosomes can change rapidly over a few generations. Plants can inherit extra chromosomes if they inherit recurrent "accidents" that occur during the division of sex cells in their parents. In other generations, chromosome numbers increase when there is a history of successful hybridization between two different species, leaving fertile offspring with a legacy of extra, mismatched chromosomes. Many species of dock *(Rumex),* hop vine *(Humulus),* and cinquefoil *(Potentilla)* have accumulated extra chromosomes over time.

There is also evidence that some plants have "reduced" the number of chromosomes in their cells. Microscope studies show that the few big, fat chromosomes in the cells of Christmas mistletoes (Viscaceae) were probably derived from many smaller chromosomes that linked up together like cocktail wieners, fusing to form one great "frankfurter."

Most plants manage to avoid gender confusion even though they accumulate lots of extra sex chromosomes. In one variety of the beer hop vine *(Humulus lupulus* var. *cordifolium),* males are XXYY and females are XXXXX. In some populations of sheep dock *(Rumex acetosella),* males are XXXXXXXY and females are XXXXXXXX.

Plant gender can also be determined with only one chromosome. In some wild yams *(Dioscorea)*, the Y chromosome has fragmented and its genes have been absorbed by other chromosomes in the same cell. Whether a yam seed grows into a "boy" or "girl" vine depends on whether it has inherited a single X chromosome.

The mere presence of sex chromosomes doesn't always guarantee that plant gender will be fixed. Remember, flower buds are not found inside seed embryos in the way genitals are found inside human embryos. Most plants begin to make flower organs only after they've sprouted and reached a certain size. Deprive marijuana seedlings of water and daylight and those destined to grow up to be females will produce male flowers instead.

Sickness will also change a plant's sex if the disease finds a way to harness flower development. An example can be found in the red campion *(Silene dioica)*, a European member of the carnation family (Caryophyllaceae). A plant of red campion should make either male or female flowers, but when a female plant is infected with smut fungus, its flower buds become bisexual. The carpels continue to grow at a depressed rate, but a ring of stamens also develops. Instead of making pollen, though, these diseased stamens spew smut spores. The fungus enslaves the female plant by sending its threads into the flowers' cells and scrambling the original hormone message. The irony is that by the time the disease has given its host perfect flowers, it has transformed its once female victim into a sterile, bisexual "nanny."

Botanists now understand that in the course of evolution, various plants have altered both the presence and the number of different organs in their flowers. The big question is, Has evolution ever caused different organs in the *same* flower to switch places?

Had you asked this question as late as 1988, most plant anatomists would have laughed at you. The relative positions of sepals, petals, stamens, and carpels in all flowers were considered to be as fixed as the constellations in heaven and as constant as the arrangement of eyes, nose, ears, and mouth on the human face. Granted, plant breeders could market a Pink Perfection camellia in which both stamens and carpels had been completely replaced by extra petals. However, different organs in a flower could never swap places . . . right?

Given enough time, nature will humiliate a botanist. In 1989, Esteban Martínez and Clara Ramos stunned the botanical community with the description of a leafless climbing plant from a Mexican jungle. *Lacandonia schismatica* looked like other members of the *Triuris* family (Triuridaceae) until the buds opened. When the petals expanded, the two scientists were astonished to see that the stamens sat smack in the center of the flower, surrounded by a circle of many smaller carpels! These little climbers bloom year-round, as if to remind all botanists of their former arrogance. In all fairness, though, no other wild plant has been found, to date, in which circles of organs have exchanged positions.

Molecular geneticists also seem to enjoy making fools of botanists. They are learning to read and control the genetic message that determines the relative positions of organs in flowers. Since every flower is a reduced branch, it was only a matter of time before someone isolated and identified the genes that control the positions of flower organs. More important, it was only a matter of time before someone identified the proteins those genes use to decide whether a developmental bump should become a petal or a stamen.

At the California Institute of Technology, the laboratory of Dr. Elliot Meyerowitz uses thale cress *(Arabidopsis thaliana)* in experiments. This weedy member of the mustard family (Brassicaceae) completes its whole life cycle, from sprouting seed to fruiting plant, within a month. These short generations make the thale cress as valuable to the genetics laboratory as the fruit fly.

Meyerowitz's laboratory has produced a thale cress with flowers in which the six stamens and two carpels never form. Instead, the flower consists of repeating circles of sepals and petals. The center of the flower consists of a circle of sepals, and they are surrounded by two rings of petals. If this variation doesn't tickle your fancy, how about a plant in which the flowers lack both sepals and petals? In this plant, as in the wild form of thale cress, six stamens surround two carpels. Wait a minute, what's this? Two additional carpels have developed *below* the ring of stamens. The stamens are now the "meat" in a carpel sandwich.

Meyerowitz reports that it's probably only a matter of time before his laboratory will be able to turn out flowers of thale cress resembling *Lacandonia,* since he's received genetic material of this plant from Mexico. A little DNA cutting and pasting will be in order. Furthermore, other laboratories around the world are performing similar experiments on plants that take a little longer to bloom, including snapdragons *(Antirrhinum majus)* and carrots *(Daucus carota)*.

New plants designed in laboratories are coming to our gardens, and we should realize that one day, such altered flowers may make significant contributions to basic research and to national economies. It won't be the first time this has happened. Remember that our interest in mutants began a few thousand years ago, when a rose was found bearing more than five petals.

Ut rosa flos florum sic est domus domorum.
(As the rose is the flower of flowers, this is the house of all houses.)
Anonymous inscription, York Minster and Chapter House at York

The Pig in the Pizza

The flower of a wild dog rose is like a pizza baked by an obsessive-compulsive chef. The chef uses only four toppings and arranges each topping in its own orderly circle on the sauced top of the pizza dough. Although the chef uses different amounts of topping in different circles, he makes certain that all the pieces in each circle are identical in size and equally spaced. There will be only five "pepperoni petals" on the pizza, and each slice will have the same circumference and thickness. He arranges the slices with care so that they form the outline of a five-pointed star. He then adds more than a hundred "anchovy stamens" to the pizza, all of them cut to the same length and width. The anchovy stamens are arranged like the spokes of a wheel and placed between the pepperoni petals and a central circle of "carpel shrimp."

The wild rose and this imaginary pizza have something else in common. If you want to cut either of them in half, it won't matter from which direction you start. Provided you cut from end to end, you should be left with two mirror images of the flower or pizza. If you cut straight through opposite points, you will be left with the same number of organs or toppings on each half.

Both rose and pizza show radial symmetry. Radial symmetry is well expressed in most flowers, whether they are complete, incomplete, perfect, or imperfect. The male mulberry flower, for example, shows radial symmetry because its four reduced sepals form an orderly circle around four opposing stamens. Radial symmetry is also found in the adult stage of many sea animals, including starfish, sea urchins, medusa jellyfish, and sea anemones. Perhaps that's why so many of these creatures have been named after stars and flowers.

The flower with radial symmetry is often a flower offering maximum accessibility to its pollinators. If a small bee visits a large rose to gather pollen, it doesn't matter which petal she lands on to enter the androecium. All petals are the same. The stamens she finds on one side of the flower will be identical to those on the opposite side, and the insect must crawl over the central clump of carpels to reach the stamens on the opposite side. A nodding grass flower opens early in the morning, dangling its three stamens and solitary carpel in the air. Since the stamens form a triangle around the carpel, it doesn't matter in which direction the breeze blows. Air currents either carry new pollen to the feathery stigma or blow pollen grains out of the anthers.

Some flowers with radial symmetry limit both the movement and the diversity of their pollinators by narrowing and lengthening the point of access. Sepals, petals, or both form long, narrow tubes or funnels. The bee that tramps all over the rose has only limited entry to morning glories *(Ipomoea)*. She reaches the nectar at the base of the narrowing funnel of petals by pushing her head down the floral tube and lapping nectar with the "spoon" that tips her elongated tongue. Stamens and carpel tips rub against the bee's head as she feeds. The design of the corolla of the morning glory reduces the theft of nectar and pollen by short-tongued flies and larger, sluggish beetles.

In contrast, pea blossoms in the bean family (Fabaceae) look like pizzas baked by a chef who has had too much to drink. In particular, the petals are of different sizes and shapes. One petal is so large and flaglike that it is called the banner. Two narrower petals stand opposite each other and are known as wings. The fourth and fifth petals have fused together to form a sheath known as the keel, which really does resemble the keel of a boat. The ten stamens and the style of the single carpel are not dispersed evenly around the flower. They are wrapped up in the keel.

If you take a knife to a pea blossom, you will find that there is only one direction in which you can cut if you want two identical halves. You must start cutting right through the center of the banner petal and then slice down through the center of the keel. This is a flower with bilateral symmetry. It has a recognizable front and back, as does the body of a bee, a turtle, or a human being.

While bilateral symmetry is most commonly expressed by the irregular development of petals, some plant species have altered the shape of their flowers by changing the development of organs in other floral rings. For example, the spectacular hood of a wolfsbane flower *(Aconitum)* is really a single, inflated sepal that is far larger than the four remaining sepals. Stamens of toadflax *(Linaria)* and the cigar tree *(Catalpa speciosa)* cluster on only one side of the corolla. Such stamens are far too close together to take the form of the regular, predictable spokes of a wheel.

Bilateral symmetry seems to dominate the flowers of fewer plant families than does radial symmetry. I have already mentioned the bean family, but many species in the jewelweed (Balsaminaceae), violet (Violaceae), geranium (Geraniaceae), gloxinia (Gesneriaceae), snapdragon (Scrophulariaceae), and mint (Lamiaceae) families have corollas that make their flowers look like sock puppets or animal muzzles with unequal jaws. Bilateral symmetry rules in 99 percent of the flowers in the orchid family, and that covers more than 20,000 species. Although the flowers of most orchids have the typical sock

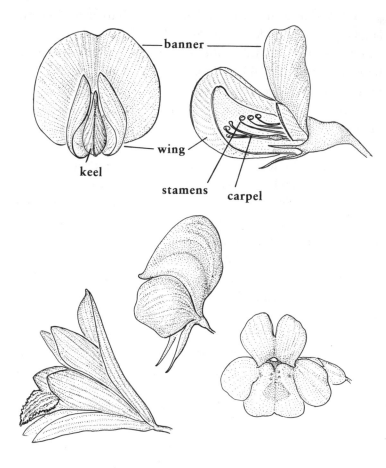

Flowers with bilateral symmetry. *Above left:* View of a pea blossom showing the unequal sizes and shapes of the petals that make up the corolla. *Above right:* Side view of pea blossom with one wing petal removed. *Below:* Variation in "sock puppet" flowers. Clockwise from far left, Chinese orchid *(Bletilla)*, wolfsbane *(Aconitum)*, catalpa tree *(Catalpa)*.

Illustrations by J. Myers.

puppet or muzzle shape, orchid fanciers see shoes *(Cypripedium)*, elbows *(Spiculaea)*, dancing dolls *(Oncidium)*, long-legged flies *(Tipularia)*, moths in flight *(Phalaenopsis)*, and even the head of a vampire *(Dracula)*.

Bilateral symmetry is likely to give a flower even greater control over the movements of pollinators than does radial symmetry. Bilateral symmetry restricts the way an animal enters and exits the flower while coming in contact with stamens and carpels.

When a bee attempts to take nectar from a pea blossom, she is most likely to reach the sweet reward if she perches directly on the keel petal. The weight of the bee's body causes the keel petal to open suddenly and explosively, swabbing the underside of the insect with fresh pollen. A tropical bee searches for rewards in a *Cattleya* orchid by landing first on a petal that is broad and thickened, like a lip or tongue. The insect then advances down the flower's "gullet," but there's no room for her to turn around inside this floral throat. As the bee backs out of the flower, her humped back knocks off the anther cap and pollen wads are glued to her thorax or head.

This means that flowers with bilateral symmetry can fix pollen to discrete parts of an animal's body instead of wasting grains by powdering the whole pollinator. Anthers of "sock puppet" flowers usually aim at the insect's back, where grains are hard for the forager to see and harder for it to comb up and brush off. The flower's style is usually curved or angled, so the stigma contacts the discrete spot where grains have collected on the pollinator's body.

The stiff, formal shapes of many flowers are maintained by the process of fusion. Instead of a bump in the bud developing into a separate organ, it unites with its neighbors, joining outer tissues together and sometimes sharing veins in common. Fusion reinforces flower shape by building continuous circular walls and allowing one circle of organs to offer support to another.

Botanists recognize two forms of fusion. Coalescence (from the

Fusion of flower organs. *Above left:* Partial coalescence in the three carpels of St. John's wort (three ovaries unite, but three styles remain separate). *Above right:* Complete coalescence of three carpels in a lily *(Lilium)*. *Below:* Adnation of a stamen to the petal of a primrose *(Primula)*. Illustrations by J. Myers.

Latin *coalescere,* "to grow together"), occurs when organs belonging to the same circle unite. Coalescence is responsible for the keel of a pea blossom and for most sepals or petals shaped like goblets, urns, trumpets, or pipes.

More important, coalescence is responsible for a trend in the development of carpels found in most of the angiosperms. Many flowers look as if they contain only one huge carpel. The gynoecium of St. John's wort *(Hypericum),* for example, looks like a single carpel with three branching styles. The gynoecium of a Madonna lily *(Lilium candidum)* looks like a single carpel in which the stigma is triangular or three lobed. If you make cross sections of the ovaries of these two flowers, you will learn the truth. Each ovary contains three separate chambers filled with ovules. In the evolution of both flowers, three carpels coalesced to form one seed-making organ. Old botany books often called such compound structures pistils because they were shaped like antique pestles (from the Latin *pistillum*).

The number of carpels that unite to form a single pistil varies among plant families. Some members of the hibiscus family (Malvaceae) form pistils based on ten or more fused carpels. The number of seed chambers in a ripe fruit may increase with domestication. Selective breeding of tomatoes *(Lycopersicon esculentum),* for example, has turned the two-chambered fruit of the wild ancestor into a broad, five-chambered descendant best encountered on hamburgers and in summer salads.

The second form of fusion is known as adnation (from the Latin *adnatus,* "grown together"). This may sound just like coalescence, but adnation has an even stronger influence on the architecture of the whole flower. When different organs from different circles fuse together, they become adnate. An example of adnation is easily observed in such garden flowers as phlox *(Phlox),* lilacs *(Syringa),* forget-me-nots *(Myosotis),* primroses *(Primula),* and mints *(Mentha).* In each of these flowers, the stamens have united with the petals, often sharing internal veins. Adnation allows very different organs to work together as a single unit. Petals become platforms or conduits supporting stamens.

Members of the milkweed (Asclepiadaceae), trigger plant (Stylidiaceae), and orchid (Orchidaceae) families go a step further. Their stamens fuse to their carpels. One would think that the sheer closeness of male and female organs would encourage self-pollination. In most cases, though, cross-pollination rules because the fused stamens and carpels, known as a column, work first as pollen traps and later as glue guns. A pollinator probing a milkweed or orchid flower is usually subjected to a two-step process. The combined design of the column and the surrounding petals usually forces the animal to deposit the pollen it's carrying on the stigma when it enters the flower. The column glues its own pollen onto the animal only when the animal attempts to leave.

Adnation ultimately determines the position of the ovary inside a flower. When only a few organs in different circles have fused, a cross section of the flower will show that the ovary has become the highest organ on the tip of the flower stalk. Botanists say that such flowers are hypogynous (Greek *hypo,* "under," the *gynē,* "woman") because the ovary sits in a superior (higher) position compared with the sepals, petals, and stamens. Maple blossoms *(Acer)* and Madonna lilies are good examples of hypogynous flowers.

In contrast, roses *(Rosa),* cherries *(Prunus),* cinquefoils *(Potentilla),* and saxifrages *(Saxifraga)* have perigynous flowers. This is another Greek word, meaning "around the woman" because the sepals, petals, and stamens all fuse at their bases without sticking to the ovary. The ovary remains the highest part of the flower, as the other organs can form only an interconnected sleeve or bowl around the base of the carpels.

That leaves the flowers belonging to members of the orchid, daffodil (Amaryllidaceae), honeysuckle (Caprifoliaceae), currant

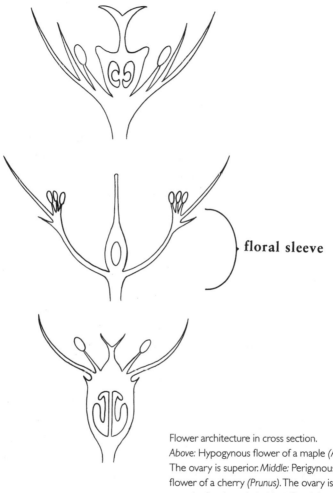

floral sleeve

Flower architecture in cross section.
Above: Hypogynous flower of a maple *(Acer)*.
The ovary is superior. *Middle:* Perigynous
flower of a cherry *(Prunus)*. The ovary is
superior but is encircled by a floral sleeve
(made of the androecium fused to the
corolla, which in turn is fused to the calyx).
Bottom: Epigynous flower of a carrot
(Daucus). The inferior ovary is buried under
adnate tissues. Illustrations by J. Myers.

(Grossulariaceae), bluebell (Campanulaceae), and daisy (Asteraceae) families. In these flowers, all circles of organs fuse ultimately to the ovary, burying it under layers of united tissue. A cross section reveals that these are epigynous flowers (Greek *epi,* "upon," the *gynē,* "woman"). The ovary is now the inferior, or lowest, organ, covered completely by the adnate circles of organs. Only the style of the pistil protrudes above the blanket of enveloping tissue.

Botanists once explained the evolution of these three forms of flower architecture as if they were telling the tale of "The Three Little Pigs." The ovary in the hypogynous flower was compared to the pig that built a house of straw. It was open to wolfish attack from ovule- and seed-destroying beasts because of the absence of tough, reinforced layers. The ovary in a perigynous flower was similar to the pig that lived in a house of sticks. It had more protection around it, but it remained vulnerable to predators entering the bowl or sliding down the floral sleeve. The ovary in the epigynous flower was likened to the pig that built a house of bricks. Protected by thickened layers, the buried inferior ovary was regarded as an early defense flowers developed to resist destructive insects, especially beetles, ants, and pests that drill holes in ovaries to lay their eggs on young seeds. It's a good story, but it is not sufficient to explain a trend that evolved independently along different lineages.

Sometimes a buried ovary is simply the consequence of so many different organs being united. An orchid flower needs a lot of fusion to hold a pollinator between its lip petal and column. This buries the orchid's ovary, but most orchid fruits are rather thin walled and tender during the earliest phases of development. Sometimes it's easier for a plant to disperse seeds that form inside a buried ovary because other flower organs remain attached to the fruit and help the seeds move away from the parent. For example, each individual fruit of a white, billowing dandelion *(Taraxacum)* rides beautifully on the wind because the dried-up sepals, still attached to the ovary, make a nice parachute.

Even perigynous flowers can put the base of that old floral sleeve to use if it continues to grow and develop after the ovules are fertilized by pollen sperm. Fetch an apple from the kitchen, and then turn the fruit upside-down and examine its scabby "dimple" with a hand lens. If you tease the dimple with a needle, you should be able to make out the tips of sepals and some dried-up stamens (the petal tips will have dropped off). The five-pointed star that makes up the hard, inedible core of the fruit is really the mature ovary, now filled with black seeds. The colorful peel and the sweet, fleshy tissue surrounding the ovary represent the base of the adnate sleeve, now swollen, juicy, and red. It's the fleshy, fused remains of the base of the sepals, petals, and stamens that attract the interest of apple-eating animals. Birds and mammals carry off the perigynous fruit of wild apples, dispersing the seeds away from the parent tree.

That also explains why there are so many individual carpels in a rose flower, yet each flower makes only one plump, seed-filled rose hip. The fleshy bowl of the perigynous flower "swallows" the hard, fertile carpels as they form seeds. The five brittle "ribbons" clinging to the base of some rose hips are all that remain of the sepal tips (the five brothers).

Some people know so little about what they eat that they try to use unfamiliar plant parts in litigation. In the late 1980s, a lawyer approached me with something "nasty" his client said she'd found in one of those apple pies that slide out of vending machines. Under the microscope, the foreign object turned out to be a bit of an apple's dimple. In fact, the shape of the sepals and the color of the stamens suggested that the pie had been filled with pieces of the most common apple, the Red Delicious. The lawyer was disappointed by my analysis, but he remained polite and paid my consultation fee promptly.

Organ numbers, symmetry, and fusion make a flower distinct, and knowledge of that combination of factors makes us wiser. The best part is that it frees us from the pretty tyranny of common names. We

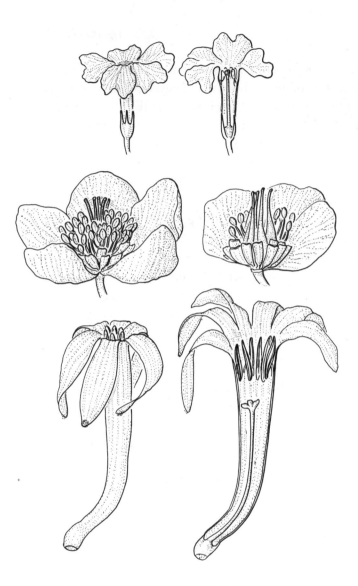

Different numbers of organs and different forms of fusion show that these flowers are not true roses, despite their common names. *Above:* Primrose *(Primula). Middle:* Christmas rose *(Helleborus niger). Below:* Tuberose *(Polianthes).* Illustrations by J. Myers.

can look at the flower of our rose and compare it with that of a primrose *(Primula)*, a Christmas rose *(Helleborus niger)*, and a tuberose *(Polianthes tuberosa)* and realize that these four flowers are rather unrelated. Their floral anatomy and modes of fusion are so different that they need never confuse us again.

Just at this time the hundred years had nearly come to a close, and the day at last arrived for Briar Rose to be awaked from her long sleep. On this very day the prince started on his enterprise and on reaching the hedge of thorns, what was his surprise to find it covered with delicately-beautiful flowers.

Jacob and Wilhelm Grimm, "The Sleeping Beauty in the Wood"

When to Bloom

A tropical tree drops all its leaves as the season turns hot and dry but quickly reclothes itself in thick clusters of flowers. A snow crocus pushes yellowish buds through defrosting soil until they reach the weak light of a February morning. Although these displays occur on different continents, both will enjoy human admirers.

Most people welcome the sight of flowering plants after a drab, uncomfortable season and are willing to extend the display by playing with plant heredity. For example, some collectors prefer the older breeds of roses, extolling their hardiness, strong scents, and fine colors. Unfortunately, most of these old forms stay in flower for just two weeks each year. Go to your local nursery and you will find it's the finicky modern breeds that sell out because they promise "repeating roses" from late spring through autumn.

Where are flowers made in a plant? They seem to rise up magically out of the bare earth or, more often, appear to emerge out of formless masses of stems and leaves.

Branches, leaves, and flowers all derive from the same microscopic source. They are manufactured by the reduced tip of a stem. This tip is hard to see with the naked eye, as it is often covered by developing leaves during the growth season or by bud scales during periods of dormancy. The tip is properly known as the shoot meristem, a name derived from the Greek word *merizein,* "to divide." By cutting thin longitudinal sections of a shoot and staining them, botanists can locate the regions of most intensive cell division, since meristems are the dominant centers of growth in plant bodies. Meristems are composed of rapidly dividing cells called initials. The shoot tip of a flowering plant is always made of layered initials.

The outermost initials form the tunica. Tunica initials are small and, as their name suggests, well organized into tight but orderly layers, like the clothes covering your body. Most tunica initials divide to make plant skin and all the hairs, glands, and bud scales on the outer surface of the plant. Below the tunica is a mass of packed, swollen initials that make up the body, or corpus, of the shoot. Corpus initials divide at various angles and planes, adding bulk to the inner parts of the plant by forming pith and vein tissues. Working together, the tunica and corpus increase the length of the primary stem and manufacture all leaves and new lateral buds. A lateral bud usually appears at the base of each new leaf. This new bud waits patiently for the central stem to age until it is permitted to sprout by itself, forming its own leafy lateral branch.

The tunica-corpus spends most of its active life adding foliage and length to the stem, until it receives signals to change production. When these signals arrive, the cells in the shoot narrow and stretch so much that leaves and lateral buds are unable to form. It's then time for meristem initials to make flowers, flower stalks, and those flat, protective enveloping structures (bracts) that appear at the base of most flower buds or their stalks.

This transition from leafy stem to flowering branch is usually per-

Cross section of a leafy shoot showing the arrangement of tunica and corpus cells in the meristem. Environmental cues encourage the meristem to stretch and make flowers instead of leaves. Illustration by J. Myers.

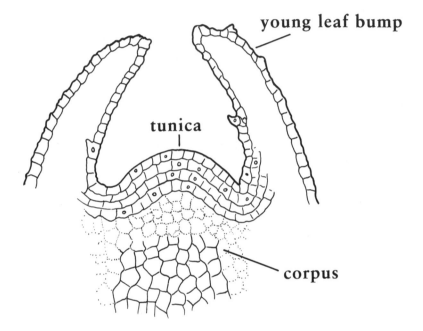

young leaf bump

tunica

corpus

manent, but there are two developmental extremes. Sex and death are linked in many of the plants sold as bedding annuals. Alyssums *(Alyssum)*, marigolds *(Tagetes)*, tufted pansies *(Viola cornuta)*, and zinnias *(Zinnia elegans)* convert all their shoots on every stem into flowering branches as they age over a single growing season. Unable to make leafy stems after reproducing, annuals die of old age even if the frost doesn't kill them. The life cycle of a zinnia, then, is similar in some ways to the lives of most insects or Atlantic salmon. That's why the only way to keep your favorite potted coleus *(Solenostemon rotundifolius)* alive indefinitely is to pick out every flowering stalk as soon as flower buds are visible. By removing a flowering stalk, you trigger the activity of lateral buds lower down on the stem, encouraging them to sprout and make new leafy stems.

At the other end of the spectrum are some Australian members of the myrtle family (Myrtaceae), especially shrubs such as bottlebrushes *(Callistemon)* and honey myrtles *(Kunzea)*. In these plants, a stem shoot converts itself into a flowering stalk, but the flowering stalk "reconverts" into a leafy stem shoot as soon as its flowers form fruits. No one is really sure how they do this. However, since these evergreen bushes usually bloom only once a year, the age of a bottlebrush branch can be determined by counting the number of hard fruit clusters on it, since each cluster represents one year of reproductive effort.

Most perennial herbs, shrubs, trees, and woody vines prefer an intermediate path to flowering. Secondary branches and twigs flower, fruit, and die, but primary stems and trunks are preserved to increase growth and extend the plant's life span. Many wildflowers return year after year because they keep their primary stems underground and poke only their seasonal secondary stems up into the air. The primary stems form rounded bulbs, pointed corms, lumpy tubers, or jointed, creeping structures known as rhizomes.

What signals "convince" a stem to make flowers? Although different plants grow at very different rates, we recognize that our local vegetation experiences peaks when the flowers of many different species bloom together. These annual miracles are so dependable that some people travel abroad just to enjoy the flowers of rural England in April, those of Mexico at Christmas, or those of South Africa in September.

Supernatural explanations for this phenomenon dominated imaginations until people began to experiment seriously with plants.

Cultures recognizing many gods or spirits assigned the annual flower show to some minor deity, often female. The ancient Greeks said that Princess Chloris became the goddess of flowers after the death of her mortal family. The Romans worshiped the nymph Flora, who exhaled petals and left flowers in her footprints. Her lively festival began on April 28 and continued for six days while celebrants played games, exchanged floral crowns, and invited prostitutes to undress in public. The Chinese Fairy-of-a-Hundred-Flowers was a strict bureaucrat who made sure that each blossom didn't open until its appropriate season. Japanese parents once told their children of Konohana-sakuya Hime (Princess Blossoms of the Trees), the lady who causes trees to bloom. A tribe of Koori people in Australia believed that flowers were a gift from the spirit of a powerful male shaman. Byamee received messages from the bees before he made the east wind blow the rain down the mountain to soften the hard ground and bring forth flowers that his bees could visit to make honey.

During the twentieth century, scientists began to understand how environmental cues stimulate flowering. Clearly, plants do not respond to external cues as quickly as animals do. Plants tend to require a rhythmic, repetitive cycle over a period of weeks or months before they make buds or become ready to open them. This period, in which a plant's physiology must follow the rhythm of the cue, is known as entrainment. Eventually, flower development becomes synchronized with one or more cues that are repeated every twenty-four hours. Plants that entrain to the same cue or cues show peak bloom around the same season, regardless of species.

Cues encourage plants to make new hormones and suppress old ones. In some plants, hormones may move to and from the meristem through the cells that link up to form the young veins. Since the early 1930s, plant physiologists have tried to isolate the hormone that turns leafy shoots into flowering stalks. They call this mystery chemical anthesin, but I don't think they'll ever isolate it. Research suggests that different plants require different hormone mixes to bloom. Some plants need gibberellins, a class of hormones that make cell walls stretch. Others are content with ethylene, surely one of the shortest compounds made by a plant ($CH_2=CH_2$). Ethylene is such a lightweight molecule that it may escape from one plant only to be absorbed by another. For example, ripe apples give off ethylene, and an old but effective trick to make bromeliads bloom is to lay a piece of apple on the plant and cover them with a paper bag for a short time.

In the Northern Hemisphere, most research on flowering has concentrated on the cue of light and dark cycles. Plants that respond directly to these cycles fall into two broad categories. Short-day plants form flower buds when synchronized to a cycle of reduced critical day length. Most short-day plants bloom in early spring or fall, often requiring fewer than fourteen hours of light each day. Cockleburs *(Xanthium strumarium)*, strawberries *(Fragaria)*, primroses *(Primula)*, a type of morning glory *(Ipomoea hederacea)*, and some breeds of tobacco *(Nicotiana)* are among the best studied of the short-day species.

Long-day plants require entrainment periods opposite those of their short-day cousins. They need daylight cycles that exceed some critical interval, usually blooming during summer. Lettuce *(Lactuca)*, most of the older breeds of potato *(Solanum tuberosum)*, barley *(Hordeum vulgare)*, and spinach *(Spinacia oleracea)* are among the best known of the long-day plants.

Light cues tend to explain some odd features of agriculture and horticulture in the Northern Hemisphere. For example, few people who live in farming regions where the summer season is brief ever see the bluish purple flowers of potatoes. That's because the wild ancestor of the domesticated potato evolved in the Andean highlands of South America, where longer days are the rule.

This also explains the proliferation of greenhouses with white-painted panes that shut out much of the sunlight. Within these greenhouses are tropical plants receiving fixed cycles of lamplight so they will bloom for winter sales. The beloved poinsettia *(Euphorbia pulcherrima)* is actually a short-day plant, but it won't survive long outdoors in a November freeze. It requires the same critical intervals of light its parents receive in Mexico, so the potted plants must be placed on an artificial cycle to produce Christmas flowers.

Green leaves "measure" the cycles of light and day. This is to be expected, since it is the green leaves that capture light energy to make sugars. During the 1930s, the humble cocklebur was subjected to a series of laboratory tests. Cockleburs are so tough that they will continue to live even if they are completely defoliated. However, a cocklebur can't flower if its leaves are removed during the critical cycle of short days. Scientists snipped pieces off cockleburs' leaves and learned that only one-eighth of a mature leaf on a stem was needed to receive the light cue and trigger the flowering process.

The response of leaves to light cycles seems to be very localized. *Kalanchoe blossfeldiana* is a succulent from Madagascar popular as a houseplant because it produces reddish flowers in winter. You can take a single plant and expose its leaves to two separate light cycles by shutting different branches of the plant in separate light boxes. Flowering stems will develop only near those leaves that receive a short-day cycle. Flowers won't form on shoots whose leaves are exposed to a long-day cycle.

Many plants require two periods of entrainment, and that often means exposure to two different cues at two different times. The first cue induces the development of flower buds, while the second cue encourages the buds to swell and open. Many trees and shrubs of the Northern Hemisphere respond to light cycles, producing their flower buds by late summer or autumn. The buds of lilacs *(Syringa)*, ornamental quinces *(Chaenomeles)*, and breeds of Asian magnolia are easy to find on autumn branches once the leaves have fallen, but they remain as buds until spring. Having produced their buds, the plants require entrainment by a cycle of low temperatures. After a couple of months of cold weather, they will be ready to swell and pop as days grow warmer.

There are problems with this double cycle when plants are grown outside their natural distribution. In the St. Louis area, fruit crops are more likely to be devastated by mild seasons than by frigid weather. Buds start expanding during extended thaws in early March, but opened flowers are slaughtered if hard frosts return unexpectedly in April. Cinema fans may remember the Sardinian peasants in the beautiful film *Padre Padrone,* whose hopes for a better life are crushed after a mild winter. They lose a year's olive crop when the early flowers are killed by a freeze so hard it turns a pitcher of goat's milk into sorbet.

Temperature cues are all some plants need to stimulate flowering. This helps explain how bulbs and tubers ready their flowers, since these underground stems lack aerial leaves for most of the year. Daffodils *(Narcissus),* tulips *(Tulipa),* hyacinths *(Hyacinthus),* and bulb iris *(Iris reticulata)* are descended from wild plants native to true Mediterranean zones. These regions experience hot, dry summers and cool, wet winters. The commercial bulbs gardeners purchase each autumn have already received their first hot cue. In some cases, the bulbs were dug up after the spring leaves withered and stored in a dark, dry warehouse for a week or more at 80–85 degrees Fahrenheit. That's all that is needed to simulate the natural conditions of clay and sandy soils baking under a Mediterranean sun. Cut a heat-treated bulb in half lengthwise and you'll find embryonic flower buds embedded inside.

Planted in the moist autumn soil of a temperate garden, a bulb begins to grow roots at its base. Although some grape hyacinths *(Muscari)* and hardy cyclamens *(Cyclamen)* will poke tough leaves

above the ground by late autumn, a bulb's flowers won't appear until
after a cold cue. Gardeners must remember that northern winters
are so severe that imported Mediterranean bulbs often delay flowering for weeks or months after their usual period of cold entrainment
has ended. In fact, most garden bulbs and tubers are bred from wild
ancestors that bloom best if they are entombed in frigid dirt for less
than twelve weeks. Take a winter holiday in a Mediterranean zone
and you may see that some native species complete their flowering
before spring. In Israel, for example, some *Crocus* species, the mandrake *(Mandragora officinarum)* and the red windflower *(Anemone coro-
naria)*, are flowers of mid- to late winter. The native vegetation of
southern California also evolved in a Mediterranean climate. Guides
to California wildflowers mention that some mariposa lilies *(Calochortus)*, blue dicks *(Dichelostemma)*, and mission bells *(Fritillaria)* start
flowering as early as February.

What about the vast majority of plants inhabiting the Tropics?
Since the earth tilts on its axis, both day length and temperature
should become less important as flowering cues as we approach the
equator. This is, in fact, the case. The plants of equatorial deserts, savannas, and monsoon forests appear to use water as a cue. Their entrainment reflects annual changes in the moisture level of thin soils.

It may seem like a contradiction, but some trees wait for the beginning or end of the dry season to bloom. Heavy, warm rains are
believed to promote fungus infestations and other flower diseases
while suppressing the movements of pollinators such as flying insects, birds, and bats. Since flowers are short-lived and lack breathing
pores on their petals and sex organs, they don't waste as much of a
tree's stored supply of water as one might think. Therefore, the dry
season in lowland coastal forests from Mexico south to Panama is
often the most colorful time of year. Trees belonging to the bean
(Fabaceae), trumpet vine (Bignoniaceae), dogbane (Apocynaceae),
cola nut (Sterculiaceae), and kapok (Bombacaceae) families deco-

rate the dry countryside in rich shades of yellow, ivory, purple, and hot red. Wet and dry cycles also entrain some shrubs and many smaller plants such as bromeliads and begonias. In western Africa, though, most orchid species ignore the expected pattern and flower during the wet season.

Some temperature cues can be expected even at the equator. Mountain ranges host many tropical plants at different altitudes. The higher the altitude, the more the temperature will fluctuate over the year, and many montane plants respond to the most subtle cues of low night temperature. Among these plants, the orchids receive the most attention, as the corsage industry demands precise results. Tropical slippers *(Paphiopedilum)*, moth orchids *(Phalaenopsis)*, Cooktown orchids *(Dendrobium)*, and miltonias *(Miltonia)* are just a few of the orchids that refuse to bloom without a cycle of cool nights.

Understandably, the flowering periods of trees in lowland equatorial rain forests have been less easy to predict, since the cycles of light, temperature, and rainfall seem so monotonous. Some trees appear to stay in flower almost all year once they've reached a certain size and girth. This is common in some members of the Brazil nut (Lecythidaceae) and cocoplum (Chrysobalanaceae) families. A feature of such trees is that they appear to stagger their buds, opening only a few each day to replace those that die or mature into fruit. They dribble their flowers over the year instead of massing them into one grand show.

In my opinion, the most surprising and dramatic of all flower shows belongs to vegetation that has evolved with fire. We usually think of fire as one the greatest of plant enemies, and in most environments, that is true. However, plants belonging primarily to Mediterranean woods and shrublands are often exceptions to this rule, as bush fires are incorporated into their long-term cycle of regeneration and reproduction. Before human beings altered the vegetation of southern Australia, southern California, southern Africa, and the

Mediterranean basin, lightning strikes made dry tinder go up in flames every few years.

Yes, a Mediterranean shrubland appears violated after a summer fire, but the majority of plants are probably still alive. Certain shrubs and trees will sprout from their stumps or rise again from "emergency" rootlike bodies known as lignotubers. The heat also cracks the coats of seeds buried a few inches down in dirt and duff, making them receptive to rainwater and germination. The cleansing fire frees bulbs and tuberous plants from unequal competition with overshadowing bushes. Within a few months, autumn and winter rains leach minerals from the burnt wood and ash, returning these essential nutrients to living roots in the soil. By spring, new growth and flowering become intense, often with rare species that may not have been seen for decades blooming in lush colonies. In Australia in particular, the spring following a bush fire provides the best excuse to take a "sick day" and search for unusual lilies, carnivorous sundews *(Drosera)*, orchids, and rare members of the daisy family.

For most Australians, the real sign that fires have stimulated optimal flowering is seen in the twenty-eight species of grass tree *(Xanthorrhoea)*. Grass trees look as if they are wearing hula skirts made of grass blades, but they are really asparagus-like plants thought to be related to our potted snake plants *(Sansevieria)*. In the absence of fire, the largest species of grass tree tend to bloom rather sluggishly and sporadically from late spring to autumn. The spring after a fire, though, each mature tree will have lost most of its "skirt" and its trunk may wear clots of hard, red resin. The center of the burnt plant grows a thick, erect stalk resembling a giant asparagus spear covered with black, bristly bracts. In some species, the flowering branch may be more than six feet tall, with some parts of the spear thicker than a man's arm. Grass trees are among the plants that hurry into bloom on exposure to ethylene, which must be released in great quantities as vegetation burns.

Which large plant lives after flowering? *Left:* The grass tree *(Xanthorrhoea)* of Australia blooms after bush fires and lives to bloom again and again. *Middle:* The maguey *(Agave)* of Mexico dies after blooming. *Right:* The silver-sword *(Argyroxiphium)* of Hawaii is a giant tarweed that dies after blooming. Illustrations by J. Myers.

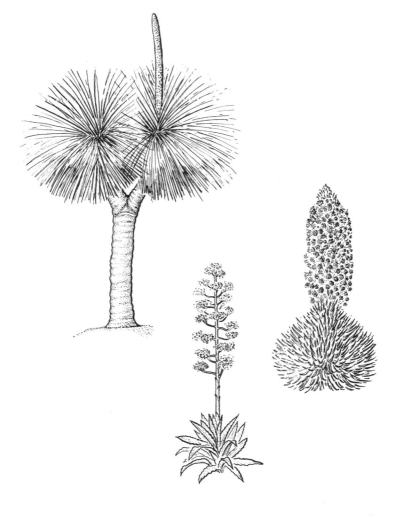

Surprisingly, the flowers of grass trees are small, cream-colored stars arranged in spirals along the dark spear by the hundreds of thousands. A spear may stay in bloom for weeks, perfuming the mid-morning air with scents evocative of honey and musty old books. Grass trees are living reminders of how dynamic a plant can be once it is committed to reproduction.

Has science spoiled the beautiful mystery of flowering with its experiments on tissues, hormones, and entrainment? In my opinion, the ancient Greeks would have been pleased with the results of modern scientific investigations. The name of Chloris, goddess of flowers, refers to the first green shoot, and the old myths say that she was helped by the Horae, the daughters of Zeus, who controlled the seasons and represented the hours in a day. As the developing meristem responds to cues of light, water, or temperature, the pagan faith in natural order is vindicated in every garden.

Let us crown ourselves with rosebuds,
before they be withered.

The Wisdom of Solomon 2:8

When to Die

Dying flowers have inspired poets since Homer likened the head of a fallen warrior to a poppy beaten down by rain. William Shakespeare, John Milton, William Blake, Robert Herrick, François de Malherbe, Henry A. Dobson, Oscar Wilde, and Edna St. Vincent Millay are just a few of the Western authors to mourn the fading rose. A bloom fallen from the bush is a metaphor for the untimely loss of a child, for the loss of love, courage, and joy.

In the East, the Japanese have a long history of *hanami,* or flower viewing. A party assembles before dawn to watch the unfolding of summer lotuses *(Nelumbo nucifera)* or braves the cold of a winter's day to admire the blooms on an ornamental apricot tree *(Prunus mume).* The Japanese believe that each season has flowers worth admiring, but they find the cherry blossom, or *sakura* (Prunus x yedoensis), most deserving of praise and attention. Television footage shows Japanese corporations closing early on April afternoons so that hourly workers, salarymen, and executives can all gather under the trees to drink beer and sing traditional songs.

Japanese loyalty to cherry trees is based in large part on the sheer brevity of the flowers, since a grove rarely stays in bloom for much more than a week. Buddhism and the samurai philosophy stressed that a few hours of glory made the impermanence and uncertainty of life worthwhile. Unlike westerners, the Japanese watch falling petals with a sense of approval and confidence.

If you want to find, grow, or study any living thing, you must first become familiar with its seasons of activity. That is why flowering plants are such important components in the science of phenology. The word *phenology* is derived from the Greek *phaino,* meaning "to show" or "to appear." A phenologist records when critical events occur during the life cycles of different species.

European scientists often insist that modern phenology grew from the writings of the Reverend Gilbert White (1720–1793), who kept records of the seasonal activities of plants and animals in Selborne, England. Calling White the Father of Phenology reflects another Western bias. The Japanese can point to more than five hundred years of written records on the flowering periods of cherry groves. Such information was of immediate interest to the aristocracy, imperial families, and certain monastic orders.

While East and West quibble about the symbolism inherent in a withered flower or who invented phenology, most botanists can agree on one thing. Specifically, we've observed that most flowers are designed to live a short time, but this brevity is probably as old as the first flowers. This is easiest to explain by returning to the "primitive" flowers introduced in chapter 1. Phenologists note that the vast majority of magnolia-like plants produce individual flowers that live for two to twelve days. Although it's true that some magnoliid plants of the Tropics remain in bloom for many months, most do so by replacing each withered flower with a fresh bud every few days.

For example, although the giant waterlily *(Victoria amazonica)* blooms constantly (at least until its pool or tributary stream dries up), each of its flowers is entitled to just two days of life. The huge bud that opens Friday at dusk will have deteriorated and collapsed by Saturday afternoon. Indeed, the flowers of many primitive species are on such a narrow, stereotyped regime that an individual blossom concludes all its business within twenty-four to thirty-six hours.

This evidence makes botanists suspect that modern flowering plants are descended from extinct ancestors that restricted their blossoms to brief moments of glory (less than two weeks of life). However, as genes have changed over millions of years, flower durability has grown increasingly diverse and flexible.

Compare the lives of flowers in different plant families and you must conclude that their fates are far more variable than in the saddest ballads of our favorite poets. Individual blossoms produced by members of the spiderwort (Commelinaceae), morning glory (Convolvulaceae), water hyacinth (Pontederiaceae), and damiana (Turneraceae) families are among the most ephemeral, rarely lasting as long as twelve hours. In contrast, the pineapple (Bromeliaceae), mint (Lamiaceae), and iris (Iridaceae) families contain some species whose flowers survive almost three days. Meanwhile, the blossoms of milkweeds (Asclepiadaceae), stonecrops (Crassulaceae), and elephant apples (Dilleniaceae) may live a full week.

At the other end of the spectrum are the flowers whose life span exceeds one or even two weeks. They are most likely to belong to some species in the rhododendron (Ericaceae), myrtle (Myrtaceae), or foam flower (Saxifragaceae) family. The orchid family must also be included within these longer-lived groups, as some of its species bear the Methusalehs of flowers. The record for longevity is held by *Grammatophyllum multiflorum,* an orchid of tropical Asia. When a bud of this plant opens in a greenhouse, it lives as long as nine months!

Flowers that live the longest tend to have the most heavily reinforced organs. All flowers wear a waxy cuticle, but those of tropical orchids are unusually thick. This helps slow the loss of water vapor and may help the blossom resist invasion by microbes that thrive during warm, rainy seasons. The veins in orchid flowers also tend to be unusually fibrous and "woody." Without this branching internal skeleton, the loose, succulent tissue in orchid flowers would be unable to hold such exaggerated shapes. It's no wonder that one of novelist Raymond Chandler's wealthier characters detested orchids, as the texture of the flowers reminded the old man of the clammy touch of human flesh.

The variation in life span of different flowers might seem capricious and unfair until the flowers are studied in their natural habitats. A blossom's long-term survival depends in large part on the resources the plant invests in response to environmental conditions. Stonecrops and cacti (Cactaceae) are most common in dry regions, but a stonecrop flower endures for more than nine days, while a cactus bloom is dead at three. A stonecrop flower rarely contains more than twenty-five organs that need to be pumped up with succulent tissue and dressed in a thick coat of wax. By comparison, a cactus flower consists of hundreds of individual parts, and there just isn't enough succulent tissue, fibrous veins, or thickened cuticle to make every organ strong and stiff.

Moreover, the life span of a flower often correlates with its breeding system and pollinators. Plants that pollinate themselves don't have to wait for the arrival of pollen from other plants. Flowers that belong to inbreeders self-pollinate within a matter of hours and often wilt long before the sun sets. On the other hand, the flowers of most tropical orchids demand cross-pollination. As you will see in a later chapter, the pollination of such flowers often depends on deceit. Therefore, some orchid blooms last for weeks, waiting for the arrival of an appropriate insect that is sufficiently "gullible" to fall for the orchid's trickery.

Flowers that are pollinated by a wide range of animals don't have to stay open for very long, either, since the environment is usually well stocked with many creatures willing to act as pollen taxis in exchange for a tasty reward. The white flower of a giant saguaro cactus *(Carnegiea gigantea)* lives for only one day and one night, but it is visited by many different bees, flies, wasps, moths, bats, and hummingbirds over those twenty-four hours.

Conversely, flowers pollinated exclusively by a few strong animals with chewing or piercing mouthparts require extra reinforcement and tend to outlast the flimsier blossoms of neighboring species. The cup gum *(Eucalyptus cosmophylla)* and yellow gum *(E. leucoxylon)* are two trees of southern Australia pollinated primarily by native songbirds. Some of these birds are larger than American robins and wield sharp, probing bills. The flower of a cup gum or yellow gum lives for three or four weeks, while the blossoms of eucalypts pollinated by small bees and flies die within twelve days.

The life span of an individual flower is often very different from the length of time its plant remains in bloom. It all depends on how a plant synchronizes the opening of its flower buds. The order in which buds open on a flowering stalk is rather predictable. Buds organized along a skinny, linear stem usually open in sequence from the bottom to the top. Since the lowest buds on the stalk were made first by the meristem, they open before the buds at the tip. Now, what about plants that pack their flower buds onto fat globes or onto flat-topped heads? The flowering head of a sunflower *(Helianthus)* or a common thistle *(Cirsium)* is really an expanded branch on which thousands of tiny individual flowers line the surface of a broad, green tray. In these plants, the meristem manufactures the outermost buds in the tray first. The buds massed along the rim open first, and flowering follows a continuous spiral progressing toward the center of the tray.

This means that the length of time a plant stays in bloom depends ultimately on how quickly its buds follow one another in bloom from bottom to top or from outside to inside. Some plants restrict this natural progression by halting the maturation of young buds until older flowers have withered and fallen. Plants on such a slow cycle of replacement may stay in bloom for weeks or months. Other plants, however, continue to pop open buds while the oldest flowers on a branch are still fresh and whole. Bud development is so rapid and well synchronized on such branches that dozens of flowers open within a few minutes of one another. These plants rarely remain in flower for more than a week.

According to the logic and observations of Al Gentry (1945– 1993), a curator at the Missouri Botanical Garden, the blooming regimes of most plants fall within one of two broadly overlapping categories. The Japanese cherry is a "big bang strategist." It remains in flower for a short time, offering minute quantities of pollen and nectar in each of its hundreds of thousands of tiny blossoms. The cherry tree attracts lots of different opportunistic insects that have rather short lives and attention spans but greedily mob mass-flowering trees for their fleeting rewards.

An example of the second category is the calabash tree *(Crescentia alata),* which stays in bloom for most of the year in lowland forests from Mexico to Costa Rica. It is a "steady state strategist," producing many buds on both its older branches and its trunk, but it opens only a few short-lived blooms each evening. The large, dark purple flowers appeal to a few bat species that are willing to visit the same groves each evening to take nectar from a few large, fresh flowers on each tree. The "steady state" plant is more likely to cater to more specialized, physically stronger, and longer-lived animals that have good memories and nomadic habits. These animals revisit the same plant every day because the plant replaces its spent flowers. An animal willing to move great distances daily for a limited but sustainable reward is like a fur trapper who is committed to rechecking his trapline. "Trapline" pollinators are especially useful as cross-pollinators in the Tropics, where there are usually thousands of different plant species in the same forest but only a few members of the same species per acre. This explains the daily dribble of open flowers produced by some rain forest trees, as mentioned in chapter 4. These species are pollinated consistently by birds, mammals, or even long-lived moths that are faithful foragers on select groups of trees.

The life span of an individual flower can also promote and exploit cross-pollination. For example, the organs in a flower often live for different lengths of time. Stamens and carpel tips (stigmas) may age differently even though they are packed into the same flower. On the first day that the bud of a mandrake flower *(Mandragora officinarum)* is open, the swollen tip of the carpel is ready to receive pollen, but the five stamens stay shut and "refuse" to release their grains. On the second day of the floral life span, the neck of the carpel twists until the dried-up tip of the carpel hangs upside-down. At this point, the female organ is no longer able to receive fresh pollen, but the stamens are ready to stretch out, open, and release their grains. This means that no matter how slow or sloppy a bee may be, she can never pollinate a mandrake carpel with pollen produced in the same flower. When female organs in a flower mature and collapse before the male organs do, botanists say that the blossom is protogynous. That's a Greek term that means the females are ready first.

Cross-pollination is also encouraged when male organs develop before female organs. When the flower buds of the death camas *(Zigadenus nuttallii)* open, the six anthers are ready to brush incoming pollinators with fresh pollen, but the three carpel tips can't receive pollen. The three carpel necks are clenched together and their stigma surfaces are closed. Over the next couple of days, the anthers dry up and snap off, and any remaining pollen grains left in the flower will contain dead or dying sperm. At this time, the carpel necks curve apart and their tips "pucker up" and expand to secrete chemicals that will help them process any incoming pollen introduced by tiny bees and rather large flies that have been visiting other flowers. Botanists describe the death camas as protandrous, a term referring

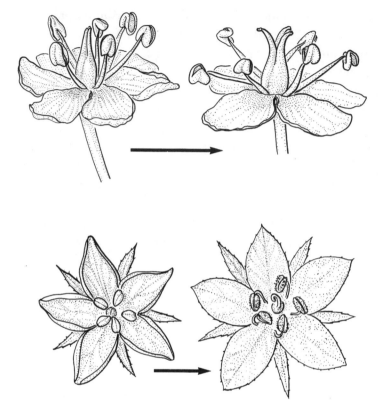

Above: On the first day the death camas *(Zigadenus nuttallii)* is open, the anthers release pollen but the three styles are closed and locked together. A day or so later, the anthers dry up, but the styles bend apart to receive incoming pollen. *Below:* On the first day the petals are open, the stigma of the mandrake *(Mandragora)* is receptive to pollen, but the anthers are pressed shut around the style neck. On the second day, the stigma is dried up and has curled upside-down, but the anthers release pollen. Illustrations by J. Myers.

to the fact that the male organs "ripen" and release pollen before the female organs are ready.

This means that the same bisexual (perfect) flower can go through both a male and a female phase by simply staggering the jobs performed by stamens and carpels. The male and female phases are isolated from each other and can last for different lengths of time. Remember, fruits and seeds are expensive to make and protect, so the flowers of some long-lived plants devote more time to fathering seeds than to accepting pollen from potential mates. Acacia flowers *(Acacia),* for example, are protogynous, but the female phase lasts for only a fifth of the flower's life span. In some acacias, only one in five hundred flowers will set a seedpod. When it comes to pollen, some plants find it more blessed to give than to receive.

Even plants with male and female flowers on the same branch can further their chances for cross-pollination by staggering the opening of blossoms. In most members of the jack-in-the-pulpit (Araceae) family, male and female flowers occupy different positions on the same fleshy stalk. Male and female flowers usually mature and open on different days, lowering the chance that a carpel will receive pollen from a male flower on the same stalk.

Sometimes the life of a flower or of a stalk packed full of blossoms is independent of a prescribed blooming season. Weed species often produce several generations in one season when growing conditions are good. Every gardener has seen how the bud on a dandelion *(Taraxacum officinale)* can survive both late spring freezes and summer droughts, opening when conditions turn mild and moist. Dandelions, shepherd's purse *(Capsella bursa-pastoris),* and plantains *(Plantago)* are just a few of the species that colonize lawns and formal beds without our permission. The weedy patches we uproot in autumn are often the grandchildren of plants ignored in spring.

Many desert wildflowers in the United States are annuals that complete their life cycles only through the largesse of heavy seasonal storms. Each new generation of seeds remains dormant until the drought breaks. Outside Tucson, drip irrigation installed on the grounds of the Arizona-Sonora Desert Museum explains why new generations of desert daisies, poppies, and mallows bloom on while just across the road, the trails in Saguaro National Park are lined with dead, brittle stalks.

Subtle changes in the environment may encourage erratic flowering in larger, woodier plants. While collecting specimens in the tropical Americas, Dr. Gentry was unable to predict when some species in the trumpet vine family (Bignoniaceae) would bloom. He called such trees and woody vines "intermittent big bangs," as they could flicker briefly into flower more than once a year without obvious cues.

The flowering habits of a single species may also change radically over its natural distribution. Regard the creeping guinea vine *(Hibbertia scandens)* of Australia, which produces flat, yellow flowers resembling large golden coins, or guineas. It's a welcome sight in the spring woods of temperate southeastern Australia, where hikers photograph its flowers from mid- to late spring. When the same species colonizes sand dunes along the tropical northern coast, it is even more generous with its golden coins. These vines bloom during the austral spring, as usual, but then they provide a second, independent display after the hot, dry summer yields to the cooler, wetter days of autumn.

Likewise, the mandrakes of Europe bloom in autumn. Cross the Mediterranean and visit Israel in winter and you will see these mysterious herbs offering their silky, purple bouquets through Christmas and the dreary days of midwinter. Differences in local climates must play an important role, but research has been meager, leaving many unanswered questions. Botanists are still not sure whether changes in flowering seasons affect the life spans of individual blossoms.

What would happen, though, if the "bloom and die" tactics of an annual weed were combined with the slower, massive growth of a shrub or a tree? The result would be plants that botanists call mono-carpic perennials. This long-winded term refers to plants that live for many years (they show perennial growth) but flower and fruit only once in their lives (they are monocarpic). Puberty is ultimately fatal to a monocarpic perennial. The plant uses up its cell divisions to make flowering branches, literally burning up the resources it has stored for years to enrich fruit and seed. Sex is an explosive Pyrrhic victory in monocarpic perennials.

Some members of the carrot (Apiaceae), daisy (Asteraceae), lily (Liliaceae), and partridge pea (Caesalpiniaceae) families are mono-carpic perennials. The largest plants to flaunt this lifestyle are usually found in deserts and tropical belts. For example, the giant silver-swords *(Argyroxiphium)* of Hawaii are really huge tarweeds that sur-vive only at high altitudes. One species actually grows in the arid cinder cones of the Haleakala Crater. Monocarpic perennials tend to have set flowering seasons, but in any given population only a few plants will bloom each year. For example, to see a couple of Hale-akala silverswords in flower, you must visit Haleakala National Park in mid-July.

The most popular of the monocarpic perennials are probably the maguey *(Agave),* zacate *(Nolina),* and cabuya *(Furcraea)* plants from the hotter, drier regions of the Western Hemisphere. These darlings of desert gardens are often called century plants, even though most species bloom and die within ten to twenty years. Magueys are the most favored by humans, as they are sources of such Mexican drinks as the beerlike pulque and the potent, refined tequila. The manufac-ture of pulque and tequila requires that different things be done to two different maguey species, but the results are the same. To make an alcoholic drink, each plant must be killed just as it is preparing to bloom.

When magueys are ready to flower, they convert all the resources stored in their thick trunks into watery sugars and vitamins. These nutrients would normally fuel cell division and nourish young seeds. Tequila is made by cutting down the whole maguey trunk before it can bloom, roasting it, and then shredding the cooked pieces to remove the three or four quarts of sweet sap. The liquid is then fermented and distilled.

The next time you mix a tequila sunrise, submarino, bloody bull, monja loca, or granada punch, consider the central ingredient. It came from a mighty plant just on the verge of blooming for the first and last time. Its reproductive energy has been turned into the chemical blaze of alcohol. The Reverend White would have been shocked by such a carnal exploitation of phenology, but a little tequila might please the Japanese still toasting the drifting cherry petals.

CHAPTER 6

I am passionately fond of the Rose . . . when the gray
dawn breaks sadly over the wood, and my eyes are closing
in sleep, then she will open her breast, and the Bee will be
welcomed with the dainty pollen from the lips of her lover.
　J. J. Grandville, "History of a White Blackbird,"
　　in *Scenes from the Public and Private Lives of Animals*

Of Pollen, Perpetrators, Politics, and Piety

Pollen is so important to the function of a flower that a rosebud develops its pollen grains weeks before the petals open. Pollen is manufactured while the bud is a blunt, greenish blob barely visible to the human eye.

The process begins with formation of the anther sacs, which will contain one to thousands of large, plump pollen-mother cells. In most cases, each pollen-mother cell goes through two divisions to form a quartet of young pollen grains. The stages of division in a pollen-mother cell are usually so precise and dependable that scientists dissect, squash, and stain them for chromosome research. During the earliest phases of division, pollen chromosomes are so large and well formed that they are easy to count, measure, and examine for defects or breakage.

Some species vary the number of divisions needed to make pol-

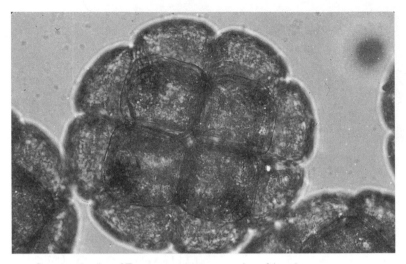

Compound pollen of *Zapoteca amazonica*, a member of the mimosa
family, showing twelve grains united to form one platelike unit.
Photograph by P. Bernhardt.

len grains. This is especially common in members of the mimosa
family (Mimosaceae), as all grains in the same anther sac remain interconnected at maturity, like an oblong tray of freshly baked buns.
For example, every pollen-mother cell in the anther sacs of a hedge
wattle *(Acacia paradoxa)* undergoes three consecutive divisions to
make a compound clump of eight pollen grains. Pollen-mother cells
inside the buds of some rain trees *(Albizia)* endure five divisions to
make thirty-two pollen grains in all.

After cell division stops, every new pollen grain must protect itself. In most cases, the young grain surrounds itself with a protective
wall it manufactures out of coiled tubes made of cellulose. However,
a grain enclosed in a cellulose wall is only half finished. The final
architecture of each pollen grain is determined by a layer of tissue in
the anther sac known as the tapetum.

Tapetum, derived from the Latin word *tapete,* meaning "carpet" or

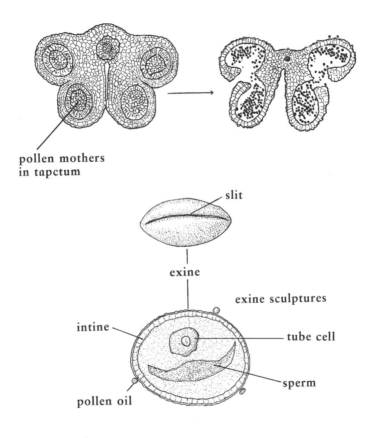

pollen mothers
in tapetum

slit

exine

exine sculptures

intine

tube cell

pollen oil

sperm

Above: Most anthers contain four anther sacs in which pollen-mother cells are nourished by tapetum tissue. The tapetum is all used up by the time the sacs split open and release new pollen grains. *Below:* Typical lily-type pollen grain with a wrinkled outer wall and a single slit from end to end. Inside the grain are one sperm cell and one tube cell. Illustrations by J. Myers.

"tapestry," is an apt name for this layer of tissue, which carpets the surface of young pollen grains. The tapetum feeds the young pollen grains but also builds their outer walls. The most important product of the tapetum is a natural plastic called sporopollenin, a unique substance that biochemists believe is similar to vitamin A. Sporopollenin is a true self-repeating polymer, like Teflon, and it is just as tough as any industrial plastic. The tapetum attaches this plastic to the cellulose wall of each grain, building a harder, sculpted outer wall. Therefore, each pollen grain is like a house constructed with two different but interconnected walls. The inner wall (intine) is made of light, papery cellulose, and the outer wall (exine) is made of dense, rigid plastic.

The surface pattern of the outer wall is based on a series of plastic rods the tapetum attaches to the grain much as ornamental pins might be affixed to a pincushion. The rods of the pollen grains of monocotyledon flowers are tipped with narrow, rounded heads that link together to form squiggly ridges. Under the microscope, a monocot's pollen grain resembles a planet covered by a continuous Great Wall of China or a human brain covered with wrinkles and convolutions.

The rods on the pollen grains of dicotyledon flowers are often very different. Each rod is usually tipped by a broad, flattened structure resembling a nail or tack head. Sometimes the nail heads fail to fuse with one another and the surface of the grain resembles a cratered moon. These nail heads may be further decorated with minute hooks, points, and jagged crusts. Such sharp structures have been shown to help attach the grain to the hairs or plumes of a pollinator. Within the daisy (Asteraceae) and mallow (Malvaceae) families, the pollen grains appear to be so wickedly armed as to resemble medieval weapons or instruments of torture.

The tapetum has one last gift to give to pollen grains before it dries up and dies. It releases oil globules that fill craters and adhere

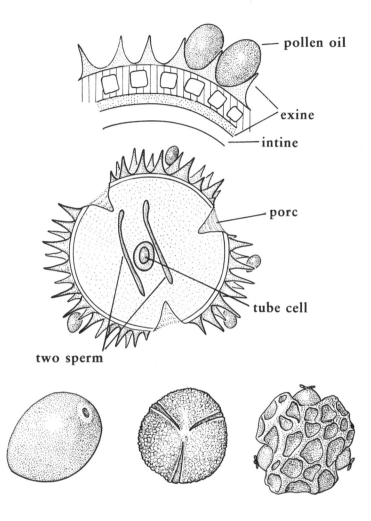

Above: Cross section of the wall of a daisy pollen grain.
Middle: Exterior and interior of a daisy pollen grain
with pores and extra sperm cell. Below: Variation in
pollen grains. Left to right, Festuca grass, beech (Fagus),
Barnedesia.

to surface ridges. Greasy grains appear to have been inventions of the first flowering plants. The pollen of the most primitive flowers remains oily, but the grains made by cone-bearing trees (pines, spruce, cycads, etc.) are always grease free.

The pollen oil of many flowering plants contains pigments. Although we expect to see pollen in various shades of yellow, orange, and cinnamon, other tints are common. A bee that has spent the morning visiting dog roses carries greenish grains on her hind legs. The pollens of squills *(Scilla)* and mignonettes *(Reseda odorata)* are blue. Black grains are found in lesser bindweed *(Convolvulus arvensis)*, and tobacco flowers *(Nicotiana)* have tan pollen. In contrast, the greaseless pollen grains of pines and spruces lack pigment, appearing white to the human eye.

Now you know the real reason why some florists "castrate" lilies by nipping off their anthers before selling them. The flowers' colorful, greasy pollen would smear and stain a white Communion dress, wedding gown, or tablecloth.

Many botanists think that pollen color is important to successful reproduction. Some pollinating animals are attracted to this visual cue, and, more important, the tint might act as a sunblock, screening out ultraviolet rays that would sterilize the sperm inside each grain. Oil globules have other duties as well. Some retain scent chemicals that give pollen grains distinctive odors to attract bees. It is also suspected that globules act as water-repellent "oil slickers," since water vapor and raindrops make pollen grains swell and burst prematurely. Most important, these oil molecules are dense, adhesive, and not easy to digest. When a dead pollinator is examined with a scanning electron microscope, it is easy to see how this oil-based "glue" has cemented pollen grains to the smooth beak of a bird, the outer shell of a beetle, or even the shingled scales on the wing of a moth or butterfly. The sheer stickiness of tapetum glues must be a major factor in pollen transport, considering the strength of the breeze made by the blurring whir of pollinators' wings and the simple fact that such animals often encounter head winds as they dart from flower to flower.

A pollen grain loses water before it leaves the anther, as the grain must lighten its load to ride easily on a breeze or cling to the body of an animal. When the "dry" grain lands on the stigma of a carpel, it must absorb water before it can release its sperm by sprouting a pollen tube. How do fluids enter and exit a pollen grain that is locked inside two complex, protective walls?

Fortunately, most pollen grains come equipped with a number of sculpted slits, pores, or both that link the living protoplasm inside them with the outer atmosphere. A slit or pore can rid the grain of unwanted fluid, allow it to absorb moisture from a stigma, and then offer an escape hatch to a sprouting pollen tube. Pollen pores are often beautifully reinforced with nipplelike rims, transparent "helmets," or pinched "collars."

Just as the surface patterns of pollen grains differ between monocot and dicot flowers, so do the prescribed numbers of sculpted slits or pores. Usually, only one pore or one slit is found on the pollen grain of a monocot. A slit may extend from pole to pole, so monocot grains often resemble deflated footballs or creased loaves of bread.

The pollen grains of dicotyledons are far more variable in shape, and one to many openings may be found on the grain's surface, depending on the species. The pollen of the dog rose, for example, forms a ball that bears three short, equidistant slits. The triangular grains of eucalypts have three pores. The grains of many members of the mint family resemble wagon wheels marked with six spokelike slits. The pollen grain of an Australian banksia bush *(Banksia)* is either bullet or kidney shaped and has only two pores. The spherical grain of *Pupalia,* a genus of tropical pigweeds, has more than a dozen pores, each one rimmed and reinforced by a six-pointed star.

Pollen grains vary greatly in size. The grains of forget-me-nots

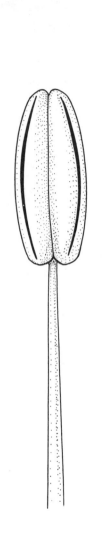

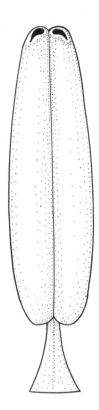

Left: A short anther that releases pollen through slits is often attached to a longer filament. *Right:* In contrast, a long, inflated anther that releases pollen through pore tips is often attached to a shorter filament.

(Myosotis) and gromwells *(Lithospermum)* are the smallest in the plant kingdom, measuring barely more than 5 microns in length. That's a bit longer than the larger rod-shaped bacteria. In contrast, the pollen grains of hibiscus plants *(Hibiscus)* and other members of the mallow family may reach 200 microns in length. Individual pollen grains of *Hibiscus* species can be seen with the naked eye if placed under a very strong light.

In most flowers, by the time an anther sac opens, each pollen quartet has broken apart into four separate grains. However, there are some exceptions to the rule. The flowers of flaxes *(Linum)*, rhododendrons *(Rhododendron)*, sundews *(Drosera)*, southern heaths *(Epacris)*, Winter's bark *(Drimys)*, and trees of the genus *Zygogynum* keep their pollen quartets together, releasing them in their original packets of four. Members of the mimosa family take togetherness one step further, uniting grains in units of four, eight, twelve, sixteen, and so on.

The flowers of most milkweeds and orchids unite *all* the pollen grains together in one anther sac. Each pollen lump, or pollinium, consists of thousands to millions of grains forming a structure so large it can be seen without any magnification. The shapes of pollinia differ from species to species. Their forms have been compared to those of pills, scaly wafers, and legs of mutton. Pollinia are so large and ungainly that the flower comes equipped with special structures that glue, plug, or stamp them right onto the body of the pollinator. This means that in some orchids, all the fertile seeds ripening in a flower's ovary have the same father, as they were all fertilized with sperm from a single pollinium.

How does pollen leave the interior of the protective anther sac and gain exposure to the air? I can illustrate the concept with a dramatic family anecdote. Years ago, my father had coronary artery bypass surgery. A few days later, he coughed so hard that the sutures in his chest opened. His surgeon called this splitting open of the chest thoracic dehiscence. Similarly, botanists call the splitting open of anthers staminal dehiscence. As layers of tissue in the anther dry out naturally, internal pressure causes the sacs to split open along designated weak points or sutures. In tulip and magnolia anthers, this drying process is so violent that the whole stamen curls up, wringing pollen out of the sacs. The sacs of some other flowers dry out from bottom to top so that the pollen is squeezed out of the anther like gel, cream, or paste from a roll-up tube.

The pollinia of some orchid species of the genus *Catasetum* are under such intense pressure that they are literally shot out of the anther when the sensitive tips of the columns are touched by a bee. Tickle a column of one of these flowers with your pinky and you'll feel the pollinia whack hard against your fingernail.

In most cases, though, pollen release is a more gentle process in which the anther sutures separate by means of a snap-lock mechanism similar to the clasps found on an old-fashioned pocketbook. The pollen grains stay inside the shallow anther sacs, like coins stuffed into an overfilled purse. Insects may use their mouthparts or clawed feet to scratch or pry the grains out of the open sacs, or breezes may carry them away. In some flowers, though, the sutures will close up again or refuse to open if the environment is too wet or frosty. This prevents the complete wastage of pollen sperm in bad weather. If pollen is kept cool, dry, and protected within a microenvironment such as the anther sac, the sperm remains viable for a long time. Experiments with low temperatures have kept some lily pollen grains alive for a decade. Expensive medical techniques used to store the semen of men and bulls also work well on pollen, but I've kept mistletoe pollen alive for four months just by storing it in a clean, dry vial in the kitchen freezer.

Damp climate may be one reason why the flowers of flax lilies *(Dianella)*, shooting stars *(Dodecatheon)*, blueberries *(Vaccinium)*, potatoes *(Solanum)*, and cassias *(Cassia)* refuse to expose their pollen to the atmosphere. Their tubular anthers are inflated, retaining the pollen grains inside deep, dry interior chambers. When the anther is "ripe," it opens one or two holes at its narrow tip. The pollen escapes when the anther is shaken vigorously and grains bounce out of sac pores like pepper particles out of a pepper shaker. This is accomplished by a bee or a hover fly *(Volucella)*, which grabs the anther with its feet and uses the flight muscles in its thorax to vibrate grains out of the anther's pores. An observer can often hear the high-pitched buzz made by the insect's muscles and see the anther "ejaculate" pollen in discrete, smoky puffs. It's all a matter of vibrating at the right pitch. I make the anthers of tomato *(Lycopersicon)* and chili *(Capsicum)* flowers release their pollen by touching them with a vibrating C-register tuning fork.

Although pollen sperm is usually short-lived, the wall of the pollen grain will last indefinitely if it escapes attack by microbes. Pollen grain walls can resist temperature extremes, the slow but continuous pressure of layers of mud, and many acids. In 1948, a Russian expedition to the North Pole found a frozen mammoth on Taimyr Peninsula. Even though this beast perished 30,000 years ago, scientists were able to determine what it ate before it fell into a crevasse. The pollen in its stomach suggested that it died in early spring after grazing on timothy grass *(Phleum)* and browsing on the blooming twigs of birch *(Betula)* and willow *(Salix)* trees.

Of course, pollen grains are among the most common "microfossils" in some soils and quarry deposits, and some recognizable forms date back to dinosaur days. Since the distinctive anatomy of the outer wall is fixed by plant genes, you can identify most pollen grains down to the level of family (and often down to genus) once you learn the appropriate terminology and learn how to clean, section, and observe the grains.

Serious attempts to draw and classify pollen began early in the nineteenth century. Major advances were made around World War I as Scandinavian botanists found that fossil pollen survived the acidic water of peat bogs. These early scientists would have been astounded to see how their studies benefit people today.

For example, fossil pollen gives a paleontologist a useful profile of how the vegetation of an area has changed over millennia. Today, some mining companies make a point of examining the fossil pollen in drill cores. The grains of extinct plants may offer clues to the depth and location of different grades of peat, petroleum, and coal.

Pollen identification also helps people who suffer from allergies and other respiratory ailments, but I will address this topic more fully in a later chapter. For the moment, I'll concentrate on some of the more interesting aspects of pollen classification.

Although honey and pollen are stored in separate wax cells in the same beehive, worker bees can't help dropping some pollen grains into their honeycombs. Therefore, the purity of commercial honey is tested by centrifuging out and identifying grains found in jars of honey from the supermarket. When there is truth in advertising, a bottle of "pure" clover honey will be free from heavy deposits of pollen from dandelion or apple blossoms. The expensive spice known as Spanish saffron *(Crocus sativus)* is examined under the microscope to make sure that the precious colored powder has not been adulterated with cheap substitutes such as the golden pollen and anthers of safflowers *(Carthamus)* or cotton thistle *(Onopordum acanthium)*. Are you suspicious of the origin of the dried plant materials used to stuff your cushions and furniture? Examination of the pollen clinging to the stuffing fibers can help determine their origins.

Pollen identification may enter the forensic laboratory when an act of murder, rape, or suicide takes place outdoors. Rare types of fossil pollen mixed with the dried mud on a suspect's shoes or clothing might help indicate whether he or she visited the site of a recent crime. Samples on the clothing of the deceased may help determine whether the body was moved.

In chapter 4, you learned that certain plants obey a flowering calendar. Since pollen is released when flowers open, pollen grain identification can also help establish the date of death for a body found in a field or forest. For example, if a decaying corpse is discovered in a woodland during autumn but clothing remnants are saturated with the pollen of resident willows or birches, the body has been there at least since last spring.

On occasion, pollen has mortified bureaucrats. Perhaps you remember the U.S. Department of State's reports of "yellow rain" back in the early 1980s? These reports insisted that people in refugee camps in Southeast Asia were being subjected to aerial bombardment with an unidentified yellowish chemical. Eleven samples of the material, found staining rocks and leaves in Thailand and Laos, were rushed to laboratories in the United States.

The funny thing about those yellow stains was that they seemed to be filled with particles resembling pollen. A full analysis was published in the journal *Nature* in 1984 by Dr. Joan Nowicke, a pollen specialist at the Smithsonian Institution, and Matthew Meselson, a Harvard biologist. The yellow rain turned out to be a mixture of pollens from tropical trees and wildflowers in various stages of decomposition.

"Aha!" said some people in the State Department and at the Pentagon. "The communists mix pollen with poison to give the poison extra ballast when it is sprayed from airplanes." However, the samples contained no pollen from agricultural sources. They were mixtures of grains from tropical Asian forests. It was unlikely that communists were climbing trees just to comb pollen from yellow blossoms of elephant apples *(Dillenia)*.

In fact, the samples looked suspiciously like the dung of two species of large tropical honeybee. Tropical honeybees have a unique way of lowering the temperature of their hot, busy hives. At some time during the day, a chemical message runs through the colony encouraging thousands of workers to leave their combs and fly up into the sky. Once airborne, the bees defecate. This lowers the temperature of the hive, since each bee reduces her body mass by excretion. Entomologists call this a "mass cleansing flight," and the rain of yellow drops can last for a few minutes. Bees swallow pollen whole, so there are plenty of empty but recognizable grains in a sample of their dung.

The color of the "yellow rain" came, of course, from the indigestible oil coating the pollen grains. Since the refugee camps were set up in forest clearings, the people and property in the camps were spattered with greasy dung that ordinarily would have fallen on the blanket of canopy leaves. It now appears that the trace amounts of toxins detected in the samples came from threads of fungi that were scavenging these tropical wastes.

Of course, information gathered from pollen analysis can't answer every question about the age and origin of things. That is because grains produced by closely related plants are often so similar to one another in size, shape, and sculpting that it is impossible to identify isolated grains down to the level of species. For this reason, I am highly suspicious of reports claiming that pollen grains found on the Shroud of Turin help prove its authenticity.

Dr. Max Frei removed about two hundred pollen grains from the surface of the shroud in 1973 by touching the surface of the shroud with sticky tape to snatch up particles of plant debris. This is a fine technique that I've used to remove pollen from the head and breast feathers of live birds (my birds were released unharmed). When Frei concluded his analysis, he insisted that some of his samples matched the pollen of thirty-nine species found in "the lands of the Bible." Is this really compelling evidence of the authenticity of the shroud?

Remember that the church has encouraged the veneration of holy relics with fresh flowers. Worshipers who left bouquets on or near the shroud also would have left a history of pollen contaminating the exposed cloth as the stamens dried. In addition, there is an ancient belief that linen can be protected from pests if it is stored with strong-smelling herbs and sweet flowers. Generations of Italian caretakers may have tried to protect this beloved cloth by secreting both local wildflowers and imported herbs in its folds.

Israel is just one small country within the Mediterranean basin. The shroud came to Italy by way of Turkey, and both of these are Mediterranean countries. Shouldn't we expect the pollens on the shroud to come from similar types of domesticated and wayside flowers that are well distributed through this vast region? After all, it *is* the Shroud of Turin, not the Shroud of Brooklyn.

When Frei identifies pollen grains of scabiosas *(Scabiosa)*, hill rues *(Haplophyllum)*, or rock roses *(Helianthemum)*, I accept his analysis. However, there are 80 species of scabiosa, 70 species of hill rue, and a whopping 110 species of rock rose in the Asian, African, and European continents surrounding the Mediterranean. How can such superficial techniques distinguish between the pollens of Israeli and Italian rock roses?

One disciple has been thrilled by Frei's identification of pollen of prickly tumbleweed *(Gundelia tournefortii)*. These plants grow around Jerusalem and may be the rolling things mentioned in the Psalms and the Book of Isaiah. The problem is that the pollen grains of *Gundelia tournefortii* look exactly like those of thousands of other species in the daisy family. This tumbleweed also grows all the way from southwestern Asia through Iran (remember the Turkish connection?). Therefore, as useful as pollen analysis can be, I am forced to conclude that the only relevant information regarding the Shroud of Turin must come ultimately from forensic laboratories that can establish the age of the cloth and tell us how the facial and body images were produced.

Pollen is such an important and fascinating component of life on this planet that it really deserves a popular book of its own. In the next chapter, you will see how pollen grains are permitted to complete their most important function.

CHAPTER 7

There is a garden in her face
 Where roses and white lilies grow;
A heavenly paradise is that place
 Wherein all pleasant fruits do flow.
There cherries grow which none may buy,
 Till "cherry-ripe" themselves do cry.
  Thomas Campion, "There Is a Garden in Her Face"

Fruitful Unions

The manufacture of pollen is only half the story of the sexual assembly line inside the rosebud. While anthers box up sperm, ovary chambers are lined with those unfertilized seeds called ovules. Each ovule is connected to a stalk of placental tissue that attaches it to some inner portion of the ovary. The way in which stalks attach ovules to ovary chambers differs within plant families, so botanists use placentation to help classify plants.

Every human has a belly button to mark where an umbilical cord once connected him or her to the placenta in the mother's womb. A mature seed wears a similar scar that shows where the stalk once connected it to a part of the ovary chamber. The "belly button" of a seed is properly known as the hilum. *Hilum* is Latin for "trifle," as the hilum appears to be just a trifling scar on the hard seed coat. It's easy to see the narrow or eye-shaped hilum on a kidney bean or a black-eyed pea. The hilum on a loose, dry seed is often more functional than the human navel. In some seeds, the hilum acts as a duct, channeling rainwater to the dormant embryo and encouraging the seed to sprout.

To make a seed, an ovule must first contain an egg cell. Egg production starts long before the flower bud opens. Every healthy developing ovule inside a flower bud contains a large cell called the megasporocyte buried under layers of protective and nutritive tissues. The word *megasporocyte* refers to a producer of big reproductive cells. In most ovules, the megasporocyte starts the developmental sequence required to make an egg.

The megasporocyte undergoes two divisions to make a chain of four interlinked cells. Three of the cells shrivel and die, but the fourth thrives and expands, undergoing a series of internal divisions to form an embryo sac. Embryo sacs differ greatly in different species of flowering plants, but they all share one thing in common. Once development is complete, every embryo sac must contain at least one living egg cell.

By the time the flower opens, every anther should contain pollen grains and every ovule should contain an embryo sac. During the life span of the open flower, the tip of the carpel (stigma) must be ready to receive and process incoming pollen. When a lucky grain adheres to this stigma tip, it absorbs sugar water released by the stigma's surface. The grain swells up and sprouts a pollen tube that pushes itself into the stigma and grows down the carpel's neck, searching for ovules hidden in the ovary. The pollen tube contains sperm cells that left the inside of the pollen grain when the tube sprouted.

If a pollen grain lands on the right stigma at the right time, it may absorb sugar water within twenty minutes of contact. Pollen grains of wild tomato *(Lycopersicon peruvianum)* and Canola *(Brassica)* plants sprout tubes within two to three hours of drinking up this stigma fluid.

Pollen tubes are made of callose, another plant plastic, which is formed by a complex of sugar molecules. In some plants, the callose tube penetrates the stigma quite violently, puncturing the skin that lines the surface and then drilling through layers of tissue. In other species, the tube appears to search for narrow, moist gaps between the cells of the stigma's skin. These gaps act as "docking sites" for pollen tubes.

It's relatively easy for a pollen tube to grow through the neck (style) of a carpel, since the central cells lining the neck are usually soft and loosely packed. The necks of rhododendron and azalea pistils don't even bother with a cellular lining. Their pollen tubes grow gracefully through canals filled with soft jelly.

A pollen tube makes rapid progress as it grows down the carpel neck, even though most tubes grow in fits and starts. They progress nicely for a few micrometers, but then they must stop and rest, as tube growth uses up energy and callose. While at rest, the tip of the pollen tube puffs up to shelter the sperm complex. Under the microscope, a pollen tube looks like a string of unequally spaced hollow beads. The beads are callose plug "blips" that testify to spots where the tube stopped growing and allowed its sperm to rest. How long must an ovule wait for sperm? Tube growth is so fast in Canola flowers that a few lucky tubes reach ovules within only six hours of the pollen grain hitting the stigma. The pollen tube of a wild tomato can reach an ovule sixteen hours after pollination.

To most people, a carpel sitting smack in the center of a flower looks like a sitting duck for incoming pollen. After all, the carpels of a rose are completely surrounded by ring after ring of stamens. You'd think that a rose would be self-pollinated every time a breeze tickles the ripe anthers or the hairy foot of a bee tracks grains across the center of the blossom. That's why botanists once believed that stamens "married" the carpels in the same flower.

In fact, self-pollination can lower the quality of seed production in many plants, as it is just another form of inbreeding and can lead to genetic problems similar to those found in animals that are the result of incestuous mating. Consequently, most plants employ a couple of mechanisms to discourage self-pollination.

You've already seen how a few of these mechanisms work. Oaks *(Quercus)*, birches *(Betula)*, willows *(Salix)*, and marijuana plants *(Cannabis)* avoid self-pollination because they make imperfect (unisexual) flowers. The perfect (bisexual) flowers of mandrakes, death camas, and many other species force stamens and carpels in the same blossom to mature at different times. In some wild capers *(Capparis)* and evening primroses *(Oenothera)*, the carpel necks are so elongated that the receptive stigma avoids contact with the shorter stamens by sheer distance. All these tricks stop self-marriage in the same flower. However, they can't always prevent the wind or an animal from transferring pollen from one flower to another on the same plant. No matter what prophylactic measures are taken, it still looks as if every individual plant that makes pollen *and* ovules is doomed to produce a certain amount of inbred seed. Right?

Wrong. Let me share some information that is well known by most professionals working in agricultural research, conservation, and the breeding of garden plants. It is estimated that almost 66 percent of all flowering plant species produce seed almost exclusively by cross-pollination. Self-pollination and inbreeding are not such terrible problems in the wild. In fact, Charles Darwin and other eminent Victorians conducted early experiments on plant breeding systems and found that nature abhors continual self-fertilization.

It's true that some plants can't always prevent their carpels from receiving pollen produced in the same flower. However, many carpels are chemically equipped to stop inbreeding in its tracks through a mechanism known as self-incompatibility. A self-incompatible plant is in no danger of becoming both mother and father of the same seed because its carpels can identify and reject sperm produced by the same plant. A self-incompatible plant is literally immune to its own pollen.

The ability of a plant to recognize and reject its own pollen has a strong genetic basis, so this recognition system has one big added benefit. A self-incompatible plant can also recognize and reject much of the pollen offered by its grandparents, parents, and siblings. This lowers genetic mistakes caused by inbreeding when several generations are clumped together in the same field or forest.

Most plant ovaries refuse to make fruit if they receive sperm from self-pollination or from a close relation. The ovaries of star anises *(Illicium)*, tulip trees *(Liriodendron)*, and some magnolias *(Magnolia)* will go through a "false pregnancy" if self-pollinated, producing undersized fruits with hollow seeds that are of no use to gardeners. Successful false pregnancy occurs in breeds of edible banana *(Musa)*. The result of past hybridization, these plants carry unequal numbers of chromosomes. The female flowers of domesticated bananas don't need sperm to form fruit. As their ovaries age, they just keep adding layers of fleshy tissue. Slice a banana onto your breakfast cereal and look for the black dots in the yellowish white pulp. Those are the remains of unfertilized seeds.

Self-incompatibility influences the way many domesticated plants are grown, especially those with commercially valuable fruits. Members of the same breed of apple are almost identical genetically, so a Red Delicious tree will not set fruit if it receives pollen from another Red Delicious tree. The next time you drive by a commercial apple orchard, note how the growers usually plant at least two different breeds in alternating rows. As a college student in New York State, I learned that an older generation of farmers referred to two breeds of cherry in the same orchard as "cock" and "hen" trees. The "cock" breeds were poor producers of cherries, but farmers kept a few in each grove to get maximum fruit production from the "hen" trees.

Farmers and plant breeders hate self-incompatibility for two reasons. First, it lowers the yield of fruit and seed crops when unfavorable climate or the absence of pollinators curtails cross-pollination within a plantation. Second, although cross-pollinated crops enjoy greater genetic diversity, individual plants in the same crop flower or fruit at different times, so it is harder to predict the growth and harvest time of all the plants in the same field. Until late in the nineteenth century, much of the history of plant breeding reflected an unconscious attempt to reduce the gene pool of crops. Breeders preserved mutations, or chromosome errors, that suppressed the genes controlling self-incompatibility. Uniform crops were easier to harvest, since all the plants matured at the same rate. More important, a poor farmer who owned a field of self-pollinating plants enjoyed increased yield without having to put more land under cultivation.

Conservationists have learned, too, that self-incompatibility isn't always their friend in attempts to save endangered species. When habitat destruction shrinks wild populations, governments and naturalists try to save the survivors by turning a few areas into reserves. Unfortunately, the few surviving individuals are such close kin that they have inherited the same genetic warning system. For this reason, certain rare palms and some trees in Fiji, Brazil, and Madagascar now fail to set any seed because they refuse to accept the pollen of their parents or siblings. Conservationists have similar problems in attempting to increase the numbers of some endangered wildflowers native to Utah and California. Yes, some of the plants can be increased by taking cuttings and making clones, but is it really saving a species to replicate the same individual again and again?

There are two basic forms of self-incompatibility in nature. The first one, which I like to call the "sloppy system," is found in most orders of flowering plants and has been best studied in clovers *(Trifolium)*, true lilies *(Lilium)*, and many members of the nightshade family (Solanaceae). With some very important exceptions, the sloppy system is easily recognized by using a microscope and backing up observations with breeding experiments.

A plant with a sloppy system produces a pollen grain that contains only one sperm cell connected to a tube cell. When the stigma is ready to receive pollen, its skin becomes unusually greasy or slimy. The stigmas of petunias, for example, produce an outer layer of liquid fat, and the stigmas of most of the remaining "sloppy system" species turn into a slime bath or a swamp of leaky cells. Pollen grains adhere to this sloppy surface like victims trapped in quicksand. There's plenty of surface fluid, so the grain has no problem in swelling up and sprouting its tube. Pollen tubes grow down through the carpel neck before it can recognize a self-pollination. However, a sloppy self-pollination never reaches the ovule. The carpel chemistry may simply force the pollen tube to stop growing, in which case it appears to dwindle away. In other cases, the carpel sends the pollen tube false messages. A "fooled" tube starts growing in the wrong direction or explodes, releasing the sperm before it ever reaches an ovule. The sloppy system has the most trouble recognizing inbreeding. As many as half of all crosses between "parents" and "children" or between "brothers" and "sisters" may result in the production of some inbred seed.

The second form of self-incompatibility, the "neat system," is much more precise because it employs an early warning device. Neat systems are less common in nature and have been studied most often in the daisy (Asteraceae) and cabbage (Brassicaceae) families. Under the microscope, the pollen grain can be seen to contain two sperm cells attached to a single tube cell. The stigma surface is dry, with surface cells wearing only a thin film of protein. Botanists are not sure how pollen grains become attached to such a dry tip. Static cling may help, or the protein film on a stigma cell may act as a fine adhesive. If a flower with a neat system receives its own pollen, the grains are recognized and rejected by the dry surface. Rejected grains often fail to swell, or they become covered with a crust of callose or produce puny tubes that coil up and are unable to pierce the carpel tip. Plants with neat systems spurn their parents' pollen and

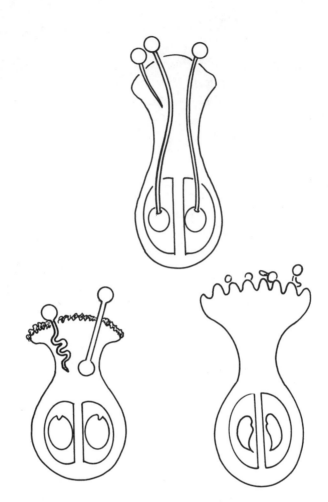

Above: When a carpel accepts pollen, the grains expand, sprout tubes, and grow down the style neck until they penetrate the ovary. There, a tube delivers the pollen's sperm by entering the ovule through a channel on the surface. *Below right:* Plants with "neat" self-incompatibility systems have dry stigmas and an early warning device. The grains of self-pollination or incestuous crosses fail to expand or sprout, or they produce tubes that fail to penetrate the stigma's surface. *Below left:* Plants with "sloppy" self-incompatibility systems have gooey or greasy stigmas. The grains of self-pollination and incestuous crosses expand and sprout tubes but are rejected by the carpel as they push down the style. Illustrations by J. Myers.

can recognize and reject the grains sent by three out of four of their siblings.

It appears that plants with neat systems are so efficient because their pollen grains wear a protein "identity card" on their outer walls. The protein molecules may be stored in the craters on the wall of the pollen grain until the grain touches the stigma's surface. The skin cells of the stigma learn the origin of each grain as molecules exit the craters.

Plant breeders have discovered a few useful techniques that deceive carpels of self-incompatible plants. These may include mutilating stigmas or swabbing them with chemicals to destroy the recognition response. Some growers place pots of self-pollinated plants in chambers enriched with carbon dioxide because self-incompatibility often breaks down in such an atmosphere. To make a prize cauliflower self-pollinate, a grower must open the youngest flower buds by hand and dab the immature stigmas with pollen before their self-recognition systems have a chance to mature.

All these methods are time-consuming and expensive, and the results are unpredictable. Sometimes, though, nature is generous, as when the self-incompatibility response shuts down when daily temperature increases. Some apple blossoms start accepting their own pollen on unseasonably hot spring days when temperatures exceed 80 degrees Fahrenheit.

When the union of sperm and egg is compatible, an embryo starts forming. However, flowering plants are unique in that most species require two sperm cells to make each seed. This means that the solitary sperm cell in the pollen tube of a buttercup, a lily, or a nightshade divides into two sperm cells as its tube takes it down to the ovary. Examination of the sperm units of Canola plants, *Plumbago* species, and some grass flowers suggests strongly that the tube cell acts as if it were a donkey dragging two sperm "carts" down the pollen tube. Once the tube finds the entrance pore on the surface of the ovule, it delivers two sperm cells to the patiently waiting embryo sac.

One sperm cell unites with an egg to start the seed embryo. The second sperm cell usually fuses with two "polar" cells in the same sac. This odd triple union makes all the cells that will become the starchy food tissue that supports the young embryo. A cell containing a tripled nucleus grows and divides rapidly, which explains why the seeds of most flowering plants mature within a couple of weeks or months after fertilization. This means that throughout history, all the great civilizations supported by the cultivation of grasses with edible seeds (wheat, corn, rice) have depended ultimately on one sperm cell uniting with two polar cells.

Fertilization is quite different in cone-bearing plants. Although a single sperm cell unites with the egg just as in flowering plants, the food tissue receives no sperm at all and matures rather slowly. The seeds of many cone-bearing plants often wait for more than a year and a half before they contain enough food cells to leave their parent trees or bushes. Pine seeds are tasty, but no large civilization has ever depended on the contents of tree cones to support its citizens.

Double fertilization in an embryo sac has given flowering plants the ability to spread quickly, since they can produce more generations over shorter periods of time. This helps to explain how mere refuges of flowering plants expanded suddenly after northern glaciers retreated following the last ice ages, recolonizing the barren earth.

Pollination is often defined simply as the act of dropping pollen onto a stigma surface. In fact, successful pollination really means that the right pollen grain has found the right stigma at precisely the right time. The history of evolution shows that flowering plants have invested considerable time and resources to make this process efficient. In the next chapter, you will learn about the effort that goes into successful pollination.

CHAPTER 8

O, how much more doth beauty beauteous seem
By that sweet ornament which truth doth give!
The rose looks fair, but fairer we it deem
For that sweet odour which doth in it live.
The canker blooms have full as deep a dye
As the perfumed tincture of the roses,
Hang on such thorns, and play as wantonly
When summer's breath their masked buds discloses;
But, for their virtue only is their show,
They live unwoo'd and unrespected fade,
Die to themselves. Sweet roses do not so;
Of their sweet deaths are sweetest odours made.

William Shakespeare, Sonnet 54

The Primary Attractants

Ugly names have been given to some pretty flowers. In Shakespeare's day, the dog rose was also known as the canker bloom (yes, the words *canker* and *cancer* have the same Latin origin). People must have compared the flower's reddish petals to running sores or rusty iron. Sonnet 54 condemns the wild canker bloom because its flowers lack the intense scents of the damask rose *(Rosa damascena)* and old breeds of Gallica rose *(R. gallica)* then under cultivation.

Elizabethan society used roses to give aroma to food, drink, and an early toothpaste. Roses perfumed the ancestors of modern laundry soaps, air fresheners, and cold remedies. Women washed their faces with rosewater in the belief that it would restore youthful luster. A rose without scent was like beauty without truth.

Poets and garden writers love to debate the relative merits of flower color versus flower scent. Tastemaking is fun, but it overlooks the real function of floral pigments and essences. In earlier chapters, you've seen how a flower may discourage self-pollination in order to decrease the production of inbred seed. To encourage cross-pollination and increase the production of outbred seed, a flower requires a different set of adaptations.

Cross-pollination occurs when a plant entrusts its pollen to a mobile pollinator, which transfers the pollen grains to flowers of different plants of the same species. The vast majority of flowering plants depend on foraging animals to serve as pollen "missiles," with flowers employing color displays and scent to stimulate the movement of pollinating animals. That is why botanists call flower color and scent the primary attractants.

With such a wide range of floral colors, from subtle to gaudy, it is surprising that all flower pigments derive from just four major chemical classes. Furthermore, the painted patterns of a flower often represent a frugal example of recycling. Often, the same pigment is used in different parts of a plant during its life cycle.

For example, every spring we admire the green dots and flecks on the flowers of snowdrops *(Galanthus),* and then in summer we welcome the emerald blossoms of spurges *(Euphorbia).* These flowers are tinged with the same chlorophyll that fills leaf cells and makes much of the plant's food.

Now consider the great range of buff, yellow, and orange flowers. Golden tones are made by carotenoid pigments. Carotenoids also aid leaves in the capture of sunlight and the manufacture of sugar by photosynthesis. When carotenoids are present in flower skin, they are seen as yellowish pigments dissolved in oil droplets or frozen in crystals suspended in cells. However, carotenoids are so versatile that flowers also use them to help build the outer walls of pollen grains.

The two remaining classes of pigment show how different chemicals often make the same colors. The betalains are a rare group of compounds restricted largely to families of true cacti, spring beauties (Portulacaceae), bougainvilleas (Nyctaginaceae), and ice plants (Aizoaceae). Some betalains produce yellow tints, overlapping with carotenoids, and the remainder are expressed as reds or purples. However, reds and purples are also made by the larger, more widespread class of chemical known as flavonoids. Human eyes can't really distinguish between a crimson shade made by a betalain and one made by a flavonoid.

More important, flavonoids are also responsible for all the blue shades we see on petals. As flavonoid pigments are soluble in water, they are mixed in the water sacs (vacuoles) found inside the living cells that make up petal skin. Flavonoids are uncommonly sensitive to changes in water chemistry and react as litmus paper does. Acidic water in a flower cell encourages the expression of pink or reddish hues, while neutral water results in purple displays. Blue tones require alkaline solutions, a fact that may help explain why some of the bluest wildflowers on this planet are restricted to rocky soils rich in deposits of iron, aluminum, and copper.

There is a special side to flavonoids that human beings can't see without the aid of sensitive photographic film and computer enhancement. Certain flavonoid pigments are sensitive to ultraviolet light and have been called "bee-blues" or "bee-greens" by various scientists. In fact, most insects see well into the ultraviolet range of the spectrum, as do many birds, small mammals, and goldfish. Humans appear to have lost the ancient ability to see an ultraviolet world, unlike most of the "lower animals." Why this is so remains a mystery unanswered by ophthalmologists.

Of course, this really means that there are very few true white

Three common ultraviolet patterns. *Above:* The star,
represented by a mallow *(Malva). Middle:* The bull's-
eye, represented by a mullein *(Verbascum).*
Below: The lobed or irregular blotch, represented by
a parrot flower *(Alstroemeria).* This pattern is most
common in flowers with bilateral symmetry.
Illustrations by J. Myers.

flowers, aside from the mutations and selected breeds propagated and pampered in our gardens. When we see a chalky or ivory blossom in the wild, our eyes receive the white light that has bounced off the starch granules in the storage cells of the flower tissue, but animals may see a completely different pattern, dyed with flavonoids. At one time, botanists thought that some wild night-blooming flowers lacked pigment and offered pure white displays. That theory has recently been set aside, following tropical research in which photographs taken with ultraviolet-sensitive film showed flavonoid designs on the flowers of some trees and vines that are pollinated by nocturnal moths.

The way flowers organize and exhibit their colors seems more important than the actual pigments they use. Professor Bastiaan Meeuse pointed this out in 1961 in his witty book *The Story of Pollination*. Things are seldom what they seem, he observed, as the most striking effects achieved by flowers look very different under the microscope.

Are the petals of a red rose pure red in color? Peel off the flower skin with a razor blade, mount it on a glass slide, and you will see that the skin is not uniformly red. Cells filled with pink water sacs are interspersed with cells filled with purple sacs, producing a blended mosaic that appears red to the human eye. Meeuse compared it to the work of French painter Georges Seurat (1859–1891), who achieved similar effects by combining dots of different colors on the canvas. We credit Seurat with the perfection of a painting technique known as pointillism, but flowers probably perfected this design more than 80 million years ago.

Consider the black blotches on flowers of different species of melanium pansy *(Viola)* or the ebony smudge at the base of each petal of an oriental poppy *(Papaver orientale)*. How does a flower wear "mourning"? Meeuse sectioned the flowers and found that different colors were produced in different layers of skin. The cells in the

Orchid flowers alter the texture of their lip petals by adding sculptures, hairs, or both to the petal skin. *Above:* An old man orchid *(Calochilus campestris)* of Australia. *Below:* A bee orchid *(Ophrys holoserica)* of Israel. Both flowers mimic the bodies of female insects and are pollinated by male insects that attempt to copulate with the dummy female on the lip petal. Illustrations by J. Myers.

upper surface of poppy skin contain purple sacs, and those in the layer directly underneath contain blue sacs. Working together, the two different but interconnected layers of color absorb most of the white light, giving a portion of the petal a blackish tone. This layering of colors is known as superposition.

Botanists now understand more about how color is influenced by the outermost layer of skin cells. The size, length, and shape of these cells determine how a sunbeam will be reflected or refracted. Some cinquefoils *(Potentilla)*, jonquils *(Narcissus)*, and bromeliads produce flowers with petals so glossy that they appear to have been polished. Under the microscope, their skin cells are seen to be low, tightly linked, and rather uniform. Meeuse compared them to interlocking ceramic tiles. A thin coat of cuticle wax over these "tile" cells completes the varnished effect.

In contrast, consider all the roses and other flowers whose petals can be compared to swatches of felt or velvet. The microscope reveals that such flower skins are composed of cells of irregular sizes and shapes. Some are domed and finely ribbed, some end in cone-shaped tips, and others are slender and angular, resembling prisms.

The petals of other flowers appear to be subdivided into zones, with smooth and wrinkled sections alternating on the same petal. For example, the lip petals of bee orchids *(Ophrys)* and bearded orchids *(Calochilus)* have dense, woolly margins, yet the central portion of the same petal is often so shiny and metallic that botanists, claiming it resembles one of those inspection mirrors used by physicians, call it a speculum. Why does the terrain of some petals vary so much?

After thirty years of experimentation, scientists in Canada, Israel, and Germany have come to similar conclusions. Skin texture appears to combine with color patterns to help produce raised visual cues that attract pollinators and direct them to the center of the flower. Since the flower's sex organs lie in these centers, the texture and color patterns encourage animals to make contact with anthers filled with pollen and stigmas waiting to receive pollen. Patterns tend to reflect both a flower's shape and the relative positions of sex organs in the open blossom.

Since most flowers are shaped like bowls, funnels, tubes, or bells, the patterns on the flower skin resemble bull's-eyes or stars. Circular patterns of contrasting colors or arrowlike streaks work equally well to direct the pollinator from the outer rim of the flower into the center, where the sex organs cluster. Think of a circular flower as a living compass. Since the same kinds of sex organs are arranged equally around the floral center, it really doesn't matter in which direction the insect enters or leaves the blossom. The organs it encounters when entering the flower from the north or south will be the same sorts of organs it will bonk against when it exits from the east or west.

Irregular flowers shaped like sock puppets, animal muzzles, or dangling aprons must use different patterns to lure pollinators. These flowers, which show bilateral symmetry, have their sex organs angled and slanted in one direction. There is usually only one "legitimate" way for an insect to enter and leave the flower while contacting both anthers and stigmas. The entry pattern is found on only one side of the flower, the side that contains a platform or perch on which the insect can land. As in flowers with radial symmetry, the sex organs swab or rub against the pollinator as it enters or exits the flower. An entrance pattern based on color may be made more obvious through texturing of the skin cells. For example, some members of the snapdragon family (Scrophulariaceae) decorate the lower lip of the flower with a thickened crease or a fuzzy patch. This is the lip a heavy bee depresses to enter the flower's throat.

As mentioned earlier, texture patterns are most dramatic in the orchid family (Orchidaceae), as a pollinating insect must be positioned precisely under the solitary, narrow column if it is ever to receive or transfer blobs of pollinia. The lip petals of orchids are often decorated with enlarged pads, warts, ridges, or fins that hold the attention of the pollinator long enough for the column to attach pollinia to the animal's body or mouthparts. In a later chapter, you will see how lip sculptures on orchids "seduce" pollinators.

Different flower colors may occur at different frequencies in populations of the same species. For example, even though *Anagallis arvensis* is called the scarlet pimpernel, in some European meadows it is possible to find pimpernels with scarlet flowers growing side by side with pimpernels that have pink or blue flowers. I think that *Thelymitra epipactoides,* a rare sun orchid confined to a few sites in southern Australia, has the finest wardrobe. Illustrations and modern photographs indicate that these orchids have been found with aquamarine, dull slate, chartreuse, pink, or bronze petals. Why should natural selection encourage members of the same species to vary their flower colors so dramatically?

It has been shown that different colors appeal to different animals. Butterflies adore the flowers of lantanas *(Lantana camara),* but the nymphalid butterfly *Precis almana* prefers lantanas with orange flowers, while swallowtails and skippers visit the pink forms. A rarity of orange lantanas in a particular field may ultimately reflect a period of many years in which nymphalids were rare visitors but swallowtails or skippers were active and faithful.

Plant breeders know from painful experience that flower color is often controlled by more than one gene. Wild pansies *(Viola tricolor),* for example, may need as many nine genes to determine whether the flower will have a yellow face with black borders and red streaks. Perhaps we should be more tolerant of nursery owners who fail to sell us flats containing plants with flowers all of the same color.

Flower color may also change with the age of the individual flower. *Brunfelsia australis* is a native of South America sold as the "yesterday, today, and tomorrow plant." When the petals opened yesterday, they were royal purple, but these pigments broke down within a short time. Today, the purple blossom has faded to a powdery blue. By tomorrow, the dying petals will have blanched to a drab off-white.

Other flowers darken with age. Some populations of white trillium *(Trillium grandiflorum)* in northeastern woods of the United States have petals that blush pink as they dry and curl. This has been interpreted as part of the dynamic partnership between flowers and their pollinators. The bumblebee associates changes in trillium color with a decline in good things to eat or drink.

English poet and satirist Andrew Marvell (1621–1678) wrote a poem titled "The Mower against Gardens" in which he accused humankind of corrupting innocent plants. Gardens were evil dens in which freaks were whelped by unnatural means. Worse, humans passed on their addiction to luxury to innocent flowers. "With strange perfumes he did the roses taint, / And flowers themselves were taught to paint." Yes, horticulturists exploit flower color, but in most cases, all they really do is harness the natural variation once maintained by natural selection.

Humans are innocent, however, of tainting roses with strange perfumes. Flower scent is as variable in nature as is flower color. Before examining the diversity of fragrance, we must ask an important question. Where in the flower is fragrance produced?

Earlier, I mentioned that some scent molecules are dissolved in the dense oil droplets adhering to the outer wall of the pollen grain. These pollen scents are not terribly strong and may be most noticeable to animals that come to flowers specifically to collect or eat the grains. The odors we smell in a bouquet tend to be manufactured by special cells on the flower's skin.

In the 1950s, Professor Stefan Vogel, an Austrian botanist, became interested in locating the sites of scent production on flowers. He soaked whole live blossoms in a solution of 1 percent neutral red, a dye that stains positively for volatile reactions such as the explosive release of scent molecules. Flowers with a strong odor showed a reaction within hours of application. Vogel concluded that different parts of different flowers become aroma factories at critical moments in the life of the blossom. Even closely related plants often place their perfume patches on different flower organs. Within the bean family, for example, the lupine species *Lupinus cruckshanksii* wears perfume cells on the center of its broad banner petal, but Spanish broom, *Spartium junceum,* carries scent on its two wing petals. Floral biologists are still unable to explain these subtle differences.

Vogel calls these perfume patches osmophores, after a Greek word that means "scent bearer." He went on to examine more exotic species, especially members of the birthwort (Aristolochiaceae), philodendron (Araceae), milkweed (Asclepiadaceae), and orchid families. He found that their osmophores are often large and extravagant, forming at the tips of much elongated petals or along the irregular margins of sepals and bracts. Some look like feathery wands, furry fingers, the teeth of combs, or fleshy pillars. These fantastic structures expand the surface area devoted to odor release, increasing the flower's ability to broadcast scent particles into the air.

How do osmophores know when it's time to release their fragrance? Vogel's microscope showed that only the cells in the layer of skin exposed to the air function as perfume bottles. This outer layer always sits on top of a special inner layer of cells packed with starch granules. When the flower digests the starch in these inner cells, the chemical energy released "uncorks" the aroma in the perfumed skin.

Recent research by Dr. Heidi Dobson of Whitman College, in Washington State, and her Swedish coworkers suggests that much of Vogel's work may represent extreme cases in evolution. Dobson notes that the majority of flowers on this planet lack big, bizarre osmophores. She devotes her time to studying the circular blooms of more common species such as the yellow buttercup *(Ranunculus acris)* and the Japanese rose *(Rosa rugosa)*. These flowers allocate scent production all over the flower's surface. When we smell a rose, we are actually inhaling concentrations of various chemicals made by different organs in the flower. The stamens of a Japanese rose release molecules of eugenol, a spicy scent reminiscent of cloves. The petals make no eugenol, but they secrete lots of geraniol and nerol, the sweeter "notes" associated with favorite roses. If Dobson is correct, sepals, petals, stamens, and carpels are like the string, brass, wind, and percussion sections in an orchestra, with each set of organs playing different scent notes at different volumes. The "music" of one rose is measured by the way the different fragrances mix, modify, and balance one another at different concentrations.

Ancient frescoes discovered in Egypt and on the island of Crete suggest that humans have farmed flowers for their fragrance for more than five thousand years. The Madonna lily *(Lilium candidum)* appears to be one of the oldest perfume crops in the Mediterranean region. Some paintings in Egyptian tombs depict ladies of the pharaoh's court wearing unguent cones on their foreheads. Recipes for making these scented cones have been translated from surviving scrolls. In most cases, pounded or chopped petals were mixed with ox fat.

The perfume industry guards its secrets jealously because they are so lucrative. This makes it harder for science writers to piece together a natural history of flower scents. Scientists do know, however, that fragrant chemicals make up only a fraction of a live flower. Scent compounds make up just 0.075 percent of the weight of a fresh rose. As odors escape into the air, some cells work hard to replace them over the flower's life span. A tuberose replenishes its scented oils so often that each flower produces as much as twelve times the amount of fragrance with which it started.

More than 700 different compounds have been identified in the floral fragrances of nearly 450 flower species. Some biochemists have

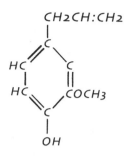

CH2CH:CH2

Eugenol

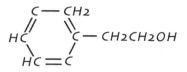

Phenethyl

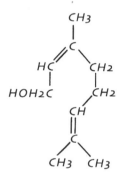

Geraniol

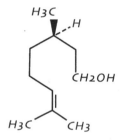

Citronellol

The molecular skeletons of four scent "notes" produced by some roses are all based on a central ring of six carbon atoms.

Illustrations by J. Myers.

tried to simplify this bewildering range of molecules, breaking the scents into three major categories. A full and fair analysis of these categories would require a separate book. Here, it is sufficient to say that all scents share one important thing in common. They are made of such small, lightweight molecules that they boil at extremely low temperatures. Most, in fact, explode into airborne particles at room temperature. The warmer the environment, the more quickly the particles diffuse into the atmosphere. A rose garden seems almost odorless in the middle of the hottest summer day, so field laborers for the perfume industry start harvesting flowers in the cooler hours before dawn.

Compounds as different as esters, aromatic benzene rings, ketones, alcohols, and terpenoids are often lumped together under the common name of "essential oils," as they become invisible but strongly scented essences in warm air. Some flowers release their essences over prescribed periods. Research by Ralph Holman at the Hormel Institute, a research center of the University of Minnesota, shows that night-blooming orchids release their scent in timed pulses as the sun begins to set. These pulses stop during daylight hours.

Flower scents discernible to insects may be produced at such low concentrations that humans can't smell them even at close range. Dr. Stephen L. Buchmann of the Carl Hayden Bee Research Center in Arizona has some excellent advice on how to smell "odorless" flowers. He recommends placing a small bouquet of the flowers in a small, clean, dry bottle with a tight lid. Leave the bottled blooms in a warm, sunny window for thirty minutes to an hour, and then open the bottle and inhale. You may be surprised. I can vouch for this technique, as my colleagues and I used it to sample the apparently odorless flowers of snottygobble bushes *(Persoonia)* in Australia. With the "bottled" flowers, we were able to distinguish five different scent types produced by the flowers of ten different species of snottygobble.

People use complimentary words such as *sweet, fruity,* and *spicy* to describe flower scents, but some members of the birthwort, philodendron, and milkweed families release compounds containing atoms of nitrogen. These chemicals reproduce the odor of proteins deteriorating into ammonia, so the flowers often stink like carrion, mildewed clothes, or fresh dung. The various odors they mimic are often quite distinct. For example, I think I can recognize the smell of bad beef in the stench of starfish flowers *(Stapelia)* and the essence of old herring in some cobra lilies *(Arisaema)*. In chapters 11 and 14, you will see that such flowers attract insects with rather different tastes.

The way in which people respond to floral scents often depends on the concentration of certain compounds and their modifiers. For example, the flowering branches of one species of Australian acacia are so rich in pyridine that the sheer bitterness of the smell makes some of my colleagues gag. On the other hand, pyridine is made artificially by the scent and flavor industry. Added to food and drink in minute amounts, it lends a pleasant "roasted" aroma to some inexpensive chocolates and instant coffees. Preferences for natural odors are often personal. My wife, Linda, loves the scent of privet *(Ligustrum vulgare)* and wants me to appreciate what she calls "that velvety smell." Frankly, the smell of privet flowers disgusts me, producing the olfactory equivalent of wailing sirens at four in the morning.

Pollinators appear to be as picky about the way a flower smells as humans are. Within the same population of wildflowers, botanists can find scent forms, just as naturalists have recorded color forms. For example, *Polemonium viscosum* is a species of Jacob's ladder distributed throughout the mountains of the northwestern United States. Two of every three Jacob's ladder plants growing on the lower, shaded parts of wooded slopes have flowers with a nasty, "skunky" smell. At this altitude, most of the flowers are pollinated by flies. Higher up the same slopes in open alpine meadows, two of every three Jacob's ladders have a honeylike scent. Queen bumble-bees are very active in these sunny areas, and they clearly prefer flowers that smell like candy.

Our knowledge of the relative importance of primary attractants is the result of experiments performed on such pollinators as bom-byliid flies, honeybees, hummingbirds, sphinx moths, and hairy scarabs. Since the 1920s, scientists have found that these creatures will visit models made of paper or plastic when real flowers are denied, can follow a scent trail in a wind tunnel, and can locate live blossoms isolated under bell jars. These animals tolerate our crude attempts at manipulation because they are motivated by hunger or an innate drive to provide their offspring with food.

Of course, experiments on moths can't explain why humans so admire the tint and fragrance of a rose. How can one possibly explain thousands of years of painting and poetry produced by a species with no pollinators as ancestors?

Tropical biologist Dr. Daniel H. Janzen offers a provocative the-ory that I find irresistible. Humans, he suggests, descend from a long line of primate ancestors that relished fruit. The pigments and es-sential oils that plants employ in their flowers also cue the ripening of berries. In particular, the esters and alcohols in the aromas of soft fruits are often identical to floral scents. Janzen argues that flower appreciation is just a happy by-product of evolution, a refinement of the senses we need to find and select a ripe banana.

Indeed, some flowers' aromas are so appealing precisely because they remind us of something good to eat or drink. The blossoms of species of *Michelia*, for example, have such a mouthwatering smell that these shrubs are often called port wine magnolias or bubble gum bushes. We pick a yellow rose with enthusiasm, inhaling its phenylethyl alcohol, nerol, and linalool. That rose is the same color as the peel of a ripe banana, and two of its essences are also found in oranges and fortified wines such as muscatel.

Janzen sees tremendous irony in some of the fads in human fashion and courtship. The woman who wears perfume and brightens her face with cosmetics, he suggests, is not emulating a blooming rose bursting with sexual allure. She is mimicking a plump, juicy rose hip bursting with vitamin C.

CHAPTER 9

Upon the roses it would feed,
Until its lips ev'n seemed to bleed,
And then to me 'twould boldly trip,
And print those roses on my lip.
But all its chief delight was still
On roses thus itself to fill

> Andrew Marvell, "The Nymph
> Complaining for the Death of Her Fawn"

Rewards

Christian Konrad Sprengel (1750–1816) studied theology and languages and became rector of the Lutheran school of Spandau in the district of Berlin, Germany. While there, he developed a passion for flowers, publishing his original observations as a book in 1793. *Das entdeckte Geheimnis der Natur im Bau und in der Befruchtung der Blumen* (The secrets of nature revealed in the design and befruiting of flowers) suffered from one of those long German titles. It was not a commercial or critical success, either.

Some historians blame the book's lack of commercial success on a combination of bad timing—few people living in war-torn countries buy books—and the limited tastes of the privileged classes. Toward the end of the eighteenth century, there was a steady market for flower books provided they were folio volumes containing color portraits of rare species. Instead of prettily composed plates, though, Sprengel crammed his book with black-and-white drawings of common field flowers and close-up diagrams of bug heads.

The book's lack of critical success may reflect the fate often suffered by writers who challenge orthodox opinion. Naturalist philosophers of the day, such as Goethe, largely dismissed Sprengel's book, deriding it as a daydream. Just imagine some schoolteacher insisting that nature prevents flowers from fertilizing themselves! This unscientific nobody believed that flowers rewarded insects with nectar for their services as pollen porters. Sprengel's most outrageous assertion, however, was that the contrasting patterns of color on a geranium told insects where nectar was to be found in the flower!

Real botanists knew, of course, that stamens and pistils married each other in the *same* flower. Bees were nectar thieves. Experts insisted that nectar was like the fluid in a woman's womb, lubricating delicate organs, aiding in the transfer of sperm, or nourishing baby seeds. Poor Sprengel lost his rectorship in 1794. Some said he paid more attention to his garden than to his students, but I'll bet the school board simply didn't like his radical notions or enjoy his sarcastic critiques of famous savants.

Today, C. K. Sprengel is regarded as a founding father of the science of pollination biology, while few people read Goethe for botanical insight. Sprengel's best ideas endured because his book was passed down and appreciated by a few discerning naturalists. Charles Darwin had become a public defender of *Das entdeckte Geheimnis* by the 1860s, and Darwin's own publications on pollination inspired a new generation of German and British naturalists. Research conducted since the early 1880s has vindicated Sprengel's interpretations of contrasting flower colors. They really do function as signposts, leading insects to nectar hidden within a blossom. In fact, modern studies in which floral parts are photographed using ultraviolet-sensitive film show that some of the most important flower signs are invisible to the human eye. Honey guides or nectar guides are the names most textbooks give to these streaks, speckles, and blotches.

Why are most of the animals that pollinate flowers so eager to find nectar? After all, 60 to 95 percent of the volume of most nectars is nothing more than water. Well, water is the easiest thing for an animal to drink, and as it is the universal solvent, plant nutrients dissolve in it. The primary nutrients in most nectars are sugars, the simplest carbohydrates to digest. Most pollinators run on liquefied energy.

Nectar sugars are usually small molecules. In fact, most nectars are based on the same sucrose molecule that makes up the refined white sugar in the bowl on your kitchen table. Some flowers break the sucrose molecule in half, offering nectars rich in glucose and fructose, which are even easier to digest. In addition to these sugars, most nectars contain small but consistent quantities of amino acids and vitamins. These are the nutritional building blocks most insects need as short-lived adults.

Different flowers secrete nectars with different kinds of simple sugars at different concentrations. These variations in chemistry are often reflected in floral form. Although there are exceptions to the rule, flowers are more likely to hide high concentrations of sucrose-rich nectars at the base of unusually long tubes or in extravagant petal pouches, hollow spurs, or "chins." Flowers concealing sucrose nectar may also guard the liquid with petal tips shaped like hinged lids or puckered lips. That is because animals on a sucrose diet either have very long, fine mouthparts or are so big and strong that they can push open the petal lids or lips. An animal designed to dine primarily on sucrose is on a most specific diet, requiring both specialized behavior and particular anatomical equipment to exploit limited food sources.

In contrast, flowers with nectar made of low concentrations of glucose and fructose may offer their drinks in shallow bowls or broad goblets. Their nectar is often available to a much wider range of animals, including pollinators with shorter mouthparts, smaller, flimsier bodies, or both.

Until the invention and widespread use of hand lenses, naturalists believed that flowers caught rainwater, fog, or mist in their petal cups and converted the drops or drizzles into nectar. That idea persisted until Flemish botanist Charles de l'Écluse (1526–1609) began serious studies of his living collection of exotic bulbs that he'd dug up or purchased in Mediterranean countries. In 1601, he published a treatise that included a description of the flowers of the crown imperial *(Fritillaria imperialis)*. He had examined these flowers' petals under magnification, finding "little tubercles" that wept sweet tears.

All flowers that secrete true nectar contain one or more nectar glands. The position of a nectar gland, or nectary, inside the flower is determined by genes, so the nectary should be found in the same place in each flower of the same species. The nectaries of some members of the buttercup (Ranunculaceae), cabbage (Brassicaceae), macadamia (Proteaceae), violet (Violaceae), and oxalis (Oxalidaceae) families are so big that taxonomists have used their shape, position, and number to help classify plants. In other families, nectaries are much harder to detect, as they blend in with the surface texture of the flower skin. Their presence is known only because discrete parts of the flower become moist.

Nectar glands may form on the bottoms of sepals, petals, or stamens, or they may nestle between carpel grooves. Sometimes they form on the floor of the flower and make puddles between the outer circle of petals and the inner circles of sex organs. In flowers of citrus trees, houseleeks *(Sempervivum),* and cheesewoods *(Pittosporum),* the nectar gland is a fleshy or bumpy disk between the ring of stamens and the carpels. Nectaries located toward the base of flower organs force the pollinator to bump against the tips of the sex organs while it probes for something to drink. Pollen is then brushed onto

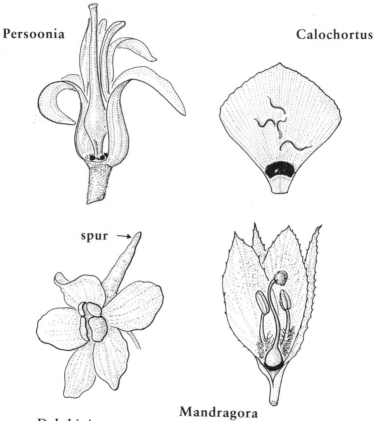

Persoonia

Calochortus

spur →

Delphinium

Mandragora

The locations of nectar glands (darkened areas) are different in different flowers. *Above left:* Four nectar glands (three are visible) under the ovary stalk of a snottygobble *(Persoonia). Above right:* Gland at the base of a petal of a mariposa lily *(Calochortus). Below right:* Nectar disc under the ovary of a mandrake *(Mandragora). Below left:* Nectar is secreted inside the tip of a hollow sepal spur of a larkspur *(Delphinium).* Illustrations by J. Myers.

the animal's body or grains carried by the pollinator are rubbed off onto receptive stigmas.

However, fresh nectar puts pollen sperm at extreme risk. Remember, pollen grains swell or explode on contact with sugar water. If nectar and pollen combine in the same flower, the sperm may be activated prematurely or the pollen grains may swell and drown. A honeybee can carry a lot of dead pollen in the baskets on her hind legs because she has mixed the pollen with nectar to help glue and pack the grains onto her basket hairs.

This means that a flower must satisfy a pollinator's hunger while "keeping its powder dry." The crucial distance between nectaries and anther sacs is measured in millimeters. Some flowers in the meadow beauty (Melastomataceae), milkweed (Asclepiadaceae), and violet families are among the few species that dare to attach nectaries directly to their anthers. These glands are so cunningly placed, though, that they usually drip their contents into petal pouches or canals, carrying the nectar away from the vulnerable sacs of pollen.

Nectar glands can afford to secrete watery food because they interconnect with strands of phloem, the fine, sievelike pipes that conduct nutrients within the plant. The phloem usually harvests sugar made in green leaves and transports it to stems or taproots for storage. It also penetrates the flower, bringing sugars and other foods to the nectar glands.

The concentration of nutrients in nectar may differ among flowers on the same plant. For example, the male (imperfect) flowers of cashew trees *(Anacardium occidentale)* secrete slightly more sucrose and amino acids than do the bisexual (perfect) flowers sharing the same twig.

The flowers of different species have different ways of secreting nectar. Nectar gushes out of open pores dotting the glands of nasturtiums *(Tropaeolum)* and dead nettles *(Lamium)*. Minute hairs dribble nectar inside the flowers of honeysuckles *(Lonicera)* and Indian mallows *(Abutilon)*. The nectar glands of elderberry blossoms *(Sambucus)* and most cacti loosen up and fragment, releasing their sweet fluids in a cellular slush.

Nectar secretion often changes over the life span of a single flower. In some larkspurs *(Delphinium)* and fireweeds *(Epilobium)* of the western United States, more nectar can be found in an old flower than in a young one. When a bee visits the youngest flowers on a stem, she finds only pollen, while mature blossoms offer a drink long after they've been emptied of grains. Since the oldest blossoms are at the base of the flowering stem, bees land on the lowest portions of the stem to drink first. With a stomach full of sugar water, a bee has enough energy to climb up the stem and scrape pollen out of the younger flowers. When the bee becomes thirsty, she glides down to find the old flowers on the stem of another plant. This process promotes cross-pollination.

Pollen is also a reward for many animals. Although the greasy globules on the outside of a pollen grain are hard to digest, the fats, amino acids, and trace minerals inside are very nutritious. Analyses show that 20 to 30 percent of the contents of pollen grains can sustain some hungry beetles, bees, hover flies, and bats. Even humans have learned that pollen is a nice treat if one has the patience to collect it. The pollen grains of cattails *(Typha),* for example, have few amino acids and little fat, but they are crammed with starch granules. The Maori people of New Zealand and some tribes of American Indians once harvested cattail pollen in spring, moistened it with water, and baked the mixture as cakes. British explorers wrote that this pastry tasted like gingerbread.

In contrast, the pollen packaged in capsules and sold in health food stores was stolen from the legs of honeybees as they tripped on wires set up at hive entrances. Advertisements claim that bee pollen will give you more energy. This may be so, but I've dissected pollen pellets, and I know they'll also give you bee lice and leg hairs.

If the wall of a pollen grain is a natural plastic impervious to most digestive acids and enzymes, how do pollinators extract the goodness inside the grain? In fact, most butterflies, moths, and birds are unable to digest pollen and avoid swallowing it when they probe a blossom for nectar. As you will see in the next chapter, only a few insects have mouthparts designed to bite through the tough outer wall. Bees, hover flies, lorikeet parrots, and bats are pollen eaters that handle the pollen grain's wall in much the same way. They drink lots of nectar first and store the sugar water in their crops or stomachs. Once swallowed, pollen soaks in these nectar-filled "tummies." The grains expand and split open, yielding their edible contents. The pollen eater's digestive system then absorbs the nutrients and excretes the deflated, emptied grains. That's why it's possible to identify the last meal of an adult honeybee by carefully examining her dung.

Honeybees won't feed hard pollen to their offspring until the grubs are at least four or five days old. For the first three to four days, nurse bees coax the babies along on a liquid brood food made of honey, digestive enzymes, and secretions from the nurses' jaws and throats. In contrast, most solitary bee species have a much cruder but more direct method of introducing their children to pollen. A mother mixes pollen and concentrated nectar into a loaf or pudding and lays an egg on it. Before the grub hatches, the grains absorb the nectar, "cooking" the pudding. The process requires perfect timing. If the bee makes the pudding too soon, the food will be attacked by microbes and will ferment, spoiling before the grub hatches.

In Central and South America, some butterflies of the genus *Heliconius* have evolved a novel way to enrich their diet by exploiting the reaction of pollen in sugar water. These butterflies are especially fond of visiting male flowers of *Psiguria* vines and other tropical members of the pumpkin family. The butterflies use their coiled tongues to knock pollen into the nectar and stir the mixture, encouraging the grains to rupture. This gives the butterfly a cocktail rich in sugars *and* proteins. Female heliconiids spend more time at *Psiguria* flowers than do males because a pregnant butterfly needs the extra nitrogen in the pollen to lay healthy eggs.

In the twentieth century, scientists have learned that some flowers offer foods more diverse than nectar or pollen. Unusual rewards often reflect unique relationships between flowers and certain pollinators. Consider the blossoms of some primitive plants that are pollinated by beetles. These insects have retained their cutting and chewing mouthparts and often prefer "salads" that are both succulent and starchy. The flowers of an Australian spice bush *(Eupomatia laurina)* and those of some members of the custard apple (Annonaceae) and magnolia (Magnoliaceae) families offer beetles extra stamens to munch. Some of the stamens inside the flowers of spice bush and *Talauma* trees fail to develop and make pollen. These "eunuch" stamens exist only to serve as beetle snacks. As the insect gnaws the snack stamens, it bumps into receptive stigmas or brushes against fertile stamens that are shedding pollen.

The stamens of California allspice *(Calycanthus occidentalis)* wear edible "pimples," while thick, starchy pillows emerge between the stamens and carpels of giant waterlilies *(Victoria amazonica)*. Scientists interpret these extra food bodies as payoffs that encourage beetles to graze contentedly without spoiling too many sex organs in a flower.

Many South American members of the nance family (Malpighiaceae) and some southern African members of the snapdragon family (Scrophulariaceae) have replaced their nectar glands with oil glands that secrete a strong-smelling grease. These flowers are pollinated by members of two different bee families that raise their young on a fatty diet rich in the diglycerides and triglycerides your family doctor wants you to avoid. The oil glands of African snapdragons are usually knobs attached directly to stamens that are industriously mopped by *Rediviva* bees (Melittidae) using their elaborately hooked forelegs.

Each nance flower *(Byrsonima)* bears a pair of large, exposed oval-shaped glands on its sepals. In South America, *Centris* bees (Apidae) scrape nance glands for oil, and the female bees hollow out wood chips to house their offspring. Each egg is laid in its own chamber, packed with pollen from different tropical trees and a slick of nance oil. To "plug" the nursery, the female bee fills the hole with an oil-and-wax mixture that has the consistency of mayonnaise. The grub reaches winged adulthood devouring the "lube job" inside the wooden "crankcase."

The startling news of the past four decades is that some pollinators forage for inedible rewards. Devil's apples *(Clusia)* are tropical trees on which each flower contains some reduced stamens that disintegrate into a pitchlike resin when the petals open. This sticky substance hardens with time and is gathered by some tropical bees,

This male *Euglossa* bee was netted while he was scraping fragrant oils from a *Trichopilia* orchid. He is wearing the slender pollen masses of the orchid on his head (the two white "horns"). Note the hairy "perfume flask" on his hind leg.
Photograph by R. Dressler.

which use it as a nest cement. Beeswax absorbs water, encouraging the growth of bacteria and fungi, so this hard, dry resin makes a superior mortar in warm, humid climates.

The tropics of the New World are rich in species belonging to the orchid (Orchidaceae), philodendron (Araceae), nightshade (Solanaceae), and gloxinia (Gesneriaceae) families. Their flowers often have unusually rich, spicy fragrances based on the essential oils known as terpenes and terpenoids. Tropical flowers that smell like cloves or menthol usually contain no nectar. These terpenoid flowers are pollinated almost exclusively by special groups of male bees that scrape, collect, and then modify the plants' strongest perfumes. To complete their life cycles, the male bees need flower scents to blend into personal colognes. The full story of this strange behavior, which refutes the old truism that all male bees are lazy drones, is told in chapter 12.

The most recently discovered reward seems so basic and useful to cold-blooded insects that it's surprising it received so little attention for so long. Some flowers reward their pollinators with warmth. A large blossom or a stalk of tiny flowers can produce a temperature higher than that of the surrounding atmosphere. The phenomenon was first noted in some wildflowers on the Alaskan tundra whose dark petals act as solar panels, absorbing the sun's heat. A warm flower offering a little nectar or pollen is a preferred site for a fly or small bee whose ability to forage declines on days when the air is cold.

Warm flowers are also common outside the Arctic Circle. Even in temperate and tropical zones, a cozy, heated chamber attracts beetles and flies. These insects often prefer to eat and mate in the flowers or flowering branches of some palms, waterlilies, philodendrons, and voodoo lilies *(Sauromatum)*. What all these different plants share in common is that their blossoms or flower stalks warm up without the direct blaze of the sun. Instead, they increase their temperature for brief periods by digesting starch hidden in storage cells and absorbing oxygen from the air. These processes produce a chemically generated heat, warming up floral organs.

Plants that keep their flowers toasty are more likely to cater to insects that prefer to forage in the evening or at dawn, when air temperatures drop a few critical degrees. A plant offering prewarmed flowers to a chilled insect may stand a better chance of attracting pollinators and setting seeds.

The Asian sacred lotus *(Nelumbo nucifera)* has long been admired for its large pink-and-white flowers, but botanists now know that each flower has its own thermostat. A single lotus bloom can produce and sustain a temperature of more than 80 degrees Fahrenheit even when the air temperature sinks to 50 degrees.

Half of the heat in a lotus flower is generated by a spongy, cylinder-shaped structure in its center known as the receptacle. It is called the receptacle because the flat surface of the cylinder forms a platform that holds the many carpels. The remaining warmth is made by stamen tips and petals. A lotus "fires up" when it is a mature bud, just before its petals expand. Temperature equilibrium is reached when the rate of heat production in the flower equals the rate of heat loss. For a few days, the flower regulates its temperature as would a small warm-blooded animal such as a hummingbird or shrew. Scientists believe that a floral temperature of 80 degrees Fahrenheit may make it easier for a cold-blooded insect to activate its flight muscles. This would speed up the rate of cross-pollination, allowing warmed, energetic beetles or bees to hurry from bloom to bloom even when the weather is cool and uninviting.

We now have a fresh interpretation of all those paintings that depict the Buddha or one of the Hindu gods seated on a lotus blossom. Nirvana must be a cold place. Beetles, great sages, and deities all agree, then, that eternity is best contemplated in comfort. I hope that the soul of C. K. Sprengel reposes on a lotus bloom.

CHAPTER 10

And mid-May's eldest child,
The coming musk-rose, full of dewy wine,
The murmurous haunt of flies on summer eves.
John Keats, "Ode to a Nightingale"

Unloved but Efficient

Insects on prized roses receive more hateful and suspicious glances than would a swineherd attempting to court a princess. We protect our favorite flowers the way European aristocrats once guarded their family honor. Honeybees and butterflies make tolerable consorts, but other insects are executed in a cloud of toxic fumes mixed with vengeful enthusiasm.

As evolution rarely reflects good taste, many wildflowers are pollinated by insects loathed by gardeners. Consider the woody vine *Uvaria elmeri,* a member of the custard apple family (Annonaceae) from the dense lowland forests of Indonesia. The plant's tan buds open from midnight until morning, and a single blossom lives for about three days, smelling like rotting wood and ripe mushrooms.

The first day the *Uvaria* flower is open, its carpel tips produce a clear, watery gelatin. This goo is not a true nectar, but it is a favorite food of tropical cockroaches, which consume the secretion without harming the flower. A day and a half later, this stigma goo dries up, the stamens shed their grains, and the roaches return to nibble pollen. Field experiments show that *Uvaria* flowers must be cross-pollinated to set seed. Adult roaches act as pollinators when they dine on pollen in an old blossom and then fly to a younger flower on a second vine to slurp stigmas. A cockroach may carry as many as twenty-one grains of pollen on its "chin" as it flutters between flowers.

Although these insects have also been observed visiting blossoms of tropical trees in the ginseng family (Araliaceae), cockroach pollination is uncommon in nature. In contrast, consider two other insect orders that are unloved by most humans. Beetles (Coleoptera) and flies (Diptera) have quite an influence on plant reproduction. An understanding of the range of interactions between these insects and their flowers helps in distinguishing the behavior of a true pollinator from that of a blossom vandal or a nectar thief.

Beetles would appear to be unpromising pollinators. Their thick, heavy armor ensures slow movement, unsteady flight, and legs too stiff to manipulate the sex organs within flowers. How could their smooth, polished shells carry pollen grains? Their mouthparts seem better designed for slashing and chopping than for precise consumption of nectar and pollen.

The common names given to some coleopterans often reflect our worst expectations. In Europe, for example, most beetles of the genus *Cetonia* are popularly known as rose chafers because of the rough way the insects treat our favorite flowers.

In all fairness, every vegetarian beetle can't be accused of floral murder. The order Coleoptera contains at least a quarter of a million species, and some entomologists insist that the count will shoot into the millions if collection efforts are extended into tropical forest canopies. Coleoptera is the most diverse order of animals on this planet, in part because the evolution of beetles reflects their exploitation of many different food sources. That's why interactions between beetles and blossoms are so variable. A beetle may destroy the flowers of one plant and then play the role of gentle pollinator on blossoms of a different species.

In Missouri, a blister beetle, *Chauliognathus marginatus,* appears in

July, shearing off the petals of cinquefoils *(Potentilla)* and mincing the stamens of yellow lotuses *(Nelumbo lutea)*. I've watched this beast's behavior alter, though, the minute it lands on the tiny flowers of a moonseed vine *(Menispermum canadense)*. The beetles carefully take pollen from the stamens of male flowers, delicately flicking the grains from the anther tips. Then they lick nectar from the base of the female flowers without harming the ovaries.

Yes, there are beetles dependent on the fat and protein in pollen. Some rose chafers, long-horned beetles (Cerambycidae), and soft-winged flower beetles (Melyridae) have broomlike tufts of bristles on their mouthparts that sweep pollen grains down their throats. Beetles of the family Oedemeridae fill up with flower nectar and then digest pollen by allowing the grains to soak in their gut. Some scarabs appear to be the only pollinators that actually "chew" pollen before swallowing it. These insects have pollen-cracking "molars" on their mandibles that can smash the outer wall of the grain. One tropical scarab, *Cyclocephala amazona,* swallows both the pollen *and* the hard hairs found on the flowers of peach palms *(Bactris gasipaes)*. It's believed that this beetle uses the gritty palm hairs to wear down pollen walls in the same way a chicken uses gravel to grind up corn kernels in its gizzard.

Food is not the only benefit beetles find in flowers. Since male and female insects are attracted to the same resources, some blossoms become sites in which beetles select mates. One odd aspect of studying beetle pollination is that dozens of pairs of mating insects may be found each time a flower is inspected. Two beetles may remain *en copula* for hours, with the female continuing to graze while the male clings staunchly to her abdomen. Scientists studying sexual selection in animals insist that this slow copulation benefits the male. The longer his penis blocks the female's genital pore, the more likely she will be to accept all his sperm so he can father all the eggs she lays.

During the first decades of the twentieth century, a few European scientists began studying beetle pollination in primitive magnolia-like flowers. Today, it is estimated that as many as 40 percent of all plant species with primitive blossoms require the aid of beetles in cross-pollination. Beetles pollinate many members of the custard apple, magnolia (Magnoliaceae), Winter's bark (Winteraceae), Panama hat plant (Cyclanthaceae), Australian spice bush (Eupomatiaceae), and waterlily (Nymphaeaceae) families. Without beetle pollinators, tropical orchards would never produce palm oils, and there would be no commercial nutmeg *(Myristica fragrans)* to grate into Christmas eggnog.

By the 1950s, many botanists had noted that flowers pollinated by beetles share similar features. Their floral organs tend to be well reinforced, enabling them to resist the insects' cutting jaws. Their blossoms are shaped like vases or urns, permitting the beetles to feed and copulate in the privacy of a darkened chamber. Finally, their petals lack the sharp, distinctive nectar guides characteristic of blossoms pollinated by animals with poor vision.

Entomologists also insisted that most beetles "see the world" with their sense of smell. The complex scents of beetle-pollinated flowers were compared to the fragrances of liqueurs, butterscotch, and overripe fruit, similarities that explain why pioneers in the United States once called yellow pond lilies *(Nuphar luteum)* brandy-bottles. These flowers usually lack nectar glands, so edible rewards emphasize pollen, starchy food bodies, and edible stamens. Beetles were regarded as such ancient and coarse tools for spreading pollen that one botanist described their sloppy tactics as "mess and soil" pollination.

Such vivid descriptions dominated the study of flower evolution until the 1980s. That's when scientists working independently in Israel, South Africa, and eastern Australia concluded that there are two diverging patterns of beetle pollination in nature. The thick, smelly urn-shaped flower associated with weak-eyed, "do-it-in-the-

Above: A large weevil emerges from the primitive flower of a *Eupomatia* spice bush. Photograph by T. Hawkeswood. *Below:* After eating pollen in an Israeli tulip, a hairy scarab climbs to the floral rim before launching into the air. Note the black-outlined "beetle marks" at the base of the flower. Photograph by A. Dafni.

dark" insects tends to reflect the specialized needs of some trees, bushes, and climbers native to dense forests. However, beetles live in so many different environments that pollination systems found in open woods and shrublands often differ in several important ways.

The beetle flowers of open habitats may take the form of broad bowls or platters made of thin sepals and petals, often marked with spectacular bull's-eye patterns of contrasting colors. They have a weak, sweet scent or are odorless. Pollen is the most important reward they offer, but some blossoms secrete nectar into shallow cups or troughs.

Working independently in the Australian bush, environmental consultant Trevor Hawkeswood observes and collects jewel beetles (Buprestidae), longicorns (long-horned beetles), and Christmas scarabs. By early summer, these insects are content to sip nectar from the shallow blossoms of ti trees *(Leptospermum),* eucalypts, or tree mistletoe *(Nuytsia floribunda).* Often, many beetles throng to the same dishlike flower, like cats drinking from the same milk bowl. In some Australian beetles, the cutting mouthparts have been replaced with membranes for sopping up sweet liquids.

Similar modifications have been described on the mouthparts of dozens of species of South African insects known commonly as monkey beetles (scarabs confined to the tribe Hoplini). These creatures, which appear to have a strong color sense, have hairy bodies that retain loose pollen grains and look like shaggy armpits sprayed with brilliant metallic paints. Obviously, each insect recognizes the color patterns of its own species, but how do scientists know whether a beetle can see flower pigments?

Dr. Amots Dafni of the University of Haifa and his associates studied *Amphicoma* scarabs around Haifa, Israel. These insects are always hungry for the pollen of wild poppies, tulips, anemones, and buttercups — wildflowers that all have red or orange petals in the Middle East. Dafni found that these beetles would eagerly invade a fake flower made of a red paper cup or even a child's beach bucket if it was made of a red-orange plastic.

In Israel and South Africa, some beetle-pollinated flowers can be identified with ease, as their blossoms wear "beetle marks." A beetle mark is a blackened spot or blotch surrounded by a lighter color, especially red, orange, yellow, or light purple. The dark, velvety blotch indicates where pollen or nectar is plentiful, inviting the beetle to crawl into the heart of the flower and, of course, bonk the stamens and stigmas.

One thing is certain. Ecologists have only begun to understand how these insects help seed production within vast communities of vegetation. On the sandy plains of South Africa, monkey beetles pollinate as much as a third of all the wildflowers that emerge each year from underground bulbs and tubers. A consortium of Japanese foresters studying the dense lowland jungle that spreads across the valleys of Sarawak, Malaysia, estimate that 20 percent of all trees, woody vines, and herbs require different beetles to set fruit. Their flowers welcome weevils (Curculionidae), reward rove beetles (Staphylinidae), cater to click beetles (Elateridae), or service sap beetles (Nitidulidae).

Beetle pollination is so diverse that many botanists now agree it's time to take a much closer look at interactions between flowers and true flies. These insects have also suffered from a biased press and slanted research. Granted, many flies produce maggots that eat flower bulbs, buds, and fruit. However, with more than 80,000 species in the order Diptera, it is to be expected that the tastes of winged adults often differ from those of their children.

The literature on fly pollination also shows divided loyalties. A few scientists are obsessed with the novelty of flowers that resemble hairy lumps of rotting meat and release a potent stench. These flowers are offered primarily by plants that exploit game flies (Calliphoridae), dung flies (Scatophagidae), fungus gnats (Mycetophilidae), and swarms of houseflies (Muscidae). Such blossoms are deeply colored, but their pigments tend to emphasize dull iodines, brick reds, and funereal shades of purple. Their floral scents, in turn, emphasize chemicals simulating the odors of feces, decaying organic matter, and mushroom-infested compost. Check out old wildflower books and you'll see that naturalists in the United States once called reddish brown trilliums (*Trillium sessile* and *T. erectum*) stinking Benjamins.

The nectar of flowers pollinated primarily by scavenging flies may target pregnant insects that are prepared to push their eggs into an animal's corpse or a dung heap. Many species of starfish flower *(Stapelia)* mimic the putrefaction of meat by secreting nectars rich in amino acids. The fly and midge species of corruption are most commonly associated with members of the *Rafflesia* (Rafflesiaceae), *Siparuna* (Monimiaceae), birthwort (Aristolochiaceae), milkweed (Asclepiadaceae), and philodendron (Araceae) families. Some orchids of the tropical and temperate zones are also pollinated by scavenger flies. The tiny flowers of some *Bulbophyllum* orchids are often hairy and iodine stained, and their stink reminds some growers of urine.

Carrion and dung flies are so common that the more opportunistic species of wayside flower release a few chemicals to retain these insects' interest. You will understand why bluebottles and dung flies sponge nectar from ox-eye daisies *(Chrysanthemum leucanthemum)* if you mass the flowering heads in a vase. In a closed room, daisies reek like fresh cow flops dabbed with honey.

Since the early 1920s, a few researchers have found that fly pollination can flourish without lurid colors and stinks. Many blossoms produced by other members of the daisy (Asteraceae), iris (Iridaceae), geranium (Geraniaceae), and cola nut (Sterculiaceae) families welcome flies with sweeter scents and nectar guides contrasting lighter, brighter tints. These flowers appeal to many flies for one simple reason. Unlike beetles, most adult flies lack chewing mouthparts, so all their nourishment derives from liquids, the tiniest particles, or both. Remember, even when mosquitoes and horseflies stab our flesh, they dine only on liquid plasma and microscopic corpuscles. Therefore, hundreds of plant species are pollinated primarily by flies because thousands of fly species prefer a straight and simple diet of nectar or pollen.

Hover flies (Syrphidae) must be the most commonly observed of all the flower flies, as they are found on almost every continent and have relatively large bodies. Some have abdomens decorated with bands of brown and yellow, making them easily mistaken for small bees. In the Southern Hemisphere, hover flies mass in golden swarms each spring, foraging on acacias, leek orchids *(Prasophyllum),* and many members of the eucalyptus family (Myrtaceae). In the United States and Europe, they are among the best-known pollinators of some enchanter's nightshades *(Circaea),* speedwells *(Veronica),* thrifts *(Armeria),* mayweeds *(Tripleurospermum),* and asters *(Aster).*

The drone fly *(Eristalis tenax),* a syrphid of Europe, has tasting hairs on its tongue that allow it to discriminate between the flavors of nectar and pollen. When a drone fly sees the color yellow, its instinctive response is to stick out its tongue, as yellow is one of the most common colors of greasy pollen and of the blotchy nectar guides on some flower petals.

The most spectacular flower flies are confined to the more temperate regions of southern Africa. For reasons still not understood, natural selection has encouraged the evolution of some African flies with mouthparts far longer than their bodies. This phenomenon is best observed in late winter through early spring, when tangle-vein flies (Nemestrinidae) and *Philoliche* horseflies (Tabanidae) emerge. The tangle-vein flies tuck their tongues between their legs as they rocket across the landscape. This is a most important concession for *Moegistorhynchus longirostris,* as its ten-inch tongue must be supported by a three-and-a-half-inch body! *Philoliche gulosa* has a tongue only twice as long as its body and must keep it extended in flight as if it were a javelin.

The proboscises of all long-tongued flies are too stiff to scoop up pollen. Instead, these insects land briefly on petals as their wings continue to beat and they thrust their tongues deep inside long flo-

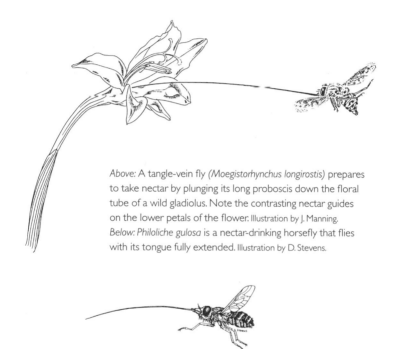

Above: A tangle-vein fly *(Moegistorhynchus longirostis)* prepares to take nectar by plunging its long proboscis down the floral tube of a wild gladiolus. Note the contrasting nectar guides on the lower petals of the flower. Illustration by J. Manning. *Below: Philoliche gulosa* is a nectar-drinking horsefly that flies with its tongue fully extended. Illustration by D. Stevens.

ral tubes and spurs. In southern Africa, tangle-veins and *Philoliche* horseflies pollinate some orchids, painted petals *(Lapeirousia),* gladioli *(Gladiolus),* and wild relatives of potted geraniums *(Pelargonium).*

These flies have excellent color vision. *Prosoeca* tangle-veins and *Philoliche* horseflies prefer blooms with purple or violet borders, while *Moegistorhynchus* flies prefer flowers with red flecks on a cream background. Different color preferences such as these may lower competition for nectar among different fly species.

Flies are naturally tolerant of damp environments that receive few bright days and endure temperature extremes. Small bees, by comparison, often are sluggish in the same habitats or are not commonly found there. I've mentioned the trend favoring fly pollination in the misty woodlands of Colorado mountain slopes, but fly pollination is also common in forests of the eastern United States. There, spring buds open against a background of dark, soggy humus on cold mornings. In southern Africa, wet, cool winters favor both the emergence of long-tongued flies and the blooming of bulbous herbs with narrow, tubular flowers.

The lowland forests around the equator endure extended rainy seasons. There, some smaller trees and tropical shrubs must flower under a hot, humid canopy that permits only snatches of sunlight to reach the forest floor. This is an environment much favored by true flies that are only a few millimeters long.

We would have no chocolate without these insects. *Theobroma cacao* and its allied species are members of the cola nut family. Cocoa bushes bloom twice a year, and their pollination depends on biting midges (Ceratopongonidae) and gall midges (Cecidomyiidae). Despite a domestication process that began with the Aztecs thousands of years ago, most cocoa bushes still require the services of their wild pollinators.

Cocoa seed develops best when the flowers receive pollen by early morning. The problem is that most cocoa flowers recognize and reject self-pollination. Genetic rules of mating are so strict that a plant often refuses pollen from a brother bush planted in the same row. Growers who fail to appreciate the wandering midge laborers find that the predicted crop of cocoa seed never materializes.

Botanist Allen Young learned that a productive cocoa plantation is a messy plantation, as growers must copy the decay in a tropical forest to please the flies. Compost and rotting banana stems must be strewn beneath the cocoa bushes to provide midge mommies with maggot nurseries. Moldy fallen fruits are left on the ground, as adult gall midges like to eat fungus spores.

Young found that some of the newer breeds of cocoa plant made fewer seeds because they had lost crucial characteristics that keep flies faithful to wild bushes. Some new breeds bloomed when most flies were still in the maggot phase. Midges always prefer wild *Theobroma* flowers that have a musty, almost bitter, scent, but the flowers on some new breeds had such faint fragrances that midges ignored them. For this reason, growers who tinker with cocoa genes must always remember to retain the features that appeal strongly to polli-nators.

Although distinctions among animals that ignore, spoil, and pol-linate flowers are minor ones, those differences affect both the range of natural diversity and the human economy. Therefore, let's start regarding flies and beetles as something more than one of nature's nastier jokes. It's all right to prefer butterflies to blowflies as long as we remember that important services are rendered by creatures that lack pleasing forms.

CHAPTER 11

The Moth's kiss, first!
Kiss me as if you made believe
You were not sure, this eve,
How my face, your flower, had pursed
Its petals up; so, here and there
You brush it, till I grow aware
Who wants me, and wide open burst.
    Robert Browning, "In a Gondola"

Psychoanalysis and Serenades

Butterfly houses are under construction in shopping malls, city parks, zoos, and botanical gardens all over the world. People actually pay good money to walk through a cage containing colorful insects. Tourist dollars aside, why raise flocks of hardy, fast-growing lepidopterans?

The answer is that an imprisoned butterfly ignores sightseers and prefers to pass its final days probing flowers. It's so much easier to watch these insects in captivity. Poets insist they are aimless, lazy creatures (Emily Dickinson compared a butterfly's flight to the "purposeless circumference" of fashionable people). However, our prisoner seems committed to investigating every zinnia before it dies. In the wild, with a wider choice of dining sites, the same insect would wander widely and capriciously, darting over the landscape and un-coiling its proboscis only after selecting the most suitable flower.

One inspirational writer turned these foraging insects into sym-bols of redemption, declaring that butterflies provide "hope for the flowers." This metaphor is supported by Western civilization, as *psy-che* is the ancient Greek word for both a butterfly and a human soul. Ancient symbolism also survives in the languages of modern medi-cine and botany. A troubled soul visits a psychiatrist, while butter-flies visit psychophilous (Greek for "butterfly-loving") flowers.

What are the distinctive features of psychophilous flowers? Care-ful studies of butterfly pollination began in the nineteenth century, and by the 1950s, scientists had concluded that some blossoms depended far more on butterflies for pollination than on any other insect. A butterfly flower stays open during daylight hours, releasing sweet scents. Its petals emphasize bright colors, especially yellowish orange through red, light purple, and blue shades. Most important, a butterfly flower stands erect on its stem, taking the shape of a stiff funnel or tube. There is enough space on the funnel's rim for the insect to perch comfortably. Access to nectar is through an unusu-ally long and constricted canal that accommodates only long, thin tongues. Botanists note how the sex organs of the flower extend above the funnel's rim. As the butterfly takes nectar, its head or body is brushed with pollen or combed by waiting stigmas.

As interest in butterfly pollination has increased, botanists have learned surprising new truths. Field research since the late 1960s has shown that comparatively few flowering plants are pollinated exclu-sively by butterflies. Of course, scientists still accept that lantana and *Psiguria* vines, mentioned in earlier chapters, demand butterfly pol-linators. To that list can be added some North American dogbanes *(Apocynum)*, fringed orchids *(Platanthera)*, phloxes *(Phlox)*, wild car-nations of Europe *(Dianthus)*, Asian buddleias *(Buddleja)*, and a few others. However, as the evidence continues to mount, it is also be-

Above: The *Sabatinca* moth lacks a coiled tongue but can scrape and grind pollen. Photograph by G. Gibbs. *Below:* Note how the stiltlike legs of this yellow butterfly (Pieridae) prop up the insect's body as it takes nectar from each of the tube flowers in the head of a *Brachycome* daisy. Photograph by T. Hawkeswood.

coming clear that the majority of butterfly flowers depend on a much wider range of insects. The same floral features that attract butterflies also attract plenty of other animals. When different insects forage on the same flower, the drab bees and flies may do most of the "hard work," even though observers tend to give the flashy butterflies all the credit.

There are two interlocking reasons why many butterflies may be indifferent or undependable pollinators. First, most of these insects have narrow bodies and long legs and hold their wings upright while feeding. Their bodies are too trim and angular for them to make adequate contact with the sex organs of flowers. Working in northern Australia, Trevor Hawkeswood found that when butterflies prance on blooming heads of *Acacia,* their proplike legs hold their bodies higher than the tips of the sex organs in the little flowers.

Second, the scales on a butterfly's wings can act as solar panels, absorbing the sun's energy. When butterflies sun themselves, they are not quite so dependent on the calories in nectar as are other insects. Therefore, a butterfly in the wild can afford to be picky about which flower it visits next. In fact, when some butterflies need essential minerals and proteins, they may adopt diets of no use to fresh flowers. These insects dip into mud puddles, dung piles, tree sap, or fermenting fruit. Tropical hamadryads (brush-footed ithomiids in the family Nymphalidae) often take nectar from dying flowers of members of the borage (Boraginaceae) family, as the fluid of decay contains useful poisons. Male hamadryads recycle the toxins to mark their territories, and females add them to their eggs to make them distasteful to predators.

A butterfly may visit flowers faithfully without ever carrying much pollen. In Sweden, 90 percent of flower visits made by the wood white butterfly *(Leptidea sinapis)* are to two species of wild violet and a vetchling, *Lathyrus montanus.* Wood whites netted on these blooms rarely carry more than three individual pollen grains.

However, accusing all butterflies of inept pollination is like accusing all psychiatrists of inept therapy. Scientists have learned that butterfly species differ in their roles as pollen carriers. For example, British scientists caught tortoiseshell butterflies *(Aglais utricae)* and found hundreds of pollen grains deposited on hair tufts that grow between the hundreds of facets that make up each insect's compound eyes. In the United States, sulphur butterflies *(Colias)* carry masses of phlox pollen on their mouthparts. Barbados pride *(Caesalpinia pulcherrima)* is a domesticated species grown as an ornamental tree in most tropical countries. The sex organs of the flowers are so long and curved that they rub the broad wings of the biggest butterflies from behind as the insects probe the nectar tubes. Pollen grains of Barbados pride come equipped with microscopic threads that lash onto loose wing scales. Clearly, the evolution of some flowers reflects adaptations that correct natural drawbacks in butterfly form and behavior.

In a few regions of the world, butterfly pollination is extremely stereotyped and specialized. Dr. Steve D. Johnson and Professor William J. Bond of the University of Cape Town suspect that the mountain beauty butterfly *(Meneris tulbaghia)* is the solitary pollinator of as many as twenty species of the scarlet wildflowers that bloom in South Africa from summer through autumn. Mountain beauty butterflies are so sensitive to red signals that hikers have reported the insects swooping out of the sky to inspect their red hats and socks. In contrast, African bees and sunbirds are ineffective pollinators of these plants because they take nectar without carrying pollen. Crimson stonecrops *(Crassula coccinea)* share the mountain beauty butterfly with scarlet gladioli *(Gladiolus)*, fire lilies *(Cyrtanthus)*, Guernsey lilies *(Nerine)*, and red-hot pokers *(Kniphofia uvaria)*. Observations of a South African swallowtail named *Princeps demodocus* suggest that although it, too, is a summer pollinator of wildflowers, it much prefers blue blossoms and refuses to compete with mountain beauties for nectar secreted by red flowers.

Relationships between flowers and true moths are even more intimate and intricate. Moths had a head start on floral relationships, as fossil evidence shows that moths are many millions of years older than butterflies. This helps explain why moth pollination is far more common and variable in nature than is butterfly pollination.

Moths also tend to have broader, plumper bodies, shorter legs, and wings that hang down by their sides. Therefore, it's easier for the sex organs of a flower to make contact with the body of a moth than with the body of a butterfly. The main difficulty naturalists experience in studying moth pollination is that much of the process occurs under cover of darkness, so some of the most interesting interactions are difficult to observe.

Fortunately, many moth species remain active during the day. Flowers pollinated by these moths show much the same range of colors, scents, and shapes as do butterfly flowers. In fact, while butterflies and day moths often drink from the same "trough," they make different contributions to the pollination of the same blossom.

Charles Darwin noted the unequal division of labor between moths and butterflies in the 1860s when he received a box of pinned lepidopterans. The moths and butterflies had been collected by a man who netted every specimen on day-blooming pyramid orchids *(Anacamptis pyramidalis)*. Since orchids release their pollen masses as paired blobs, it was easy for Darwin to see which type of insect carried the biggest load. Each pinned butterfly in the box carried a maximum of two or three pairs of orchid pollinia on its tongue. In contrast, one pale shoulder moth *(Acontia luctuosa)* wore seven pairs on its tongue, and a *Caradrina* moth carried eleven. Darwin was so impressed that he drew and published a posthumous portrait of the pale shoulder moth.

Another reason why the role of moths in pollination is underemphasized is that these insects are easily mistaken for other animals. Burnet moths *(Zygaena)* of Europe, for instance, are found on many wildflowers, but people mistake them for butterflies because of their showy black wings spangled with red or yellow dots. In the United States, people sometimes confuse clearwing moths *(Hemaris)* with hummingbirds because of their chunky bodies and rapid, hovering flight.

Furthermore, some naturalists are unaware that many moths feed as winged adults. Children who enjoy rearing the cocoons of cecropia moths, luna moths, and other silkworm moths (Saturniidae) know that the emerging moth lacks functional mouthparts and lives only to mate and lay eggs. It may come as a surprise, however, that other moth species will go almost anywhere for a drink.

For example, in eastern Australia, the craving for nectar hits bogong moths *(Agrotis infusa)* as they emerge from their cocoons in spring. These insects must find nectar continuously to supply the energy they need to fly up mountain peaks, sleep through the summer, and avoid the hot, dry months on the lower plains. Many bogongs lose their way during this frenzied flutter to higher ground and take refuge in cool houses, much to the annoyance of Sydney homemakers. Other species fly even longer distances in search of nourishment. In northern Africa, *Plusia gamma* also emerges from its cocoon in early spring, but it quits the country by May to migrate across the Mediterranean Sea and feed on flowers in European meadows.

The most primitive moths have eating habits similar to those of flower-visiting beetles and cockroaches. The Micropterigidae are a family of tiny moths that retain chewing mouthparts as winged adults. They even have special scraping palps on their faces to "pry" pollen out of anther sacs. On the Pacific island of New Caledonia, moths of the genus *Sabatinca* follow the flowering of *Zygogynum* trees. These insects congregate on young flowers to drink stigma goo and on older flowers to eat some of the greasiest pollen in nature. The pollen is so gluey that it clumps onto the moth's body scales. The insect then cross-pollinates flowers when it investigates young blooms on a second tree. *Sabatinca* moths are less than a quarter of an inch long, so an open flower offers a large platform on which male and female insects can dance and mate. Both sexes of the moth respond to the odor of *Zygogynum* flowers as a signal to assemble in the same place within the same dense forest.

Night moths are cold-blooded insects, but they fly at a time when it's impossible for them to harness the energy in a sunbeam, as do the day-flying butterflies. The successful foraging of a moth at night depends in part on the warmth of the evening air. Consequently, moth pollination is recorded more often in the hot, humid Tropics than in cooler temperate zones. This helps explain why some desert and Mediterranean plants, such as green daffodils *(Narcissus viridiflorus)* and many caper bushes *(Capparis),* delay flowering until late summer or early autumn, when the desert twilight is hot and muggy.

Important exceptions to this rule have been noted in the frigid woods of New England. Professor Bernd Heinrich, an authority on body temperature in insects, studies owlet moths such as *Lithophane hemina* and some *Eupsilia* species. These animals, which carry the biochemical equivalent of antifreeze in their bodies, remain active through the cold of November, gorging on the nectar of witch hazel flowers *(Hamamelis).* Dormant owlets hide under tree bark to survive the months of ice and snow, emerging after winter thaws to visit pussy willows *(Salix discolor)* in bloom.

Plants pollinated by night moths have especially fragrant flowers. Our noses recognize these piercing scents long before our eyes see the blossoms. The fragrance is released in nocturnal pulses, making it easy to identify which of our neighbors grow jasmine or Japanese honeysuckle *(Lonicera japonica)* in their backyards. Essences of night-blooming flowers have been favorites in the perfume industry for thousands of years, but many night flowers smell strongly without smelling sweetly. Some hobbyists insist that the odor of nocturnal orchids reminds them of freshly chopped green beans and other

Above: A fritillary butterfly
(Heliconius charitonius) takes
nectar from a female flower of
a *Psiguria* vine. *Below:* Relative
lengths of flowers pollinated
by moths. Left, fluttermill
(Oenothera macrocarpa),
an evening primrose.
Right, Japanese honey-
suckle *(Lonicera japonica).*
Illustrations by J. Myers.

juicy vegetables. In the hot lowlands of New Guinea, some Vireya rhododendrons are pollinated by night moths. As evening progresses, they release a fragrance surprisingly similar to that of nonprescription medicines used to soothe indigestion. At home in Missouri, I like to water my garden at sundown because my gold band lilies *(Lilium auratum)* smell of vanilla and soap, evoking the fragrance of a woman's hair washed with herbal shampoo.

What night-moth flowers gain in fragrance they may lose in color, appearing white, cream colored, or ivory to the human eye. It is suspected that moths in night flight pick up the flowers' pale images in the moonlight. A closer inspection, though, reveals that these blanched blooms should also be appreciated for their subtle tints. Look for the gold-and-green sheen on the night horse orchid *(Brassavola cucullata),* the terra-cotta stain on the petal tips of some angel's trumpets *(Brugmansia),* or the purple blush on the sex organs of capers and some swamp crinums *(Crinum).*

The size and shape of night-moth flowers tend to reflect the size and feeding behaviors of the insects that pollinate them. Field biologists discriminate between blossoms pollinated by "settling" moths and those pollinated by sphinx moths and hawkmoths (Sphingidae). Settling moths include most of the night-flying species that have small bodies and perch on flowers while they search for nectar. They crawl under, over, and between the flowers' sex organs, transporting pollen on their bodies, legs, and cloaking wings. Flowers pollinated by settling moths are small and shaped like brushes or short, erect funnels. The tiny blossoms are usually massed together at the tips of flowering branches. For example, bushes of the genus *Zapoteca,* Mexican members of the mimosa family (Mimosaceae), have congested, whitish pom-poms on which settling moths land.

Hawkmoths and sphinx moths have larger bodies, much longer tongues, and flight muscles so strong that the moths drink nectar while hovering in midair. These insects burn up a great deal of energy in flight, so they prefer flowers far richer in sucrose than those visited by most butterflies. However, flowers pollinated exclusively by hawkmoths have restricted access to the insects' bodies. A hovering hawkmoth pokes only its head into the blossom, so the flower's sex organs come in contact with only the insect's mouthparts, "forehead," and eyes.

Hawkmoths are large insects and feed on the wing, and for this reason they often visit flowers with large, solitary blossoms projecting horizontally from their stalks. These flowers remind me of instruments in the woodwind and brass sections of an orchestra. It's easy to see "clarinets and saxophones" in capers, sea daffodils *(Pancratium)*, tobaccos *(Nicotiana)*, white gilias *(Gilia)*, and woodbines *(Lonicera periclymenum)*.

Compared with other lepidopterans, hawkmoths are dependable pollinators of some of the largest flowers of tropical habitats and dry zones. These "tubas and sousaphones" include flowers of the comet orchids of Madagascar *(Angraecum)*, many climbing cacti, and such famous nightshades as desert jimsonweeds *(Datura)* and angel's trumpets.

The absurd length of hawkmoth flowers is easy to understand in light of the way their pollinators feed. Like the tangle-vein flies discussed in the previous chapter, some hawkmoths have tongues far longer than their bodies. A species of *Cocytius* moth from South America and a *Xanthopan* sphinx from Madagascar have proboscises almost a foot in length.

These insects drink while hovering, so a moth with a long proboscis can steal nectar from short flowers without ever bringing its head into contact with stamens or stigmas. Charles Darwin found that the tubes and spurs of most flowers committed to hawkmoth pollination are slightly longer than the longest tongues of their moths. Nectar is concealed at the spur's tip or at the base of a long floral throat, so the insect is forced to ram its head into the flower to claim its reward. When it does so, pollen clumps on its eyes and around the thickened base of its tongue. The impact of a hungry hawkmoth on a flower may be so violent that the insect loses some scales on the flower's petals.

The eighty or so *Oenothera* species in the United States (better known as evening primroses, fluttermills, and shepherd's dandelions) are celebrities of hawkmoth pollination. Domesticated breeds of these wildflowers with trumpets rimmed in white, light yellow, or pink have become increasingly popular since the late 1980s as perennials for rock gardens. However, in the first two decades of the twentieth century, authors and schoolteachers cited them as perfect examples of hawkmoth flowers because they were common yet dramatic wayside plants. In many species of evening primrose, the bud opens rapidly at twilight only to fade and shrivel by late morning of the following day. These flowers turned early nature writers into romantics. In 1900, Neltje Blanchan wrote, "Like a ball-room beauty, the evening primrose has a jaded, bedraggled appearance by day when we meet it by the dusty roadside."

Modern research in California, Kansas, and Missouri confirms an interdependence between many hawkmoths and certain species of evening primrose. Unfortunately, the relationship between rare plants and common moths shows signs of fraying, and humans are responsible.

People enjoy fragrant hawkmoth flowers and agree that they should be protected, and nature reserves and zoning laws make this possible. People also hate those crop-eating tomato and tobacco hornworms *(Manduca)* and believe they should be eradicated, and crop dusters and modern pesticides make this possible. When hornworms are allowed to mature, though, they develop into some of the largest hawkmoths in the United States. These insects are essential in the cross-pollination of rare evening primroses, jimsonweeds, and some cacti.

At the Arizona-Sonora Desert Museum, outside Tucson, Drs. Stephen L. Buchmann and Gary Paul Nabhan offer convincing evidence that populations of *Peniocereus striatus,* one of the most striking night-blooming cacti, are declining in the United States. The remaining plants, which grow near the Mexican border, rarely set berries. They require cross-pollination, but few of the flowers are ever visited by *Manduca* moths. Buchmann and Nabhan attribute the drop in hawkmoth pollination to uncontrolled crop dusting in northern Mexico. Winds carry the toxic droplets north, failing to respect the boundaries of property reserved for cacti and moths.

In Antioch, California, sand mining reduced the distribution of a rare subspecies of the desert evening primrose *(Oenothera deltoides)* to an area of just twelve acres. As a result of habitat destruction and a history of spraying, both *Manduca* and *Hyles* sphinx moths have been rare visitors at this site for almost forty years. When cross-pollination occurs at all, it is usually the work of a few opportunistic bumblebees finding flowers that linger through morning. However, only two of every ten seeds in an ovary are fertilized when a bumblebee visits.

You've seen how butterflies share pollination duties with flies, bees, and day moths. Could a specialized insect such as a hawkmoth share pollination duties with other insects? More important, could other flower-visiting animals help hawkmoth flowers set seed?

Remember, hawkmoth flowers secrete such rich nectar that this delicious reward could act as a powerful incentive, attracting other "musicians" with broad bodies and extended tongues. It's possible that the relationship between trumpet flowers and hawkmoths is not always as exclusive as it might appear.

I offer one anecdote. In 1992, my wife and I were guests at Camp Zama, a U.S. military base outside Tokyo. One morning, I followed a trail through a glen and found a Japanese honeysuckle in bloom. In the United States, this introduced vine has become an invasive pest, so I was interested in examining this classic hawkmoth flower in its country of origin. Even though the sun had been up for hours, the flowers' sweet fragrance remained strong.

What I did not expect was the incredible diversity of insects I found in the flowers. I saw no day-flying hawkmoths, but the range of flies, butterflies, and bees proved overwhelming. The largest patrons were Asian relatives of the big wood-boring carpenter bees found in the United States. They had such long tongues and bulky bodies that I was sure they were pollinating the honeysuckles as they drank.

Unfortunately, without equipment to collect and analyze specimens, I couldn't gather hard evidence, so the question of how exclusive the hawkmoth-honeysuckle relationship may be remains unanswered. All I have is a vivid memory of a unique day in June. The life of a naturalist is full of regrets, so always travel with a butterfly net and a killing jar. You have been warned.

CHAPTER 12

Auto-da-fé and judgment
Are nothing to the bee;
His separation from his rose
To him seems misery
    Emily Dickinson, "Two Worlds"

The Faithful and Unfaithful Bee

Writers want us to believe that bees and flowers are soul mates. A 2,400-year-old drama from India compares the hero's courtship of a maiden to a bee claiming a blossom. Thousands of years later, performers in British music halls sang about another bee that remained faithful to a honeysuckle long after the flower died.

Few poets have challenged the tradition of the manly and active bee seducing the girlish and languid flower. Even Vita Sackville-West, an author who enjoyed her share of lesbian affairs, wrote, "For every bee becomes a drunken lover / Standing upon his head to sup the flowers." Romance colors the language of beekeepers as well. Worker honeybees try to rip open buds to reach immature pollen, and their jaws leave brownish scars on tender organs. Hive owners call these wounds "bee kisses."

Depending on which entomologist is consulted, there are 20,000 to 30,000 bee species throughout the world, and we can't expect each one to play Romeo to only one floral Juliet. Consider the queen bumblebee *(Bombus pennsylvanicus)* I caught on a sensitive brier *(Schrankia nuttallii)* on a Kansas prairie. Her pollen baskets combined grains from the sensitive brier with those of wild roses and sundrops *(Calylophus berlandieri)*. On another occasion, a *Nomia* bee I netted on a guinea flower *(Hibbertia scandens)* in an Australian rain forest wore pollinia of hyacinth orchid *(Dipodium)* on her head. I often find that a single bee carries pollen grains from three or four different plant families on her body, even though these different plants may offer flowers with extremely different shapes, colors, and scents.

It is true, though, that some bee species are always associated with a narrow range of closely related flowers. Naturalists may refer to such insects as creosote bees, borage bees, or prickly pear bees to emphasize their specialized foraging habits. Conservative shopping can be taken to extremes. Take the case of the bee genus *Perdita,* which is common throughout the southwestern United States. Like their Shakespearean namesake, some *Perdita* bees show a finicky bias for particular flowers and ignore other plants blooming at the same time. *Perdita californica* restricts her visits to three species of mariposa lily *(Calochortus)*. *Perdita calochorti* is even pickier, frequenting only sego mariposa *(Calochortus nuttallii)*.

That's right—some bees have scientific names that reflect their preferred flowers. Each spring, the woodlands of the eastern United States buzz with females of *Andrena erythronii* gathering the pollen of trout lilies *(Erythronium)*. On the western coast of Australia, males and females of *Leioproctus conospermi* mate on flowering branches of smoke bush *(Conospermum),* and then the impregnated females gather smoke bush pollen.

Of course, the more we learn about the lives of these working mothers, the more we realize that some loyalties are overrated. For instance, *Lasioglossum nymphaearum* frequents waterlilies *(Nymphaea),* but some adults stray from ponds to visit wildflowers on dry land.

Earlier chapters gloried in important relationships between flowers and various insects, but now I want to emphasize the fact that we live on a planet pollinated primarily by bees. Bee pollination is the rule in most big plant families, including beans (Fabaceae), heaths (Ericaceae), orchids (Orchidaceae), snapdragons (Scrophulariaceae), daisies (Asteraceae), and others. It's virtually impossible to read current monthly scientific journals without finding some new paper that describes bees pollinating common or rare plants. Some naturalists quip that pollination biology should really be called "bee botany," as bees are a flower's winged penis.

Bees share the order Hymenoptera with their close cousins the hunting wasps and the more distantly related ants. Wasp pollination, as you will see, is important but infrequent in nature, and ant pollination has rarely been documented. How can we account for such a remarkable dependence between most flowering plants and only eight to ten families of true bees?

Motherhood offers the best clue. As discussed briefly in chapter 9, female bees are among the few insects to rear their offspring almost exclusively on floral foods. Some stingless *Trigona* bees "enrich" their offspring's diet with carrion and dung (imagine how this taints their honey), but pollen and nectar remain the basic formula for raising bees to maturity. Also recall that some bees gather floral oils to enrich infant diets. Oil gatherers are found in southern Africa, North America, and South America. To feed their grubs, they harvest grease from flowers of snapdragons, rhatany roots *(Krameria),* yellow loosestrifes *(Lysimachia),* nance trees *(Byrsonima),* and *Stigmaphyllon* vines.

True honey is a refined food for bee larvae. Workers evaporate the excess water in flower nectar to concentrate the remaining nutrients. The bees then mix their digestive enzyme, invertase, with the remaining syrup to prevent it from solidifying. The honey sold in supermarkets crystallizes because the invertase vanishes when the bottler warms the comb to remove the wax. Some adult bees also use their digestive chemistry to break down the large sucrose molecules in nectar into glucose and fructose, making sugar digestion easier for grubs. However, only a few hundred species (true honeybees, stingless bees, and bumblebees) make so much honey that they keep some on tap in communal pots or combs. The vast majority of bee species make up tiny quantities of honey each day, mixing it with pollen to produce puddings and loaves.

With the next generation to provision, bees are under far greater pressure to find flower foods than are most insects. The pregnant beetle feeds herself, but the solitary bee feeds herself and makes a pudding for children she'll never see. Depending on genetic history, caste, physical age, and community structure, a social bee feeds herself but may also shop for her children, her mother, her mature siblings, and her grub sisters and brothers.

Consider the benefits a plant population receives when flowers are visited repeatedly and consistently by animals that are zealous pollen carriers. Natural selection favors the plants with the most efficient bee pollinators, as their flowers produce the greatest number of cross-pollinated seeds.

Bee flowers are so common that they seem to lack unique features. Most of them open during the day because most bees prefer to forage under strong sunlight. These blossoms have a familiar, sweet fragrance, although acrid stinks have been recorded in the mandrake *(Mandragora officinarum)* and some wild and cultivated gourds *(Cucurbita)*. Cheerful yellows, the vast range of blues through purples, and ultraviolet shades color most bee flowers, while reds and oranges are uncommon. Until the late 1990s, scientists presumed that bees were red-blind because results of early experiments showed honeybees either ignoring scarlet models or "forgetting" the location of sugar water when it was dished up against a background of crimson paper. However, the most recent research in the United States and Germany confirms that bees' eyes can pick up red-orange wavelengths. A new generation of scientists must now explain why so many bees disdain red-orange blooms.

Bee-pollinated plants are likely to tuck their rewards into flowers with the strangest shapes. Compared with the stereotypical trumpet-shaped bloom that awaits a hawkmoth, bee flowers have a multitude of forms. It's true that some flowers offer bees diluted nectar in simple, shallow bowls. However, other bee flowers secrete rich nectars that have the highest concentrations of edible sugars (more than 35 percent). These blossoms often force bees to search for their drinks under floral hoods, inside hollow spurs, or down long floral throats. The nectar most preferred by bees is often hidden in flowers resembling sock puppets, dangling urns, teakettles, brushes, and sailboats.

Flower shape reflects the one major advantage most bees have over all other flower-visiting insects. Bees use their six legs as a human would use fingers on the same hand to investigate and manipulate floral organs. It's easy to see how a bumblebee or honeybee uses her forelegs to scrape pollen out of anthers. However, she also uses her limbs to push open petal lips and lids, to shove aside organs that cover nectar, and to carry pollen. The flowers that have evolved with manipulative bees are really designed to deny access to less efficient beetles, flies, and butterflies.

In fact, some bee flowers are unattractive to other insects because they contain no nectar at all and make it difficult to harvest pollen. In North America, bumblebees and sweat bees *(Lasioglossum)* visit wild roses with the loyalty and enthusiasm of old customers. They comb hundreds of anthers in each flower without the promise of a drink. The same bee repeats the same behavior in other "dry" blossoms, including prickly poppies *(Argemone),* bloodroots *(Sanguin-*

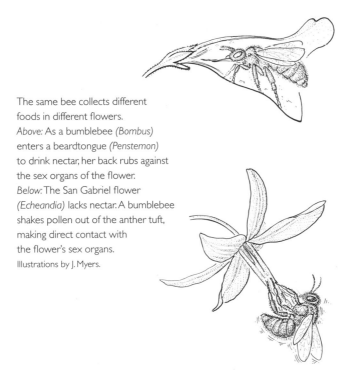

The same bee collects different foods in different flowers.
Above: As a bumblebee *(Bombus)* enters a beardtongue *(Penstemon)* to drink nectar, her back rubs against the sex organs of the flower.
Below: The San Gabriel flower *(Echeandia)* lacks nectar. A bumblebee shakes pollen out of the anther tuft, making direct contact with the flower's sex organs.
Illustrations by J. Myers.

aria), and leather bells *(Clematis).* Female bees that visit nectarless flowers sacrifice fulfillment of their own immediate needs for the benefit of their offspring or younger siblings. It's worthwhile to visit a flower that lacks an open bar provided it offers generous quantities of nutritious pollen.

The most specialized nectarless flowers have the most stream-lined forms. When they open, they often nod upside-down on their individual stalks. The petals curl backward, exposing stamens clustered together in tufts, like fancy lightbulbs below ceiling fans. Each plump anther resembles a salt shaker, with ripe pollen escaping only through terminal holes or tiny slits. These elegant flowers are seen on most nightshade vines *(Solanum),* tomatoes *(Lycopersicon),* shooting stars *(Dodecatheon),* sennas *(Cassia),* and many lily-like herbs. To harvest pollen, a bee must hang upside-down, grabbing the tuft of anthers with the claws on her legs, and then shake the tuft by vibrating the wing muscles in her thorax. Watch a bumblebee perform these acrobatics on a nightshade flower and you will probably be able to hear the high-pitched whine of muscles in her chest. As she sonicates, clouds of pollen spurt from the flower's anther holes like salt grains knocked out of a shaker.

Gathering pollen without benefit of the liquid energy in nectar sounds like an excellent way for an insect to become exhausted. How can sonicating bees "jump-start" nectarless blooms and still have enough fuel to return to their burrows or hives? In most cases, these insects interrupt their visits to nectarless, pollen-rich flowers by refreshing themselves at blossoms that secrete lots of nectar but offer meager pollen. My Kansas bumblebee scraped up pollen from dozens of "dry" roses by bolstering herself with drinks from sundrops blooming on the same prairie. Insect physiologist Bernd Heinrich, who studied this economical alternative system of foraging in the 1960s and early 1970s, calls it "majoring and minoring." Different plants benefit because they share the same pollinator without having to waste resources by duplicating rewards. Scientists now know that majoring and minoring is not confined to bumblebees and is practiced by many bee species around the world. The *Nomia* bee I caught in the Australian rain forest also carried triangular pollen grains on her hind legs, indicating that she had visited the nectar-filled cups of *Baeckea* or native turpentines *(Syncarpia)* before perusing the nectarless blooms of hyacinth orchids and guinea vines.

Of course, this also means that different wildflowers blooming together often appeal to different bees. The physical size and symmetry of bee-pollinated flowers vary because bees come in so many sizes and pack different tools for harvesting food. For example, among Wallace's giant leafcutters *(Chalicodoma pluto)*, which are confined to the Moluccas, females are more than two inches long. In contrast, *Perdita minima* of the western United States is about as big as the period that ends this sentence. The commercial honeybee is about half an inch long, but that's a biggish bee by entomological standards.

Most bees are not able to hover in midair while they drink nectar, so most bee-pollinated flowers are equipped with petals or sepals modified to form rigid landing platforms complete with runways well marked with nectar guides. That's why the flowers of so many orchids, snapdragons, mints, irises, jewelweeds *(Impatiens)*, and peas have stiff lower lips, aprons, or keels.

The length, shape, and sculpting of bees' tongues and other mouthparts differ so much that taxonomists use these organs to describe new species and assign them to appropriate families. A short-tongued bee, whose proboscis is usually shorter than her head, may have to confine her search for nectar to shallow, dish-shaped blooms. A long-tongued bee can dip into deep floral throats and spurs, as her proboscis is far longer than her head. Many gold bees and orchid bees (Euglossini tribe) of the tropical Americas have tongues that are longer than their bodies. To fly, a gold bee holds her tongue against the underside of her body by threading it between her three pairs of legs.

Specialist and generalist bees share the same deserts, bogs, prairies, and woodlands, so a single flower is often visited by obsessed fanatics *and* flexible opportunists. Along Canadian waterways, for example, pickerel weed *(Pontederia cordata)* receives two different sets of customers. Five large bumblebee species balance their trips to pickerel weed with visits to flowers of common milkweed *(Asclepias syriaca)* and other wildflowers. In contrast, smaller bees such as *Melissodes apicata* and *Duforea novae-angliae* depend on pickerel weed for almost every droplet of nectar and every grain of pollen. On

Different bees use different equipment to take nectar. *Above:* The *Amegilla* bee has a long, extended tongue. Illustration by J. Manning.
Below: The Fu Manchu bee *(Leioproctus filamentosa)* has a short tongue but can extract nectar with a series of elongated, threadlike palps.
Illustrations by J. Myers.

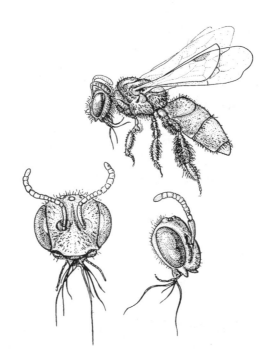

warm, sunny days, the combined work of generalists and specialists empties every open pickerel weed flower of 95 percent of its pollen by noon. Which set of shoppers, though, makes the most efficient pollinator?

Sometimes the specialist is the best "matchmaker." Most deerberry *(Vaccinium stamineum)* fruits are the result of visits by a single species of bee, *Melitta americana,* even though deerberry flowers are also visited by many generalist sweat bees and leafcutter (Megachilidae) bees. In the United States, a squash bee *(Peponapis pruinosa)* is considered the superior pollinator of pumpkin and zucchini crops because she carries more pollen into female flowers than do commercial honeybees.

On the other hand, bees can become so dependent on a single group of flowers that they evolve into sophisticated thieves. In the eastern woodlands of Australia, the Fu Manchu bee *(Leioproctus filamentosa)* lives almost exclusively on food found in flowers of snottygobble bushes *(Persoonia).* The Fu Manchu has a short tongue, so she pushes her long moustache (composed of threadlike palps around her mouth) between the snottygobble's petals to rob the flower of nectar. Fu Manchus have such tiny bodies that they are able to pilfer pollen without touching the receptive tip of the carpel. In contrast, *Exoneura* bees divide their time between snottygobbles, acacias, daisies, and eucalypt flowers. These generalists pollinate more snottygobbles than do Fu Manchus because they never rob nectar and always touch both male and female organs of the same flower while foraging.

Research indicates that the pickerel weed hedges its bets. A big, sloppy bumblebee carries more pickerel weed pollen from flower to flower than does either of the two little specialists. The problem is that bumblebees are bargain hunters that will abandon pickerel weed if something else offers a sweeter nectar or more pollen. When this occurs, the pollination of pickerel weed becomes the sole province of its smaller but more loyal fans.

I started this chapter by poking fun at a literary tradition that praises "macho" bees even though we know that worker bumble-bees and honeybees are always sterile females. Must this mean that *all* pollinating bees are always female? It is true that male honeybees spend their adult lives being hand-fed by their sisters. However, using this celebrated drone to represent the typical life of all male bees is like using the most notorious celebrity in Hollywood to represent American morals. The males of most bee species on this planet feed themselves once they've reached winged maturity. They visit flowers in search of food and receptive females. Collections and field experiments show that male bees of various species help pollinate blueberries, leek orchids *(Prasophyllum),* bluebells, and snotty-gobbles. Males don't harvest pollen for the grubs they father, but they do drink nectar, and as they feed they come in contact with the flowers' sex organs.

Pollination by male bees is especially well documented in Central America and South America. Male orchid and gold bees cross-pollinate the often nectarless flowers of some orchids, gesneriads (Gesneriaceae), tree tomatoes *(Cyphomandra),* and aroids (Araceae) such as *Spathiphyllum.* As mentioned in chapter 9, these blossoms secrete unusually complex scents that are rich in terpenoids. The male bees scrape up bits of the flowers' scent glands and store them in flasklike saddlebags on their hind legs. By blending scents of several flowers, an orchid bee makes his own distinctive cologne. Aggressive males of some species may use this perfume to mark territory, like dogs squirting fire hydrants. Others broadcast their cologne to attract other males, encouraging mating dances that may lure virgin females to a humming, fluttering circle of bachelors.

Although wasps are close relatives of bees, they would appear to be unpromising pollinators because female wasps are such well-known hunters, rearing their grubs on meaty diets of spiders or insects. Few people have observed a wasp harvesting pollen. Remember, though, that it takes a lot of energy to wrestle tarantulas and sting caterpillars, so many wasps visit flowers for nectar breaks. A few naturalists who study plants pollinated primarily by wasps believe that wasp flowers have special features that make them less attractive to most bees and hover flies. Examples are figworts *(Scrophularia),* helleborine orchids *(Epipactis),* and a few species of passion flower *(Passiflora)* that are green with brown or dirty red splotches. These flowers offer fructose-rich nectars, and some plant collectors insist that the petals exude a bizarre odor like honey mixed with human sweat or raw, aging meat.

There are some unique relationships in wasp pollination. Male wasps are the only pollinators of many Australian and Eurasian orchids, a topic explored in a later chapter. Each spring, the chocolate-colored bells of some Turkish and Persian fritillaries *(Fritillaria)* are visited by the fertile queens of yellow jackets *(Vespula)* that have overwintered beneath logs or stones. British gardeners complain of wasp queens invading their conservatories when their pots of *Fritillaria graeca* bloom, releasing scents similar to that of bad meat.

Female masarid wasps (Masaridae) actually swallow pollen and store it in a special "crop" in the abdomen. This bizarre but effective mode of foraging is a feature these wasps share with primitive hyalacinae bees (Colletidae). When the masarid returns to her burrow, she regurgitates grains and uses them for baby food. It is suspected that these insects play an important role in the lives of many of South Africa's wildflowers. Closer to home, California's masarids pollinate some beardtongues *(Penstemon).*

Fig trees *(Ficus)* and gall wasps in the family Agaonidae depend on each other in a relationship that is highly specialized. It appears that each of the 800 species of fig tree on this planet must rely on a different species of agaonid wasp for pollination. A female gall wasp rears all her children inside a succulent, flower-lined stalk that appears on a tree twig. In exchange for this nursery, the female wasp carries pollen into an immature stalk and dumps the grains onto the female flowers, ensuring fertilization. A fertilized stalk ripens into a plump, edible fig. The "seeds" in a ripe fig are really all that is left of the individual fruits of tiny female flowers.

The mother wasp encourages cross-pollination by carrying pollen from her birth tree to a second tree that bears young, green fig stalks. Each fertilized fig offers room for only one family of gall wasps to mature, so brothers and sisters must mate with each other. Each impregnated daughter then gathers fig pollen and starts the next generation on a new tree. The wasp is a child of sibling incest, but she is the only matchmaker who can ensure that each ripe wild fig is the offspring of a marriage between two genetic strangers. Can every royal house in Europe make the same claim?

There are more species of ants on this planet than there are species of bees or wasps. However, ant pollination has been documented in only a few plants, including a couple of orchids, desert spurges, and a creeping member of the mint family. Ants adore liquids that are rich in sugars and amino acids, so why have plants seemingly ignored a potentially rich source of pollinators?

It was once assumed that interactions between ants and blossoms were unsuccessful because wingless worker ants lack pollen-trapping hairs and can't fly from flower to flower. This argument is inadequate, though, in light of the diversity of ant anatomy and behavior. Different ant species have a wide range of body hairs and are often shaggier than some small bees and flower-visiting beetles. Furthermore, many ants are fine climbers. As you will see in the next chapter, you don't have to fly to be an efficient pollinator if you are agile and unafraid of heights.

Australian scientists Andrew and Christine Beattie offer a superior explanation derived from experiments conducted in the 1980s. Pollen sperm dies a quick death if the grains stick to ants. Workers secrete antibiotics from a gland on their bodies and smear themselves and their larvae with natural disinfectants. Bees and wasps can line their nurseries with antiseptic waxes, resins, or paper, but ant eggs must hatch in burrows made of dirt or dead wood. The ant antibiotics protect offspring and adults from diseases carried in soil or decaying matter. Unfortunately, the same chemicals that knock out bacteria and fungi have a devastating effect on pollen.

Although ants may be negligible pollinators, they are extremely important in maintaining and protecting generations of flowering plants. The workers of some species disperse and "plant" the seeds of many acacias, spring wildflowers, and members of the sedge family (Cyperaceae) after they eat the fleshy food bodies on the seed coats. Other ant species protect the stems and leaves of *Cecropia* trees, bromeliads, orchids, and acacias from grazing insects in exchange for more food or for hollow, chambered stems that make cozy nesting sites.

Had evolution taken a slightly different turn, our songs, plays, and poems would have different metaphors. We'd sing of the ant and *his* rose and write odes to pismires and petunias.

CHAPTER 13

*In the East, the Rose is an object of peculiar esteem.
The Oriental poets have united the beauteous Rose
with the Melodious nightingale; and the flower is
fabled to have burst forth from its bud at the song
of the warbler of the night.*

Richard Folkard Jr., *Plant Lore, Legends, and Lyrics*

The Squawking Tree

For two years, my wife and I lived in a quiet apartment in a residential corner of Sydney, Australia. Well, it was quiet until a pink-flowering gum tree *(Eucalyptus ficifolia)* bloomed outside our window. At dawn, we'd wake to the tinny shrieks of rainbow lorikeets *(Trichoglossus haematodus)*. These starling-sized parrots dress outlandishly in streaky blue, grass green, and yellowish orange plumage. Each polished, hooked bill is coral red in color and conceals a flexible, fingerlike tongue tipped with brush cells. These brushlike tongues sop up nectar and sweep pollen out of the gum blossoms. Our lorikeets insisted on arriving by the dozen and quarreling incessantly over the twigs that held the most clusters of open flowers.

The situation grew worse at bedtime, when dark phantoms with rubbery wings flopped onto the branches. Our clumsy ghosts were grey-headed flying foxes *(Pteropus poliocephalus),* and these bats ate whatever had been left by the lorikeets. They squealed and screamed until we felt as if we'd rented rooms next to a convention center for banshees. So much for the warblers of the night.

The tree and its patrons taught me one loud lesson. Some warm-blooded animals depend almost exclusively on flower foods. It appears to be the perfect association. While the animal is awake, its metabolism demands energy in the form of sugar to fuel its bony flying machine. Cross-pollination seems a sure thing, as the ravenous animal must search and forage constantly or it will starve within a day or two. Birds and bats appear to be superior pollinators compared with bees and moths. After all, the activity of a cold-blooded insect is fixed, in large part, by air temperature.

If pollination by warm-blooded animals is so efficient, why is it so rare in Canada and more than half of the United States? The ruby-throated hummingbird *(Archilochus colubris)* is the only nectar bird that nests east of the Mississippi River, and only three or four species of flower bat visit America's Southwest. Furthermore, there are virtually no bird- or bat-pollinated flowers in Europe. What factor limits the range of most flower-visiting birds and small mammals?

The answer is that these animals require habitats in which the flowering season is so long that nectar flow remains steady and plentiful. Cold, freezing winters force flower birds and bats to migrate, and extended flights burn energy. Throughout most of Canada and the eastern United States, there's no nectar to drink from mid-autumn until spring. Fast-breeding, short-lived insects are better adapted to long stretches without food than are slow-breeding, long-lived birds and mammals.

Bird and bat pollinators favor warm equatorial belts or places where mild winters encourage nomadic wanderings instead of an annual exodus. That's why tropical South America remains the center of diversity for the hummingbird family (Trochilidae). More than 200 of the world's 319 hummingbird species are distributed throughout this region, from lowland rain forests to Andean meadows 15,000 feet above sea level. There are also more than 140 species of leaf-nosed bat (Phyllostomatidae) in the Western Hemisphere. Many live primarily on flowers and fruit, and only a few species ever flap north of the Mexican border.

More is known about the relationship of birds and flowers than about bats and blossoms because it's easier to make observations in daylight. It is estimated that almost 20 percent of bird species consume nectar as part of their diet. Bird pollination occurs on every major land mass, excluding Europe and the North and South Poles. Hummingbirds are unique to the Western Hemisphere, and a new form of laboratory analysis called DNA hybridization confirms that they are more closely allied to chimney swifts (Micropodidae) than to any other family of nectar bird.

Lorikeets are true parrots confined to New Guinea, Australia, and some warmer islands of the South Pacific. All remaining avian pollinators belong to the huge order of songbirds (Passeriformes), sharing the same lineage as crows and sparrows.

Pollinating songbirds are rare in the continental United States but are common on southern continents and islands. In the New World Tropics, hummingbirds share flowers with bananaquits (Parulidae) and some oriole species (Icteridae). No bird-watcher feels deprived by the absence of hummingbirds in the Old World Tropics. From Africa through southern Asia, that characteristic shimmering, metallic plumage belongs to more than a hundred sunbird species (Nectariniidae). African sunbirds are most commonly associated with pollination of many members of the bird-of-paradise (Strelitziaceae), showy mistletoe (Loranthaceae), and macadamia nut (Proteaceae) families.

Australia and its neighboring islands are also centers for songbirds that visit flowers. Here, lorikeets compete for nectar with sunbirds, thornbills (Acanthizidae), flowerpeckers (Dicaeidae), silvereyes (Zosteropidae), and almost 160 species of honeyeater (Meliphagidae). Honeyeaters show a wide range of body size. Spinebills *(Acanthorhynchus)* are as small as chickadees, but the noisy friarbird *(Philemon corniculatus)* is bigger than an American blue jay. Most of the Australian continent is warm in winter, so there's always something tasty in bloom. Even on wet, cool mornings, these birds are observed bickering over the blooms of giant gymea lilies *(Doryanthes excelsa)*, winter banksias *(Banksia)*, native heaths *(Epacris)*, and waratahs *(Telopea)*.

The Hawaiian islands, including Laysan Island, were specialized

Relative sizes of birds that drink the nectar of Australian eucalypts and mistletoes. Follow the branch from its twig tip *(above left)* to its base *(below right)* and see the white-throated honeyeater *(Melithreptus albogularis)*, eastern spinebill *(Acanthorhynchus tenuirostris)*, white-plumed honeyeater *(Lichenostomus penicillatus)*, New Holland honeyeater *(Phylidonyris novaehollandiae)*, and red wattlebird *(Anthochaera carunculata)*. The little parrot at right is a gizzle lorikeet *(Glossopsitta pusilla)*. Illustration by W. W. Delaney.

aviaries until humans claimed them. There were a couple of native honeyeaters, but twenty-two species of honeycreeper (Drepanididae) were the dominant songbirds. This unique group evolved from finches (grosbeaks or buntings) stranded on the island chain less than 5 million years ago. Museum records indicate that half of all honeycreeper species drank nectars of ohias *(Metrosideros),* wili-wili *(Erythrina sandwicensis),* and many woody members of the lobelia (Lobeliaceae) and hibiscus (Malvaceae) families. That was before the arrival of Polynesian bird catchers hundreds of years ago. In the nineteenth century, white colonists arrived. They cleared the native vegetation to make way for sugarcane plantations and cattle and, by accident, introduced avian malaria. Today, all the honeyeaters and most of the honeycreepers are extinct. A visitor to Hawaii's forests is fortunate to see 'i'iwi *(Vestiaria coccinea)* or amakihi *(Loxops virens)* honeycreepers foraging on ohia blossoms.

Regardless of geography or plant family, most bird-pollinated flowers share the same features. They flower during the day and have funnel, bell, tube, or massive brush shapes. As all birds have sharp, probing beaks, these blossoms are protected on the outside with a thick, smooth cuticle. On the inside, the floral organs have thickened, woody veins. Most bird flowers incorporate the red-orange colors ignored by bees, so many plants of Mexico, Australia, and South Africa bear blossoms resembling scarlet bows and ribbons.

There is no evidence, though, that any flower bird is attracted to red by instinct alone. On leaving the nest, juveniles learn the best nectar sources by trial and error. This probably means that the color of pure crimson or tangerine flowers may not encourage the attention of birds as much as it discourages the patronage of bees and some other insects.

Therefore, if you ever see bees "sharing" red columbines *(Aquilegia formosa)* or scarlet monkey flowers *(Mimulus)* with hummers, note that these blooms are not pure red or orange. They are splotched with contrasting yellows or bluish purples, and some have ultraviolet patterns invisible to human eyes.

There's another reason why insects ignore bird flowers. Hummingbirds, parrots, and perching birds pollinate scentless flowers. Bees and moths may find bird flowers both hard to detect and unappetizing because their blossoms lack savory aromas.

The sex organs of a flower visited by a hummingbird or honeyeater are usually angled toward the bird's darting head or its throat. Pollen lands either on the smooth bill or on plumage. Grains deposited regularly on bills tend to be round or oval but are well coated with globules of sticky oil. In contrast, lobed, triangular, or spiny grains lodge between the interlocking feather barbules covering the birds' heads and necks.

Different flowers reward different birds with different combinations of sugar. Hummingbirds receive sucrose, while most songbirds prefer drinks that mix some glucose and fructose. Scientists suspect that some songbirds, such as orioles, lack the enzyme sucrase and therefore can't easily digest sucrose.

Many bird nectars test poorly for amino acids and fat, so how do flower-visiting birds acquire enough protein to grow feathers and lay eggs? Lorikeets are the only birds capable of collecting and digesting the important nutrients in pollen. Hummingbirds and songbirds often swallow grains accidentally, but this is regarded as an occupational hazard rather than a regular source of nourishment. Hummers, honeyeaters, sunbirds, and other nectar drinkers must augment their diet by catching fatty, protein-rich insects.

Hummingbirds feed efficiently on flowers while hovering, so they are able to visit nodding bells and horizontal funnels that lack landing platforms. In contrast, songbirds must perch to feed properly. They are more likely to frequent flowers that either grow on tough, swollen stems or mass together to form compound landing pads. In southern Africa, the bird-of-paradise flower *(Strelitzia reginae)* is pol-

linated by sunbirds that actually cling to the tough stamens. In this
rare case, sunbirds carry away the gluey pollen on their toes.

With their distinctive shapes and colors, bird flowers are easy to
identify. For this reason, you could see how important bird pollination is to native vegetation by driving across North America and
then south into tropical countries. Since the ruby-throated hummingbird is the only common hummer species in the northeastern
United States, bird pollination there is limited to wildflowers such
as red rockbell *(Aquilegia canadensis)*, trumpet honeysuckle *(Lonicera
sempervirens)*, orange trumpet-creeper *(Campsis radicans)*, some native
lilies *(Lilium)*, and flame azaleas *(Rhododendron)*.

Drive from New Mexico west to California and you'll find eleven
hummer species nesting in the region. By early spring, the valleys
are alive with scarlet flowers of hedgehog cacti *(Echinocereus)*, boo-
jum trees *(Fouquieria)*, some beardtongues *(Penstemon)*, and Indian
pink *(Silene laciniata)*. By the time the summer heat has dried up the
shrubland, most hummingbirds have raised their young, so Mom and
the kids retreat into the mountains to drink from Indian paintbrushes
(Castilleja), star glories *(Ipomopsis)*, and American fuchsias *(Zausch-
neria)*. Bee-pollinated mints and snapdragons on the East Coast that
are yellow or purple are likely to have red relatives throughout the
San Gabriel Mountains and the high Sierra.

During the first half of the nineteenth century, plant collectors
sponsored by the Royal Horticultural Society began sending seeds
to England from the West Coast of the United States. Wealthy gardeners were delighted by red novelties such as a larkspur robed like
a cardinal *(Delphinium cardinale)*, the firecracker plant *(Brodiaea ida-
maia)*, the scarlet fritillary *(Fritillaria recurva)*, and such bushes as the
fuchsia-flowered gooseberry *(Ribes speciosum)*.

Once you cross into Latin America, hummingbird species increase by the hundreds and are joined by orioles and bananaquits.
Bird-pollinated plants are found at most altitudes throughout the

New World Tropics and show an unusually wide range of growth forms. For example, in warm lowland forests, bird flowers are found on tall trees. Immortelles *(Erythrina)* post their red cigars on pole-like stalks that rise above the dense, interlocking canopy, giving birds uninterrupted access to the nectar. When storms knock trees down, the gaps in the jungle are quickly colonized by fast-growing herbs such as lobster claw plants *(Heliconia)*. Blooming in shade, they are particularly attractive to timid hermit hummingbirds *(Phaethornis)* nesting in the undergrowth. The hermits poke their sickle-shaped bills into the dramatically curved flowers of each lobster claw.

In the cloud forests clothing the peaks of dead volcanoes, many bird-pollinated plants roost on the moss-encrusted limbs of trees watered by daily fogs. The host becomes a "Christmas tree" festooned with red baubles made by *Bomarea* vines, hundreds of species of gallito (bromeliads with flowering stalks as red as rooster combs), and climbing cacti with crimson funnels. Gesneriads and the shrubby relatives of garden fuchsias *(Fuchsia)* are also common on these mountain slopes. Some of my happiest memories of Guatemala and El Salvador are of morning hikes up mountain slopes to watch colorful hummers with swordlike bills duel over fuchsias blooming along the trails.

The thought of colorful Australian lorikeets and drab flying foxes sharing the same gum tree may seem odd, but birds and bats can exploit the same plant for food because they arrive at different times, avoiding competition. In Mexico, hummingbirds and orioles probe the candelabras of magueys *(Agave)* by day, while the lesser long-nosed bat *(Leptonycteris curasoae)* takes the night shift.

A more common trend in the evolution of pollination systems is that different species of very closely related plants may be either bird pollinated *or* bat pollinated. For example, red passion flowers *(Passiflora)*, pollinated by hummingbirds, are found throughout the New World Tropics, including the islands of Jamaica and Cuba. A rare passion vine from southeastern Brazil, *P. mucronata,* opens its green-ish blossoms at two in the morning, smells like lemon cake or raw vegetables, and receives bats. The screw-pine tree *(Freycinetia arborea)* of Hawaii has been pollinated by introduced silvereye birds *(Zoster-ops)* since the extinction of most honeycreepers. A relative, the 'ie'ie vine *(Freycinetia reineckei)* of Samoa, waits for the Samoan flying fox *(Pteropus samoensis).* These days, though, 'ie'ies may wait in vain, as commercial hunters from Guam have decimated the bat roosts. Many people of the South Pacific insist that flying foxes are delectable when stewed in coconut milk.

More than a quarter of all bat species eat some flower foods. Flowers pollinated primarily by bats often "copy" the architecture of bird flowers, emphasizing bell, funnel, and massive brush forms. Bats have sharp teeth and needle-like claws on their toes *and* wings, so we would also expect protected, reinforced blossoms.

Nevertheless, flying foxes are often accused of vandalizing flowers. The great tropical botanist E. J. H. Corner was fascinated by the lurid blooms of the midnight horror *(Oroxylum indicum).* This sixty-foot tree, which is native to Indonesia and Malaysia, is a cousin of the orange trumpet creeper familiar to westerners. Corner observed bats clinging to the fleshy petals of midnight horrors and wrote, "Scratches, as of bats, can be seen on the fallen flowers next morning."

Plants pollinated by bats may also present their flowers on extended, leafless stalks that allow incoming bats to avoid the labyrinth of interfering foliage. Some *Parkia* trees, for example, mass their tiny florets into big upside-down pom-poms. These compact, flowering branches dangle beneath the umbrella of tree limbs. A bat reaches *Parkia* flowers by gliding underneath the tree's canopy and grasping a football-sized cluster of blooms. Nectars fed to bats tend to reflect differences in digestion. Leaf-nosed bats receive more glucose and fructose, while flying foxes are pampered with sucrose.

True bat flowers lack the hot colors associated with bird pollination. Whites tinged with light greens, tans, or liver browns are more often seen on flowers that entrust their pollen to nocturnal mammals that are probably color-blind. Much is made of the remarkable sonar system of bats, but echolocation is not all that useful in the attempt to find immobile flowers. Personal radar is uncommon in flying foxes, a fact that explains why the bats in my gum tree made loud, guttural calls instead of chirps too high-pitched for the human ear to hear. In general, flower bats have superior eyesight compared with bats that eat only insects, and they probably pick up some flowers' pale tones against dark backgrounds much as sphinx moths do.

More important, flower bats use their noses to find their smelly quarry. A few naturalists claim that some bat blooms smell like musk or overripe fruit, but descriptions of rancid, foxy, and sweaty stinks are more common. Butyric acid appears to be a major component in these scents. This is the same chemical that alerts our noses when milk is sour, aged cheeses have reached room temperature, and bath towels need a trip to the laundry.

The wormlike, bristled tongues of flower bats rival hummingbird and honeyeater tongues in length, but these mammals have one trick that is absent in most nectar birds. Most bats eat and digest pollen. Their snouts and "chins" wear branched hairs and whiskers that gather grains as the animals bump into anthers. Their muscular tongues then lick the caked pollen from their muzzles.

The largest, heaviest species of flying fox climb about the branches when they find food. The daintier phyllostomatid (leaf-nosed) bats will try to hover before a blossom but rarely continue this activity for more than a few seconds. Natural selection appears to have favored bat pollination in plants that are unusually massive and robust, as they must endure the punishment of clambering, clinging visitors. The Bombacaceae, the best-studied family of bat-loving trees, have dangling flowers that resemble floating parachutes. This family includes broad, often grotesque trees, including silk cottons *(Ceiba)* and durians *(Durio)* and especially baobabs *(Adansonia),* which still give children nightmares after they read *The Little Prince.*

The wild bananas *(Musa)* of Thailand lack woody shoots, but fibers in their stems make such a strong skeleton that they grow to treelike heights. Species with thick, drooping branches that bear pallid flowers are usually pollinated by bats. Even though the yellow banana familiar as a breakfast food can no longer produce seeds, its blossoms retain their batty appeal wherever they're introduced. Visit any tropical resort and sit next to a grove of bananas. Bats should start arriving at twilight while you finish your cocktail.

A small blossom bat *(Syconycteris australis)* taking nectar from a flowering branch of Australian *Banksia.* Note the bat's long, wormlike tongue and the "climbing rungs" of the massed banksia flowers. Photograph by M. D. Tuttle. Used by permission of Bat Conservation International, Austin, Texas.

Some flower bats continue to serve their plants after pollination. These mammals love fruit, and many of them prefer to carry berries away from fruiting trees, feasting on the wing or using the limbs of a second tree as a communal picnic table. They are insecure "eat and run" feeders, and for good reason, since bats lingering too long on fruit trees may be ambushed by climbing snakes. Of course, when seeds are dropped far from the parent tree, the saplings do not have to compete with the adults. Paul A. Cox, a Hawaiian authority on interactions between Pacific peoples, trees, and flying foxes, insists that the bats' role in seed dispersal is critical on the smaller islands scattered through the South Pacific. These islands have few fruit-eating birds, so bats play midwife to much of the forest.

Field studies conducted since the early 1970s have confirmed that other mammals pollinate flowers at dusk as well. Small, wingless primates, rodents, and marsupials may climb the branches of shrubs and trees or visit large flowering heads that bloom close to the ground on lax stems. In lowland forests of South America, some woody *Combretum* vines and the tree *Quararibea cordata* are pollinated by tamarin marmosets *(Saguinus)*. In Costa Rican cloud forests, rice rats *(Oryzomus devius)* climb trees to take nectar from the greenish flowers of a little vine called *Blakea chlorantha*.

In Africa, the flower clusters of bushes such as *Protea amplexicaulis* and *P. humiflora* smell yeasty, bloom at ground level, and are visited by rock mice *(Aethomys)*. The mice carry pollen from bush to bush as they nibble the sweet, fleshy leaves ringing each cluster of flowers.

On the island of Madagascar, which lies to the east of the African continent, six endangered species of lemur feed on nectar and carry pollen on their fur. The traveler's tree *(Ravenala madagascariensis),* a giant member of the bird-of-paradise family, appears to be pollinated almost entirely by ruffed lemurs *(Varecia variegata)*.

The honey possum *(Tarsipes rostratus)* and pygmy possums *(Cercartetus)* are the best studied of all the flower marsupials of Australia. No larger than house mice, they drink nectar and eat pollen of many shrubs, including banksias, some eucalypts, stick-in-jugs *(Adenanthos),* and swamp bottlebrushes *(Beaufortia).*

Honey possums have also been observed robbing nectar from flowers pollinated by birds. These marsupials, which are native to the Mediterranean shrublands of southwestern Australia, often become so glutted with nectar that they sleep through the day, curled up in cradles formed by the cupped leaves of some needlebushes *(Hakea).*

It is almost impossible to tell the difference between flowers pollinated by bats and those pollinated by wingless climbers. Naturalists have recorded subtle differences between the two, noting that flowers pollinated by mice and possums have much meatier, cheesier, or yeastier smells. Others note that flowers patronized by wingless mammals come equipped with ladder rungs that are grasped by the animal as it hoists itself up the flowering branches. For example, Australian scientists point to the "wire hooks" running up and down cobs of banksia flowers. Each hooklike rung is really a stiff carpel neck protruding from a flower. The pollen-dusted possum pollinates each ladder rung as it climbs and pokes its head into flowers, probing for nectar.

My neighbors in suburban St. Louis, Missouri, hang up fanciful feeders to attract ruby-throated hummingbirds, and in Sydney, Australia, apartment dwellers leave red bowls filled with sugar water on their balconies for lorikeets (it really works). Is there a future market for affluent homeowners in the Tropics who are fond of flower bats and climbing mammals? Will some entrepreneur sell plastic feeders shaped like baobab flowers so gardeners can sit on their patios each evening and watch flying foxes, leaf-nosed bats, lemurs, or tamarins? Of course, each feeder would have to be perfumed with the odor of smelly socks.

CHAPTER 14

God made a little gentian;
It tried to be a rose
Emily Dickinson, "Fringed Gentian"

F Is for Fake (and Flower)

Are plants generous employers of hungry pollinators? We know that roses offer bumblebees pollen but nothing to drink. However, if the same bee visits milkweed flowers *(Asclepias),* she laps up nectar and ignores the lumpy globs of inedible pollen that adhere to her legs and tongue. Different plants can share the same pollinator if their flowers offer the same animal different rewards. A bumblebee visits many different flowers in the same meadow for much the same reason we visit different aisles in the same supermarket.

Furthermore, most flowers dole out rewards in stingy portions. Paying an animal a meager wage for its services as a pollinator is a sound economic practice. If a hummingbird, lemur, or moth is glutted by a single visit to a solitary blossom, it need not visit a second plant to satisfy its hunger. Overfed animals visit flowers less frequently, lowering sperm exchange among plants. Therefore, a generous blossom can doom itself to a lower rate of seed production.

Long-lived flowers replace their rewards slowly. Sturdy flowers visited by hungry birds usually wait until night to replenish lost nectar. If red blossoms on a bush are emptied by thirsty songbirds before noon, their floral spurs or pouches may not brim with fresh nectar until dawn of the following day.

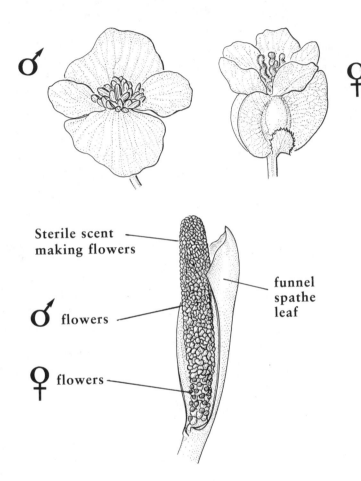

Above left: The male flower of a wax begonia (*Begonia semper-florens*) offers edible pollen. Above right: The female flower lacks pollen, but the color and shape of the stigma mimic stamens bursting with pollen. Below: Architecture of a flowering branch of *Cerceris*, with the spathe leaf "cut away" to show the arrangement of male and female flowers. This aroid imprisons flies at the base of the funnel, and their pollen-coated bodies bump against the female flowers. Illustrations by J. Myers.

In fact, every flower refuses to make more pollen after bees collect all the grains. Shooting stars *(Dodecatheon)* and nightshades retain their attractive colors and some scent after the earliest workers have vibrated all the pollen out of their anthers. Naive latecomers continue to land on these attractive flowers but shake the anthers in vain. An emptied flower continues to receive pollen carried by these diligent bees, but the faithful insects receive nothing in return.

There are plants on this planet that regularly exploit inexperienced animals. Unlike the examples just described, they do not make blossoms that simply run out of groceries. Instead, they offer flowers that look as if they are bursting with goodies even though the floral cupboard is always bare. Scientists who study flowers that offer such false promises call this phenomenon pollination by deceit.

Pollination by deceit may be partial or complete. To find a plant in which seed set depends partially on deceit, go to your favorite pot of begonias *(Begonia)* and check out the flowers under a hand lens. Most begonia blooms are imperfect. That is, the majority of flowers on a stem are unisexual. Inside each male blossom there is a cluster of plump, yellowish stamens but no carpels.

Can you find any female flowers? It's not easy to do because there are fewer of them on a stalk and they closely resemble male flowers. They have the same shape, and there is also a cluster of plump, yellowish sex organs in the heart of each female. This cluster is made of carpel necks tinted yellow and sculpted to resemble fat stamens.

I've watched the pollination of wild begonias in the tropical forests of El Salvador. Bumblebees and stingless bees visit male flowers to gather pollen to feed to their babies. A worker bee that lands on a female flower does not recognize immediately that she is foraging on a blossom devoid of rewards. Instead, she grabs the cluster of yellow carpel necks and gives them a hearty shake. The bee receives no pollen for her visit to a female flower, but she leaves some grains from male flowers on the carpel tips, pollinating the female blossom.

Begonia flowers are good examples of partial deceit. Since most of the flowers on begonia stems are male, bees receive pollen from most of the flowers they visit. It's only when they find the odd female flower that they are fooled and lose a bit of the pollen they've gathered. It's a minor loss for the insect, and the deceived bee ensures the next generation of begonia seeds. That papaya fruit *(Carica papaya)* you had for dessert played a similar trick on a night moth. Moths don't eat papaya pollen, but they transport the grains in exchange for the nectar inside male flowers. Female papaya flowers lack nectar but resemble male flowers in their pale color and their scent. Deceived moths deposit pollen when they probe the empty tubes of female flowers, ensuring fertilization of the next crop of sweet fruit. Some glory bushes *(Tibouchina),* partridge peas *(Cassia),* and even some members of the Brazil nut family (Lecythidaceae) also practice partial deceit, rewarding and fooling their bees at the same time.

Deserts, shrublands, and forests also host many con artists that trick pollinators without offering a speck of nourishment. There's nothing inside these gaudy blossoms for an animal to eat, drink, or use, so their deceit is complete. Although an insect does encounter some pollen inside a fraud flower, the grains are usually inedible or too difficult to swallow.

Some plants practice complete deceit by masquerading as neighbors that always offer real rewards. For instance, when winter rains soak Arizona soils, ghost flowers *(Mohavea confertiflora)* bloom alongside sand blazing stars *(Mentzelia involucrata).* The flowers of both plants display creamy petals with purple-orange highlights, and four bee species mistake the nectarless and pollen-poor ghost flowers for the nectar- and pollen-rich blooms of blazing stars. In another example from Arizona, eight plant species have red, tubular flowers that secrete nectar and are pollinated by rufous hummingbirds *(Selasphorus rufus).* A ninth species offers crimson tubes but lacks nectar, fooling juvenile birds too inexperienced to recognize the false promises of the cardinal flower *(Lobelia cardinalis)*.

The similarity of mimic flowers and their model flowers is astonishing, but recall how pigment and scent chemistries overlap in flowering plants. Ghost flowers, for example, belong to the snapdragon family (Scrophulariaceae), while blazing stars are members of the stickleaf family (Loasaceae). Remember, there are far more flowering plant species on this planet than there are different color effects and fragrance molecules. Both chance and natural selection have encouraged some plant populations to exploit the potential of floral masquerades.

Why are mimics at a distinct advantage in nature when they reproduce the dress and perfume of a model flower? The simple explanation is that the mimic saves sugars, fats, or proteins that its model must spend on pollinator rewards. What is not squandered on a pollinator's hunger can be either saved for the plant's personal growth needs or used to manufacture more seeds.

Let's turn the question around and ask, Why don't most flowering plants employ complete deceit? The answer is that pollination by deceit is efficient only when models vastly outnumber mimics. Since the foraging preferences of some animals are formed by experience, bees and hummingbirds soon learn to recognize and avoid fakers. Sun orchids *(Thelymitra)* of southern Australia offer multicolored, sweet-scented flowers resembling pollen-laden lilies, austral bluebells *(Wahlenbergia),* and fan flowers (Goodeniaceae). I've watched native bees attempt to harvest pollen from these deceitful flowers. After a couple of frustrating attempts, a bee learns to inspect the orchid patch, circling the seductive petals without landing on them.

Therefore, mimics produce lots of seed by cross-pollination only when there is a steady supply of naive visitors. They must bloom at a time of year when a sucker is born every minute. In some cases, as you will soon learn, this means flowering within an extremely narrow time frame.

Fungus gnats and dung flies are unusually gullible, and plants that exploit these insects are among the most dramatic fakers. Many members of the birthwort (Aristolochiaceae) and philodendron (Araceae) families, as well as such tropical milkweeds as *Ceropegia* and *Tavaresia,* are best regarded as deceitful stinkers. Now I can explain the dark, funereal colors and loathsome stenches these plants use to advertise their blossoms. They mimic the fleshy toadstools, animal corpses, and fresh feces that so many adult flies seek as food or a proper place to lay their eggs. When these flowers heat up by digesting the starch hidden in storage cells, their increased temperature mimics the warmth of fresh dung or a recently killed animal. Sometimes the illusion is so convincing that pregnant flies lay eggs in the flower. When this happens, the hatching maggots starve to death for lack of appropriate nourishment.

The architecture of most deceitful stinkers detains incoming flies for hours or overnight. The tepals of birthworts and the petals of *Ceropegia* vines form hollow traps like lobster pots. Midges and bluebottles enter through slits or petal tunnels but are unable to leave until a portion of their jail cell withers or collapses, forming an obvious escape route.

Most aroids, such as cobra lilies *(Arisaema),* lords-and-ladies *(Arum),* voodoo lilies *(Sauromatum),* and Indian kales *(Xanthosoma),* produce tiny flowers massed together along a fleshy pole. Although aroid flowers lack big petals, their pole is usually surrounded by a broad, stiff leaf. The base of the leaf forms a cone or hollow chamber around the fertile flowers. Once a fly enters this chamber, it is trapped inside, as the inner surface of the enfolding leaf is too smooth and slippery to climb. The insect is freed only after the flowering pole wilts.

Flies trapped inside the jail cells of deceitful stinkers bump about, coming into contact with male and female organs fixed inside the blossom. However, deceitful stinkers usually avoid being self-polli-nated by frantic trapped insects because their male and female or-gans ripen at different times. When most fakers open fresh, young traps, their female organs are receptive to pollen introduced by in-coming inmates. As the flower ages, these carpels dry up, the stamens open, and prisoners are dusted with pollen as they are "paroled" by their wilting prison. Without a real memory for bad experiences, gnats and flesh flies have a high rate of recidivism, carrying that fresh pollen to a second mimic and encouraging cross-pollination.

Although we may appreciate voodoo lilies and birthworts for their lurid charm, most botanists agree that true orchids are the monarchs of floral masquerade. Many orchid species reward moths with sugary nectar or give male bees spicy oils, but it's estimated that at least half of the more than 20,000 orchid species produce flowers pollinated by deceit.

Most orchids work on the same set of floor plans. Male and female organs fuse together inside a flower, forming a single unit known as the column. The column is designed to both release and receive pollinia. For a flower to attach pollinia to an insect or receive a glob of pollen, a portion of the pollinator's body must be posi-tioned *under* the column. How can a flower coerce an insect into re-ceiving such sticky, heavy, and inedible lumps?

In most cases, the column is located opposite a specialized lip petal. Lip petals are uniquely shaped, perfumed, and ornamented, and naive insects find them irresistible. A duped insect either lands directly on the lip petal or tries to probe it with its tongue while hovering in the air. This sandwiches a part of the pollinator's head or body between the lip petal and the column. The bee, fly, or moth can't back out of the flower without having pollinia dumped on its face or back.

Some lip petals are further equipped with a natural hinge. The sheer weight of an insect that lands on this hinge tips the pollinator into the column. In most greenhood *(Pterostylis)* and all flying duck *(Caleana)* orchids, the hinged lip is an irritable organ responsive to the mere touch of an insect's legs. When stimulated, the lip jolts upward violently, slamming the pollinator into the column.

Some of North America's orchids exploit their pollinators. The distinctive shoelike lip petals of lady's slipper orchids *(Cypripedium)* form inflated, colorful, and sweet-smelling chambers that never secrete nectar. To escape from the hollow shoe, visiting bees must squeeze themselves under the sex organs. Fairy slippers *(Calypso bulbosa),* rose pogonias *(Pogonia),* and false grass pinks *(Calopogon)* have open, flatter lip petals sporting yellow warts or golden tufts of hair. They bloom at a time of year when many wildflowers offer lots of pollen. Naturalists note that the orchid's inedible yellowish clump of warts and hairs mimics the ring of stamens inside meadow beauties *(Rhexia)* and true rose pinks *(Sabatia).* These orchids deceive bumblebee queens and mother *Andrena* bees that are collecting pollen for their offspring from mid-spring through early summer.

False promises of food or drink are even more pronounced in tropical orchids. The lip petals of the wild ancestors of such popular corsage and florist's flowers as Cooktown orchids *(Dendrobium),* cymbidiums *(Cymbidium),* and moth orchids *(Phalaenopsis)* either are decorated with phony pollen warts or end in hollow, nectarless spurs.

Dancing doll orchids *(Oncidium)* are among the most specialized of the tropical mimics. Two species in South America are visited by carpenter bees that mistake the orchids' sweetly scented bright yellow flowers for the fragrant, pollen-rich yellow blossoms of tree cassias. Throughout the islands of the Caribbean Sea, dancing dolls mimic the pinkish purple blooms on bushes and trees in the nance family (Malpighiaceae). These orchids exploit the *Centris* bees that collect flower oils to feed to their grubs. Duped females confuse the wrinkled, pitted wart on the lip petal of the orchid for the oozing oil gland of a nance flower.

The orchid family also contains its share of deceitful stinkers. Many of the 1,200 *Bulbophyllum* species have small green- and iodine-colored flowers and are pollinated by carrion flies and midges. Fans of bulbophyllums (yes, even these orchids have passionate collectors) insist with pride that some of the flowers smell like dog urine.

Scientists continue to speculate on the hundred species of helmet orchid *(Corybas)* distributed through tropical Asia and Australasia. These flowers are shaped like helmets or antique ear trumpets, and their moist, ribbed interiors remind some naturalists of the gills under mushroom caps. Female fungus gnats and their eggs have been found in the flowers of one species. I've smelled some helmet orchids and agree that they have an uncanny aroma, like mushrooms sautéed in butter.

One form of complete deceit seems unique to the orchid family. Most of the plants discussed in this chapter exploit the inexperience of young animals, female insects, or both, but some orchid flowers deceive male flies, wasps, and bees that are searching for mates. Instead of offering false promises of food, the lip petal forms a crude but effective copy of the bulbous eyes, humped back, hairy abdomen, and dark colors of a nubile insect. The human nose fails to catch scents in these flowers, but biochemical analyses performed in Swedish and German laboratories have confirmed that the floral organs release molecules mimicking the sex odors (pheromones) of virgin females.

These pseudocopulatory orchids are a delight to find in the wild but are a bit unnerving. Some seem to stare right back at you because the round paired glands at the base of the lip petal resemble bug eyes. Return to chapter 8 and take a second look at the polished mirror (speculum) on the furry lip petals of the bee *(Ophrys)* and bearded *(Calochilus)* orchids. The function of this strange pattern is easy to understand if you watch a male insect cover the petal with his body. The mirror copies the smooth, dark surface on the female's back where she folds her shiny, translucent wings.

Orchids that deceive males depend on precise timing to fool suitors. Male insects mature and leave their pupal cases more quickly than females, which develop more slowly because they must emerge from their cocoons with abdomens bloated with eggs. This means that male bees and wasps pass their first week of flight as lonely bachelors. They may spend these days drinking nectar and competing for territory with other males, or they may visit flowers that display dummy females. The orchids bloom just in time for the emergence of the randy males, but this must occur before any real females appear.

Some male insects are so stimulated by the dummy female that

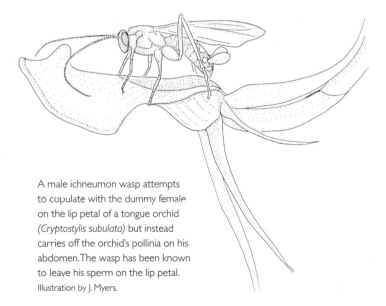

A male ichneumon wasp attempts to copulate with the dummy female on the lip petal of a tongue orchid *(Cryptostylis subulata)* but instead carries off the orchid's pollinia on his abdomen. The wasp has been known to leave his sperm on the lip petal. Illustration by J. Myers.

they ejaculate onto the lip petal. All thirteen species of Australian tongue orchid *(Cryptostylis)* are pollinated by only one species of ichneumon wasp *(Lissopimpla semipunctata).* Sperm packets left by these insects on the long, stiff lip petals were first reported by a schoolteacher, Edith Coleman, near Melbourne, Australia, in 1927.

With the specificity of false pheromones and design of dummy females on lip petals, naive males are often extremely particular and persistent about which orchids they visit. The different bee orchid species in Europe, Turkey, and the Middle East are pollinated by male digger wasps *(Gorytes) or* solitary wasps *(Argogorytes) or Andrena* bees or *Eucera* bees. Professor A. J. Richards of the University of Newcastle upon Tyne watched one male *Eucera* bee attempt to mate with a particular flower of *Ophrys sphegodes* for more than three hours!

Dozens of orchid species in southern Australia are pollinated by dozens of tiphiid flower wasps. Female tiphiids always lack wings, and the males attempt to fly away with their brides, mating with them in the air as part of a ritualized nuptial flight. Consequently, the dummy females attached to the hinged lip petals of the king-in-his-carriage *(Drakaea),* some spider caladenias *(Caladenia),* and elbow orchids *(Spiculea)* rudely catapult the wasp groom back into the orchid's column.

Some readers may be displeased by this chapter, as it spoils their original impression of animals and plants enjoying a pure relationship in which both organisms always benefit. Frankly, I think that turnabout is fair play when we consider how often animals exploit flowers. Insects chew them to bits, and some bees, wasps, and birds rob them of nectar by piercing their petals. Plenty of beetles and butterflies are small enough to help themselves to rewards without transferring pollen. Novelist and butterfly collector Vladimir Nabokov was right when he called nature the Arch Cheat. Under special circumstances, some cheating plants prosper, provided baits evolve that appeal to individual hunger, mothering instincts, or libido.

CHAPTER 15

But the breeze of the morning blew, and found
That the leaves of the blown Rose strewed the ground
  Henry A. Dobson, "Fancy from Fortunelle"

Into Thin Air

Thousands of plant species are cross-pollinated without the aid of a single insect, bird, or small mammal, making use of an almost invisible form of reproduction that dominates every grassy patch and many temperate forests. These are the plants that entrust their pollen to air currents. Wind pollination is such a common alternative to animal pollination that it plays a far greater role in American woodlands and meadows than do the cheap tricks employed by the orchids described in the previous chapter.

Wind pollination is easy to overlook because the flowers that employ this system are so diminutive. The modest bloom of a dog rose is gigantic next to most wind-pollinated flowers, hundreds of which would fit into the bowl of a wild rose. A rose is composed of hundreds of organs, while wind-pollinated flowers are such models of minimalism that the parts of a single flower can often be counted on the fingers of one hand. The rose has large sepals and even larger, broader petals. In contrast, the calyx and corolla of wind-pollinated flowers either are reduced, scabby scales or fail to form at all. This means that most wind-pollinated blossoms are incomplete. In many species, floral development is limited to the formation of only one kind of sex organ inside each bud. Consequently, many wind-pollinated plants are incomplete *and* imperfect.

Although some wind-pollinated plants mass hundreds or even thousands of flowers on their stems in imposing structures, it's easy to overlook them until their pregnancy becomes obvious. Drive past a marsh in late spring and you might miss the thin, dark candles of cattails *(Typha),* although you'll admire their swollen, fruiting clubs in autumn. We eat the yellow ovaries on corncobs *(Zea mays)* but forget the spidery clusters of male flowers tipping each tall, green stalk.

Few writers champion the spartan beauty of wind-pollinated flowers. In the 1890s, Mrs. William Starr Dana used her newspaper column to introduce New Yorkers to alders *(Alnus)* flowering in late winter. She described the catkins as "decorative as well as encouraging . . . when each little tassel enclosed in ice sparkles and quivers in the sunshine like a jewelled pendant." D. H. Lawrence referred to hazel *(Corylus)* catkins in his famous novel *Women in Love,* in which the hero, Mr. Birkin, explains the function of the "long danglers" (soft branches of male flowers) and "little red flames" (female flowers), enchanting a woman admirer.

By the end of a frozen winter, we're starved for the sight of wildflowers. There is an international market for the budding stems of two species of pussy willow *(Salix)* native to North America and Eurasia. The flower buds of female pussy willows fail to form plump tufts of silvery fur, so florists sell the twigs of male trees. If you place these male stems in water, you'll soon see yellow pollen emerge from each catkin's back. In rural England and Russia, the catkins of goat willow *(S. caprea)* were regarded as victories over winter and often replaced palm leaves during celebrations on Palm Sunday.

Field experiments show that some of the 400 species of willow employ a mixture of insect pollination and wind pollination. Two Dutch scientists "caged" branches of forty female trees of goat wil-

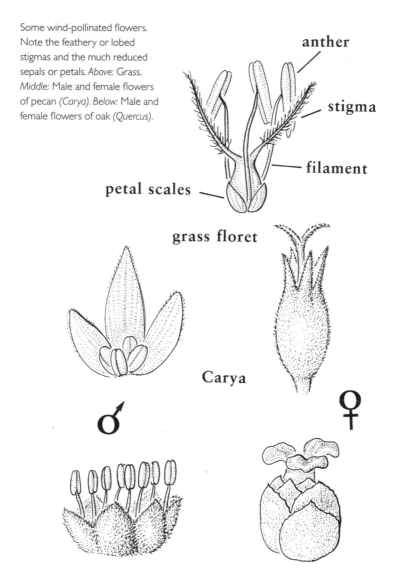

Some wind-pollinated flowers. Note the feathery or lobed stigmas and the much reduced sepals or petals. *Above:* Grass. *Middle:* Male and female flowers of pecan *(Carya)*. *Below:* Male and female flowers of oak *(Quercus)*.

anther

stigma

filament

petal scales

grass floret

Carya

♂

♀

Quercus

low and forty bushes of creeping willow *(S. repens)*. The cages were made of nylon mesh that let air currents flow through but shut out bees and flies. By the end of the flowering season, half of the female goat willow flowers had set seed, but results were extremely varied for the creeping willow. At one site, 70 percent of the flowers of creeping willow set seed, while in another part of Holland, only 20 percent were pregnant. Some willow populations must need insect pollinators more than others do.

In other plant families, there is a far sharper division between species dependent exclusively on breezes and those that require animals for pollen transport. Within the family Moraceae, for example, botanists discriminate between wasp-pollinated figs *(Ficus)* and wind-pollinated mulberries *(Morus)*. I noted earlier that 'ie'ie vines employ bats, but within the same family (Pandanaceae), the flowers of *Pandanus* trees wait for warm tropical breezes.

In some families, wind pollination dominates flower evolution. Although the 9,000 grass and bamboo species in the family Poaceae are the best studied, their pollen often shares the same air currents that transport most members of the goosefoot (Chenopodiaceae), sedge (Cyperaceae), and marijuana (Cannabidaceae) families. In North America and Eurasia, most catkin trees are wind pollinated, including birches and alders (Betulaceae), beeches and oaks (Fagaceae), walnuts and hickories (Juglandaceae), and plane trees (Platanaceae).

Therefore, much of the Northern Hemisphere is a wind-pollinated landscape, a fact that influences national economies and individual health. At the economic level, because cereal crops belong to the grass family, people expect the wind to help make their daily bread and beer. In earlier days, residents of rural communities understood the connection between crops and breezes. For centuries, laborers on British farms trooped into nut orchards equipped with long poles and an awful rhyme, "A woman, a dog, and a walnut tree/

The more you beat them, the better they be." This cruel saying contains only one kernel of truth. Gently whacking walnut branches in
spring knocks pollen out of male catkins, allowing it to billow onto
female flowers.

Of course, clouds of pollen can cause serious health problems. If
you are sensitive to pollen, you probably react to the plants most
common in your region. If you live near dairy farms or ranches,
your wheezing may be based on pasture grasses grown for stock feed.
In cooler parts of the world where the countryside is dominated by
timber plantations, tree pollens are health risks. For example, 16 percent of the people living in Sweden are allergic to the pollen of birch
trees. That statistic equals the number of Swedes suffering from food
allergies (eggs, milk, fish, etc.) and is only slightly less than the per-
centage of citizens who can't tolerate cat dander.

Although it may be of small comfort to hay fever sufferers, pollen
rarely makes up more than 2 percent of the organic particles in the
atmosphere during the growing season. Airborne spores of bacteria
and fungi are thousands of times more common in the air we breathe
than are the pollens of seed plants. During the coldest months, particles of wood ash, animal dander, plant hairs, and even the dung and
corpses of dust mites may be the real cause of our misery.

A technical interest in identifying airborne pollen actually started
as early as the 1870s, when naturalists hung greased glass slides outdoors for a few days in an attempt to determine the components of
dust. They soon learned that the pollens of different plants could be
identified by their dependable grain shapes and wall sculpting. Specialists started writing pollen atlases early in the twentieth century,
and some editions are continually updated. The crude technique of
collecting pollen by dangling sticky slides has been replaced by new
automatic devices that revolve sheets of transparent adhesive film or
use whirling rods to draw floating grains into a miniature vortex.
Since so many people suffer from pollen-related respiratory ailments,

the sampling of pollen that drifts through cities has become a lucrative and competitive industry. That's why your local weather program provides such startlingly precise breakdowns of the identities and ratio of various types of pollen during hay fever season.

To understand why pollen is so irritating when inhaled, you must first understand the natural mechanics in effect when flowers release pollen grains into the air. Although botanists call this process wind pollination, it is a term used only for convenience. After all, the longer a pollen grain spends in the grip of a strong wind, the farther it will be carried from the receptive tip of a female flower. Severe winds are actually the enemies of plants that release pollen as aerosols.

That's why the anthers of catkins and grass flowers tend to open rhythmically, whether early in the morning, late in the afternoon, or both. Pollen released at such times avoids much of the turbulence produced when the sun heats the earth's surface at midday, destabilizing the atmosphere. This also explains why most wind-pollinated plants bloom during the mild days of spring or autumn. Some grasses bloom twice each year, exploiting the biannual cycle of moderate temperatures—and, on the nicest days, sending hay fever sufferers to the medicine cabinet.

Once again, there is poetic truth in classical myth. Remember Flora, the Roman goddess of flowers, mentioned in chapter 4? Her priests insisted that she was the devoted wife of Zephyrus, god of the mild, warming west wind (far gentler than his unruly brothers). Flora's fertility depended on annual exposure to her husband's warming breath.

Of course, the direction taken by air currents is undependable, so cross-pollination is most likely to occur if a grain floats less than a dozen yards from its catkin. North America's forests and prairies favor plants that grow together in clumps. Trees in dense, monotonous stands and grasses in thick swards are more likely to exchange pollen with appropriate partners because the pollen rides on the air for only a short distance. A stigma has the best chance of intercepting a wayward grain when prospective mates grow nearby and breezes are slow.

Even under the best of conditions, though, all flowers pollinated by air currents must contend with the same disadvantage. Although both the timed release of pollen and the limited diversity of trees, sedges, and grasses can increase the potential for cross-pollination, wind pollination is at best a hit-or-miss approach to sex. Weather in early spring and mid-autumn is often unpredictable, with vertical air movements flinging pollen into storm fronts, and pollen sperm dies quickly when the grains drown in raindrops. Since the mid-1920s, ships carrying scientific equipment over the Atlantic Ocean have trapped pollen produced by coastal forests as the grains are blown more than fifteen miles out to sea. Why do some trees in particular persist in flowering so early in spring, when wintry conditions intrude? Why do some sedges and grasses bloom through tornado or hurricane season?

Since physical barriers impede the progress of airborne pollen drifting toward receptive stigmas, the catkins of most deciduous trees must open in early spring, before leaves appear. Most grasses and sedges compress their short-lived flowers into spiky clusters at the tips of flexible, multibranched stalks. These branched stalks need time to grow tall enough to rise above the dense foliage.

How do the carpels of these flowers snag pollen grains drifting by? The greater a stigma's surface area, the better its chances of catching incoming pollen. On most of these carpels, the stigma surface is much larger than other organs in the flower. The tips of the female organs of beeches and oaks, for example, wear broad lobes. Ash stigmas remind me of fans, while hickory stigmas look, improbably, like hairy snake tongues.

The female organs of grasses are the longest. Consider the long, silky tassels of female flowers on corncobs. Most grass species subdivide their stigma tips into barbs, which resemble bird plumes under the microscope. Like a feather duster lying on a shelf, the tangled stigmas of a grass flower sift the air, trapping incoming grains.

Even with these adaptations, though, most pollen grains that are shed into the air fail to land on a stigma, since an air current does not seek out receptive flowers as does a foraging animal. Plants pollinated by air currents must manufacture extraordinary numbers of pollen grains to counteract so many "launch failures."

Compare a linden tree *(Tilia)* and a beech tree *(Fagus)* growing

This scanning electron micrograph (SEM) shows how the feathery stigma of ryegrass *(Lolium)* "snags" pollen grains as they drift by on gentle air currents. SEM by Dr. I. Staff, Plant Cell Research Center, School of Botany, University of Melbourne, Australia.

together in the same woodlot. Within each insect-pollinated flower of the linden, there are 100,000 pollen grains for every unfertilized seed. This may seem excessive, but male beech flowers produce 10 million grains for every seed in a female flower. Linden pollen stands a far better chance of "hitting the right target" (despite insect appetites) than does the aerial flotsam of beech pollen.

Where does a catkin or grass stalk acquire all the resources needed to make and shed pollen clouds? This is a classic trade-off in the evolution of pollination systems. A plant pollinated by air currents avoids squandering materials on attractants and rewards, reinvesting molecules that would otherwise be used to make nectar, pigments, fragrances, and large petals. In fact, pollen grains are cheap, cheap, cheap when they must be light enough to ride the breeze. They are low in edible fats and proteins and almost devoid of gluey, chemically complex droplets on the grain wall. Pollen that is adapted to whirl in the air doesn't need heavy, sticky grease to adhere pollen to hairs, beaks, moth scales, and beetle shells. It's this generous virility of wind-pollinated flowers that makes allergy sufferers feel sick.

Pollen can be an irritant whenever it comes into contact with mucous membranes in the human nose, eyes, and lips, where watery secretions make the grains swell and rupture. The grain fragments contain substances that trigger the immune system, which mistakes pollen residue for a dangerous disease. Antibodies are summoned in defensive waves of fluid, causing runny noses, itchy eyes, tears, sneezing, and sinus headaches. Fortunately, pollen grains trapped in mucus are moved out of the respiratory system and into the digestive tract, to be neutralized by stomach acid.

In the lungs of a hypersensitive person, inhaled pollen fragments trigger an immune response in the terminal bronchiole sacs, causing an asthma attack. Medical researchers are working to identify the full range of pollen allergens that inflame the human immune system. Protein films on the surface of the grain wall may play a role, but it seems certain that something vile lurks in the starch granules that surround pollen sperm.

My late mentor and boss R. Bruce Knox (1940–1997) spent years studying this problem, leading a team of cell biologists and biochemists. Less than a decade before he died, Knox and his associates discovered a powerful connection between pollen fragments, bad weather, and hospitals. Have you ever heard that emergency wards sometimes see a dramatic increase in asthma attacks during thunderstorms? Knox and his colleagues determined that in violent weather, grains of grass pollen trapped in the upper atmosphere burst. Fragments of the grains are swept down into the lower atmosphere and then into people's airways, and the starch granules are so small that they can avoid being trapped by mucous membranes. It is when they are inhaled into unprotected lungs that the allergens in the starch do their dirty work. One severe thunderstorm in late spring of 1994 sent 640 asthmatics into London's emergency wards.

I miss Knox's intellect, support, and personal decency, but hay fever victims miss him even more as a scientist who shared their agony. He would be asked to present his research at allergy and asthma foundations every spring, when ryegrass *(Lolium)* blooms in every Australian paddock. At that time of year, his head would resemble a damp, bearded beet. He later joked that his tortured face was worth more than all the slides or movies he showed. Boards of trustees were delighted to give grants to a fellow sufferer.

When I was a child living in New York, local governments thought they were protecting citizens from allergies by spraying herbicides on stands of goldenrod *(Solidago)* and purple aster *(Aster)* before the plants could bloom in autumn. However, these members of the daisy family are pollinated by insects, not wind, so they were unjustly executed. Such attempts at community hygiene extirpated some of the last suburban populations of native wildflowers. The real culprits were opportunistic docks *(Rumex)*, ragweeds *(Ambrosia)*, and lamb's-quarters *(Chenopodium)*. These plants often avoid early detection and eradication because their flowers are so inconspicuous and the scraggliest weeds are often the most difficult to identify with field guides. More important, they share the capacity to thrive in sites of urban decay, homesteading cracks in concrete and brick.

Once upon a time, physicians in the United States told people with weak or tuberculous lungs to move to isolated towns in desert areas. These dry zones didn't receive enough rain annually to support the growth of big catkin-producing trees, grassy pastures, or swamps of sedges and cattails. The native vegetation was pollinated primarily by insects, birds, and bats.

However, conditions changed after World War II, when new water systems allowed residents of Arizona, New Mexico, and southern California to landscape their gardens as if they lived back east. With local water tables altered, desert suburbs became havens for invasive mulberries, cottonwoods *(Populus),* and weedy herbs. Just like European rats and Asian cockroaches, these plants are camp followers of urban expansion. Add the smog produced by the increased number of cars and new industries and it's easy to understand why people no longer move to Las Vegas for their health.

CHAPTER 16

Their lips were four red roses on a stalk,
And in their summer beauty kissed each other.
William Shakespeare, *Richard III*

Self-Made Marriages and Virgin Births

Abeautifully renovated farmhouse stands on the edge of the Kansas prairie where I study bees and spring wildflowers. By June, dandelions *(Taraxacum officinale)* grow so thickly around the house and old barn that they shroud the dusty lawn in white fuzz. I've watched flocks of hungry goldfinches attack the fluffy stalks before winds can free the seed parachutes. It's then the turn of the dandelion heads to be hidden under chirping blobs of black and yellow.

Death by goldfinch sounds poetic, but the lives of most seeds are short and nasty. Many succumb to disease, insects, or nematodes (parasitic eelworms) before they even leave their parent plant. Others are devoured by rodents, slugs, crickets, or birds. Those that escape predation and manage to sprout often do so in inappropriate sites and perish as seedlings.

"Infancy" is usually the weakest link in the life cycle of a flowering plant. The continuity of every plant population depends on the efficiency with which adults produce, package, and protect the next generation. The problem is that most plants have a limited time in which to make seeds and a limited budget to invest in their off-spring.

There are two overlapping reasons why some ovaries in cross-pollinated flowers fail to become fruits. First, after spending much of its resources in attracting and rewarding pollinators, the parent plant may lack sufficient reserves to provision every fertilized seed. Scientists note that tropical trees regularly abort a portion of their ovaries, especially when dry weather dominates the fruiting season.

Second, pollinators do not always fulfill their appointed tasks. Rainy days keep honeybees in their hives, and cold snaps kill some insects and make others too sluggish to fly. When too many plants in the same meadow secrete too much nectar, hummingbirds become quick learners and avoid the flowering stalks offering the least reward. Furthermore, as noted in the previous chapter, storms destroy pollen and strong winds carry the grains away from female flowers.

Although extra flowers on a stem may seem wasteful, they are far cheaper to manufacture than equal numbers of big, seed-filled fruits. More important, a plant can derive two reproductive benefits from the manufacture of flowers that never fruit. First, excess flowers enlarge the overall display of color and scent, and that makes a plant more attractive to hungry pollinators. Second, when a plant makes seeds by cross-pollination, it's just as important to father offspring as it is to become a mother. When an extra flower releases pollen, it has a chance to pass its genes on to the next generation if the sperm is accepted by a second flower.

Yes, there are disadvantages to cross-pollination when the survival of a population demands massive seed production. In particular, the self-incompatibility systems described in chapter 7 can impose severe mating barriers on some long-lived plants if their pollinators are lazy foragers. For example, if a fly visits a blooming grove of wirilda wattles *(Acacia retinodes),* it is not doing these shrubs any favor if the insect restricts its visits to a family unit consisting of a grandparent, parent, and grandchild sharing similar genes. Canola oil plants *(Brassica campestris)* live for only one season, so crosses between generations are impossible. Nevertheless, seed production drops if bees visit rows of plants that had the same two parents.

This means that those female willows in the previous chapter were unusually fertile even though their flowers were isolated in insect-free cages. When 50 to 70 percent of the flowers on a cross-pollinated tree set seed in the absence of disease and enemies, it must be regarded as a high rate of reproductive success. The literature suggests that the conversion rate of blossoms into fruits is far lower in long-lived wildflowers pollinated by animals. My own field studies have recorded that only 1 in 5 flowers on the stem of a flax lily *(Dianella caerulea)* or a San Gabriel *(Echeandia macrocarpa)* forms a fruit. In a good season, 17 in every 100 flowers of pink wood sorrel *(Oxalis violacea)* develop ripe capsules.

For more than a century and a half, naturalists have observed that the ratio of fruit set is even lower in orchids that trick insects into visiting flowers devoid of rewards. Even though a flowering spray of *Dendrobium* produces more than a hundred flowers, only one or two ever set pods. A single plant of pink lady's slipper *(Cypripedium acaule)* may have to participate in a decade's worth of flowering seasons before one of its pouched blossoms is entered by a naive bumblebee. Tricky orchids are able to compensate for infrequent insect visits because a single ovary sets hundreds, thousands, or millions of microscopic seeds once fertilization occurs. This occasional jackpot makes up for years of spinsterhood.

The problem is that not all plant species can afford to wait for the perfect flowering season, when the climate is kind and pollinators are robust and willing. Their populations experience a combination of problems due to high rates of infant mortality and limited resources to make healthy seeds. These plants reproduce within limits imposed by such factors as brief flowering seasons, too much shade, and soils poor in water and critical nutrients.

Under such inhospitable conditions, seed quantity takes precedence over seed quality. Producing inbred children is better than producing no offspring at all. These plants bear flowers that accept their own pollen and make every grain count toward seed set. If these species ever had a self-incompatibility system, it has been jettisoned in the course of evolution.

Check some of the wildflowers growing on forest floors in the United States and you'll see that some make seeds by both cross-pollination and self-pollination. For example, bloodroots *(Sanguinaria canadensis)* bloom in early spring, when the weather is rough and unpredictable. Bloodroots can be cross-pollinated by *Dialictus* bees foraging on warm days. When the weather is too cold, bee activity stops, but a bloodroot can form fat fruits without pollinators. As the white flower ages, stamens collapse onto the receptive tip of the carpel, smearing it with pollen. Fieldwork suggests that most American gingers *(Asarum)* regularly self-pollinate in much the same mechanical way when fungus gnats fail to visit the flowers.

Therefore, self-pollination often acts as a fail-safe mechanism when unpredictable weather disrupts animal activity and plants are forced to compete for a limited number of pollinators. This system has also been identified in some wildflowers of tundras and alpine zones, where low temperatures and lingering ice discourage small insects.

Let's go one step further. There are woodland wildflowers that maintain a high level of seed set by producing cross- and self-pollinated flowers at opposite ends of the same cycle of bloom. The floor of a broadleaf forest is quite a sunny place in mid-spring, when canopy leaves are just starting to appear and expand. At this time of year, native herbs under trees have large, often colorful flowers that are easily seen by insects. Cross-pollination occurs as bees and flies forage on warm days.

However, once the canopy leaves mature, the forest floor is plunged into shadow and becomes a less attractive place for sun-loving pollinators. Many species of violet *(Viola)*, milkwort *(Polygala)*, ground ivy *(Glechoma)*, wood sorrel, and dayflower *(Commelina)* continue to bloom in the gloom, but these end-of-season flowers offer smaller, duller petals. In fact, some late flowers look just like

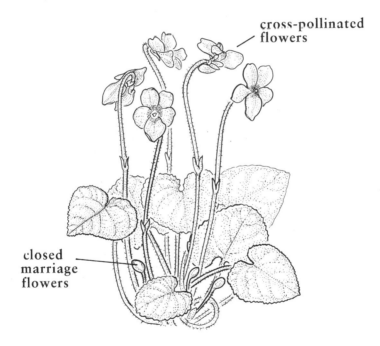

cross-pollinated flowers

closed marriage flowers

Many violet *(Viola)* species make two kinds of flowers each year. In early spring, there are the scented, colorful flowers waiting for insects on long stalks. These are gradually replaced in late spring and summer by "closed marriage" flowers that never open, resembling fat green buds on short stalks.

fat, green buds that never expand. Within each of these "buds," stamens grow just long enough to rub against the receptive tips of the carpels and release their pollen. That is why botanists call them cleistogamous ("closed marriage") flowers. The closed marriage ensures seed set because the stamen groom always weds the carpel bride locked up inside the same bud case.

In a few species of violet and milkwort, the budlike flowers of closed marriages are on such short stalks that they fail to rise above the forest litter, so the seeds are preplanted at the base of the parent plant. In time, the adult plant is surrounded by an incestuous dynasty.

It's obvious that many plant species alternate between cross- and self-pollination, combining the genetic benefits of outbreeding with the mass production of inbreeding. However, in some environments, conditions are so harsh and hostile that certain species must forsake cross-pollination just to complete their life cycles. Plants that are compulsive self-pollinators often have the shortest life spans, setting seed just before they die. These include annual herbs that appear after desert rains or endure a few months of life on an alpine slope. Other species are pioneers, exploiting land cleared suddenly by earthquakes, mudslides, bulldozers, or fires. These colonizers grow quickly, making just enough food so they can produce and release lots of windblown seeds before the original, taller vegetation regenerates and evicts weedy squatters.

True self-pollinators are easy to identify if you compare them with their cross-pollinated relatives. Since self-pollinators refuse to waste energy and resources on foraging animals, their flowers tend to be smaller than those of their cross-pollinated relatives. They are also deficient in scent and contrasting colors. Dissect these "do-it-yourself" blossoms and you will note that their nectar glands either fail to develop or refuse to secrete fluids. Male and female organs crowd together in the same flower, bonking into each other in the course of maturation.

Under the microscope, it's easy to see that the stamens of self-married flowers manufacture fewer pollen grains than do those of cross-pollinated flowers. Pollen production is much more economical in self-pollinated blooms, since every grain is destined to hit the right target. The ratio of unfertilized seeds to pollen grains is quite low in a self-pollinated flower because the anthers always dump their grains onto the receptive tip of the nearest female organ. As each ovule is guaranteed to receive sperm, every flower on a stem makes a fruit unless it is destroyed by enemies. The self-married flower is a model of safe and cautious investment.

Members of the cabbage family (Brassicaceae) have been well studied because the flowers of closely related species have such a wide range of cross- and self-pollinated forms. Wild mustards, radishes, toothworts *(Dentaria),* and dame's rockets *(Hesperis)* tint their straplike petals with yellow or purple and reward insects with nectar, excess pollen, or both. The honeylike odors of wallflowers *(Cheiranthus cheiri)* are so enticing that it's easy to understand why 92 percent of their seeds are the result of cross-pollination.

In contrast, consider the weedy species of *Leavenworthia;* the desert races of whitlow-grass *(Erophila verna);* thale cress *(Arabidopsis),* which goes from cradle to grave in a month; or even the shepherd's purse *(Capsella bursa-pastoris)* invading bare spots on your lawn. Their stubby, whitish petals make each flower look reduced and constricted compared with those mentioned in the previous paragraph. Even though insects are rarely observed visiting such mingy little blooms, their ovaries always plump up into fertile fruits. Alpine penny cress *(Thlaspi alpestre)* lives on European mountains, enduring soils contaminated by concentrations of metal ores that kill most plants. In a typical season, more than 95 percent of penny cress seeds are products of self-pollination.

Self-pollination, then, is a dependable way of making certain that children will be able to endure the same awful conditions survived by the adult. According to the mathematical rules of Mendel's laws of genetics, a seed made by self-pollination must inherit an extremely high proportion of the same combination of useful genes found in its sole parent. Ironically, a seed produced by "self-incest" is often fitter under harsh extremes than a seed made by two different parents because the inbred seed grows into a plant programmed to cope with specific, unchanging problems. That's why shepherd's purse has left its European pastures and spread all over the world. Gardeners everywhere want lawns, so shepherd's purse is as well suited to the suburban United States as to suburban Japan.

However, Mendel's laws of genetic segregation carry a fearful price, since bad combinations of genes can turn up as often as good combinations. Self-married plants must produce far more seed than their cross-pollinated relatives because of high rates of congenital defects. It's estimated that at least half of all the self-pollinated seeds of one weedy species of evening primrose *(Oenothera biennis)* die in the womb because of accumulated defects. However, since each fruit contains hundreds of healthy seeds, this plant continues to invade waste places in North America.

In fact, there's only one way a plant can make seeds that grow into almost perfect copies of the parent without fear of lethal gene combinations. This radical process is properly known as agamospermy, a term derived from the Greek *agamic,* meaning "without sex cells," and *spermy,* "seeds." Agamospermic flowers make seeds without uniting sperm and egg. The living seeds emerge from virgin ovaries.

Depending on the species, any of about five different paths of cell development in an unfertilized seed can result in agamospermy. Some embryo sacs need the chemical stimulation of incoming pollen tubes just to "jump-start" virgin birth. This accounts for almost all the seeds we fish out of homemade lemonade and fresh orange juice. Hive bees make delicious honey when allowed to forage in a citrus grove and dutifully transfer healthy pollen from flower to flower. However, most ovules in a lemon blossom become seeds *after* they refuse sperm. In other systems, pollen production is almost superfluous. You can "castrate" every flower in a dandelion and put a bag over the flowering head so bees are unable to introduce fresh pollen grains, but about 99 percent of the ovaries in the yellow disk will set seed without sperm.

Since a seed produced by virgin birth is an almost perfect replica of its mother, it grows happily under the same conditions. You could say that the embryo inside an agamospermic seed is merely a clone of its mother, but populations that consist exclusively of single parents can thrive by rubber-stamping the same tough and fertile form over and over again.

You can't always identify flowers that make seed by virgin birth just by looking at them, as some plants that reproduce this way continue to make large or colorful blossoms bursting with pollen. You have to place the pollen under a microscope to see that a majority of the grains are malformed, collapsed, or empty of live sperm. In South America, a number of wild trees and shrubs that regularly produce branches heavy with fruit belong to isolated wild strains or races of "virgin" guavas *(Eugenia),* mangoes *(Mangifera),* and prickly pears *(Opuntia).* Studies show that many native blackberries *(Rubus),* hawthorns *(Crataegus),* and shadbushes *(Amelanchier)* in suburban woodlands and city parks throughout North America and Europe reproduce by agamospermy.

This also means that under certain conditions, plants that produce only female flowers can establish thriving sororities in the absence of "husband" plants bearing male flowers. Parts of Australia's outback feature all-female woodlands of she-oaks *(Allocasuarina),* while an entire beach on a South Pacific island can be colonized by a solitary *Pandanus.* The lonely plant seeds the sand with her identical daughters, establishing female groves.

Virgin birth is scattered throughout the flowering plants but is

especially common in the grass, daisy, and rose families. Yes, a proportion of seeds inside some rose fruits are made without sex. This
means that a much admired shrub employs the same tactics as those
dandelions and crab grasses *(Panicum)* you've tried to eliminate from
your rose beds.

The very existence of a rose that produces seeds by virgin birth
may seem to contradict everything in earlier chapters about flower
sexuality and pollination. Consider, though, that different species of
wild rose thrive in different environments. Many species grow only
in stable habitats and are always cross-pollinated by insects. However, some European dog roses and briar roses also flourish as invasive weeds. European civilization has disrupted the natural succes-
sion of native vegetation for millennia, and this has encouraged the
spread of colonizing roses that exploit cemetery fences, hedgerows
bordering plowed land, and roadsides.

These opportunistic plants attract pollinators because they make
some edible pollen and sometimes advertise their flowers with color
and scent. At the end of the flowering season, though, ripening
ovaries tend to contain a mixture of seeds, some made by cross-pollination and others by virgin birth. The seeds of virgin birth thrive
best near their mother. Offspring that have a mother and a father
tolerate a wider range of conditions and can become established in
new sites when the juicy rose hips are eaten and seeds are spread by
birds.

Most farmers would be thrilled if all their fruit and seed crops re-
produced as dandelions do. If the ovary of every crop flower were
guaranteed to ripen and set seed by self-marriage or virgin birth,
we'd produce more food on only a fraction of the land now used for
agriculture. We'd be free of worries such as when to set out bee-
hives, which insecticides harm pollinators, and whether unseasonal
temperatures or wind velocity will spoil seed set.

After thousands of years of plant domestication and selection of cultivars that produce the highest yields, we can visit farms on which pollinating animals and air currents are of limited importance. Examples can be seen in the production of most commercial citrus fruits, bananas, peas *(Pisum)*, oats *(Avena)*, and strawberries *(Fragaria)*. Over the past five thousand years, though, we've had only partial success in convincing other crops to give up their pollinators. For example, while tomato breeds such as *Lycopersicon esculentum* will self-pollinate, people who grow them out of season know that fruit production is highest when bumblebees are released in greenhouses to shake pollen out of the flowers.

Meanwhile, most of the most popular varieties of melon *(Cucumis)*, apple *(Malus)*, cherry *(Prunus)*, avocado *(Persea)*, macadamia nut *(Macadamia)*, and blueberry and cranberry *(Vaccinium)* demand pollinator services in exchange for profitable yields. Developing new breeds that self-pollinate or make seeds without sex is a major responsibility of agricultural research stations all over the world, but in most cases it is a slow and expensive process. We still wait for the radical transformation of crops promised by biotechnology.

It's true that inbreeding by self-pollination or agamospermy is the perfect way for a population to endure, provided each child inherits both an unchanging environment and a genetic heritage free of lurking lethal genes. Unfortunately, the history of evolution shows that habitats and gene pools are rarely in concert. Environments change, and surviving species need generous gene banks if they are to adapt to those changes. No wonder dandelions continue to show off yellow petals and offer some edible pollen containing healthy sperm. I've watched flies and bees visit their golden heads in the United States, Australia, and Japan. Under humankind's heel, dandelions keep their evolutionary options open, with an estimated 1 percent of all the seeds in each head made by cross-pollination.

Charles Darwin was right when he noted that nature abhors continual self-fertilization. Nature hates continual self-fertilization because time loves to fiddle with the landscape. We've wiped out plenty of plant species through greed and pure ignorance, but I suspect we will always have dog roses. All these bushes have to do is alternate between hot sex and virgin birth and continue to infiltrate our graveyards.

CHAPTER 17

Each Morn a thousand Roses brings, you say:
Yes, but where leaves the Rose of Yesterday?
　　The Rubáiyát of Omar Khayyám, trans. Edward Fitzgerald

The First Flowers

When was the last time you visited a museum or private collection and saw fossil flowers displayed among slabs of trilobites and fish skeletons? Do fossils of flowers exist? A rose wilting in a gentleman's buttonhole seems a poor candidate for immortality in stone. The most distinctive parts of the rose are small and thin and fall apart within hours after the flower is plucked. Without thick shells, armored plates, or bones, floral organs are not expected to leave lasting impressions in silt destined for sedimentation.

For much of its brief history, the science of paleobotany studied the earliest stages of evolution in flowering plants without fossil flowers. The age and origin of flowers were reckoned by comparing and contrasting structures that were so tough in life that they left lasting impressions in petrified mud. These included woody stems, seeds with thick coats, nutlike fruits, fibrous veins of big leaves, and walls of pollen grains.

The fossil record shows clearly that trees started making seedlike offspring toward the end of the Devonian period (about 360 million years ago), but they were unable to enclose them inside flowers. These woody plants of the Devonian lacked both the internal plumbing and the leafy "blueprints" needed to enclose embryos inside floral rings. Instead, each seed wore a simple lobed and fleshy jacket and was attached to the base of a loose, weblike cup. In life, each pair of seeds looked like two pointy eggs inside an open, fanlike nest. Fossils of these webbed seed nests are called *Archaeosperma* ("ancient seed") and *Spermolithus* ("stone seed"). Scientists think that these organs belonged to the ancestors of the 140 surviving cycad species (Cycadophyta) and the maidenhair tree *(Ginkgo biloba)*.

To find fossils resembling flowering plants, paleobotanists must search later deposits that formed during the long reign of the dinosaurs. The evidence is scanty, but what has been recovered suggests that the ancestors of flowering plants lived between 225 and 140 million years ago. These fossils contain impressions of tissues and organs that appear to be intermediate between true flowering plants and extinct trees with exposed seeds. The best evidence was discovered in 1997 and comes from beds of Late Jurassic rock located east of Beijing, China. Nestled among impressions left by dinosaur bones, snail shells, and freshwater shrimp are the branches of *Archaefructus* ("ancient fruit"). This is the earliest fossil that shows seeds forming inside a ripe, bottle-shaped carpel. Although its stem structure suggests the architecture of an extinct seed fern tree, *Archaefructus* produced the same sort of simple but modern fruits found in many members of the houseleek (Crassulaceae), magnolia (Magnoliaceae), and buttercup (Ranunculaceae) families.

Every child who owns a triceratops or tyrannosaurus toy knows that the Cretaceous period (144–66 million years ago) was the last hurrah of the dinosaurs. However, it's time we also taught our children that the Cretaceous saw many advances in flowering plants. Fossil pollen found in drill cores of sedimentary rock (generously provided by mining companies) and veins etched on leaf fossils offer hard evidence that some modern plant families appeared more than 100 million years ago. More important, stones in Cretaceous deposits containing bits of fossil stamens, carpels, whole blossoms, and flowering stems were collected and described within the last twenty-five years of the twentieth century.

Yes, Virginia, there *are* fossil flowers, and when their remains are added to the body of information on Cretaceous plants, they tell a convincing tale of change. How did such important evidence escape our attention until the end of the twentieth century? Let's be frank. There will always be more people who scour fossil beds for dinosaurs than people who search them for flowers. Interesting plant fossils often stay boxed up in museums for decades, waiting for a sympathetic paleobotanist. More important, the earliest flowers made extraordinarily small organs that rarely exceeded an eighth of an inch in length. It's easy to overlook significant finds when you're ignorant of scale.

A chronological stroll through the garden of stone flowers will give you a feeling for major evolutionary changes in floral size, gender, and fusion. Currently, the oldest twig of a fossil flower is estimated to be more than 120 million years old. It comes from a piece of Cretaceous rock found in Koonwarra, Gippsland, a southeastern corner of Australia. To date, no flower fossil of the same age has been found in sediments from the Northern Hemisphere. Therefore, the sheer age and location of the Koonwarra specimen contribute to the theory that flowering plants first evolved somewhere in the Southern Hemisphere, spreading their seeds throughout the united supercontinent scientists call Gondwana. Many botanists believe that the flowering plants of the Southern Hemisphere migrated north as the southern plates supporting Gondwana split apart and continents such as India, South America, and Africa rafted north, colliding with North America and parts of Eurasia.

When the stem of the Koonwarra fossil was first smothered in silt, the flowers were smashed up against the leaves. Dug up in 1986, the specimen was first believed to be a fern frond wearing spore bodies.

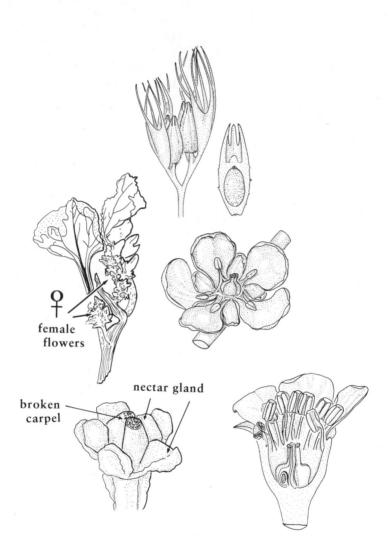

Reconstructions of fossil flowers. *Above:* Reproductive twig of *Archaeosperma* and its seedlike organ, at right (360 million years old). *Middle:* Left, Koonwarra fossil, with a cluster of tiny female flowers protected by reduced leaves (120 million years old). Right, complete dicot flower (100–80 million years old). *Below:* Left, Swedish flower with bumpy nectar glands (70–66 million years old). Right, cross section of *Paleorosa* (50–45 million years old). Illustrations by J. Myers.

That's what happens when you don't look closely. In 1990, two scientists from Yale University took a second look and realized that what looked like spore bodies are really the impressions of flower clusters the size of pinpricks.

All the flowers are females. Each tiny blossom consists entirely of a single, neckless carpel protected by a few reduced leaves. All of the flowers lack sepals, petals, and stamens. Also lacking are impressions of scars where these organs would have been attached, indicating that these early flowers were incomplete (fewer than four whorls of different organs) and imperfect (unisexual). Male flowers must have grown on separate stems or on separate plants, but fossil hunters have yet to turn up a male twig at the Gippsland site.

The Koonwarra fossil is so old that scientists can't match it with any living plant or modern family. Only an inch and a half long, the interconnecting stem and leaves blend anatomical features now found in the black pepper (Piperaceae) and yam (Dioscoreaceae) families. However, in its flower anatomy and flowering stalk, the fossil resembles the lizard's tail plants (Saururaceae) that survive in parts of Asia and North America.

In addition, fossil pollen taken from Israeli rocks about as old as the Koonwarra fossil convince most botanists that the Winter's bark family (Winteraceae) evolved around the same time. Since Israel was part of a southern plate 120 million years ago, this also argues that the earliest flowering plants rafted north with the aid of continental drift.

If we move ahead just 7 million years, we find that flowering plants have invaded a few regions in North America and Asia. These Cretaceous fossils are almost as small as the Koonwarra fossil. They still lack petals, but there have been some important additions to flower sex. Some of these specimens are the oldest known forms of perfect (bisexual) flowers with male and female organs found in the *same* blossom. The number of carpels in the flower has also increased

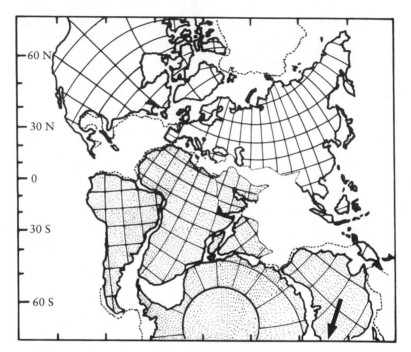

Relative positions of the continents 130–120 million years ago, modified
from *Biology of Plants*, sixth edition (W. H. Freeman and Company, 1999).
Land masses that once composed the supercontinent of Gondwana are
darkened. The general area where the Koonwarra plant once grew is
indicated with an arrow.

from one to eight. Some carpels are fused together, forming hard
nutlets.

The stamens consist only of pollen sacs inside bullet-shaped anthers that are attached directly to the floor of the flower without the
benefit of stalky filaments. Flowers from this part of the Cretaceous
period have been compared to temperate sycamores and plane trees
(Platanaceae). Some resemble the little blossoms in the makino tree
family (Chloranthaceae), woody plants that are distant relatives of
magnolias.

The next great phase of floral innovation occurred about 100 million years ago. Teeny-weeny unisexual flowers continued, but some massed together, forming modern catkins. The fossils of bisexual flowers wear both sepals and petals, providing convincing evidence that the first complete flowers had arrived. A few rocks from the Czech Republic, Nebraska, and New Jersey offer specimens with five or ten organs in each floral ring, just as in a modern dicot. The inferior ovary had also evolved by this time, with outer rings of organs fusing onto the carpels. Some of these extinct epigynous flowers shared floral features with some modern members of the eucalyptus family (Myrtaceae).

For me, the most exciting find of this time are fossils of the first really big blossoms that grew on land destined to become the Linnenberger family ranch in Kansas. *Archaeanthus* ("ancient flower") was a small tree that made each of its large flowers by organizing hundreds of stamens and carpels in a continuous spiral protected by five broad tepals. In life, an *Archaeanthus* flower must have looked like both the goblet-shaped blooms of tulip trees *(Liriodendron)* and the graceful flowers we prize on some Asian magnolias.

Flower fossils from Sweden and Spain indicate that between 90 and 75 million years ago, some ancestral bushes grew in regions subject to smoldering forest fires. Beautifully preserved as fossil charcoal, the flowers of these plants are among the smallest blossoms ever found, with a width of only about a sixteenth of an inch. However, an examination of the shape and fusion of their organs permits us to peek at plants that could have radiated into the rose (Rosaceae), foam flower (Saxifragaceae), walnut (Juglandaceae), oak (Fagaceae), and bayberry (Myricaceae) families. Some flowers of this time were probably the first to reward animals with nectar, as lobed or disklike glands appear between the rings of stamens and carpels.

By the end of the Cretaceous period (70–66 million years ago), floral forms were changing. Flowers broke away from shallow cup and dish forms, uniting their petals to form stiff, minute tubes and funnels. Furthermore, a few fossils showed irregular development of petals and sepals, indicating the beginning of bilateral symmetry. Sock puppet flowers appeared on plants that looked like members of the ginger (Zingiberaceae) and banana (Musaceae) families.

Combining all the fossils of flowers, fruits, leaves, wood, and pollen from the end of the Cretaceous period, scientists find that the "grandparents" of many modern groups were well established. I've already mentioned the early rise of sycamores, oaks, and walnuts, but by the end of the Cretaceous, the family of palm trees (Arecaceae) had appeared in the same warm forests. Waterlilies *(Nymphaea)* were established in lakes ringed by woodlands of bayberry, magnolia, and cinnamon *(Cinnamomum)*. Leaf remains indicate that the Cretaceous period witnessed the evolution of more than 150 species of fig tree *(Ficus)*. I will leave it to your imagination as to whether these plants made a funeral wreath for the dinosaurs or a bouquet and fruit basket to welcome the Age of Mammals.

Before I attempt to generalize the most recent 65 million years of flower diversity, let's backtrack and consider a most important question. Did pollinators shape any Cretaceous trends in the evolution of flowers?

Curiously, fossils of pollen-eating insects are far older than the record of fossil flowers. For example, both weevils (Curculionoidea) and short-horned flies (Brachycera, a group that includes the modern tangle-vein flies) were visiting seed plants by the end of the Late Jurassic period, 163–144 million years ago.

However, there are even earlier records of bugs that ate pollen. Fossils of extinct insects with lacelike wings known as hypeperlids have been taken from rocks in Russia dating back to the Early Permian period, about 280 million years ago. When these insects died, dung containing pollen was squeezed from their bodies, and it eventually turned to stone along with the impression of the insects' flattened corpses.

In 1995, the scientific community was astounded by a fossil found inside a petrified log from eastern Arizona. A nest resembling the home of a solitary bee was preserved inside the stone trunk, which had once belonged to a gymnosperm tree. No bees were found, but the design of the brood chambers is almost identical to that of chambers made by modern short-tongued sweat bees of the family Halictidae. The nest is thought to be 220 million years old.

How could flower-visiting bees, flies, and beetles exist before the evolution of flowers? Biologists offer two explanations. First, based on the remains of stems and leaves, it's probable that flowers date back much further than the Cretaceous period. Scientists are still looking for their fossils (remember, the Koonwarra fossil had to wait until 1986 to be uncovered). I agree with most paleobotanists that the cradle of flowering plants lies in a geologic period far older than the Cretaceous.

The second explanation, however, is far more important to the evolutionary history of flowers. Pollen-eating insects are probably older than the earliest flower because they were content to subsist on grains made by woody plants bearing naked seeds. The earliest weevils, bees, and flies ate the pollen offered by male cones and then drank the sugary secretions that leaked from the pollination drops of naked, unfertilized seeds.

Even today, insects pollinate some plants with naked seeds. Weevils in Mexico and Florida pollinate cycads. On the islands of New Guinea and Sarawak, snout moths (Pyralidae), geometer moths (Geometridae), and representatives of four fly families pollinate melindjo vines *(Gnetum)* while they drink the sweet green droplets secreted by the exposed ovules. In Israel, small flies visit the fleshy cones of *Ephedra* bushes. This is a good thing for us, since they are

pollinating one of humankind's earliest sources of the drug ephe-
drine, best known as an early, effective treatment for asthma and
stuffy noses. This means that the story of flower evolution in the
Cretaceous period is really the story of how flowering plants "stole"
animal pollinators from the dominant forests of gymnosperms.

Some gymnosperm trees of the Cretaceous were so huge that
when they were wounded, they leaked buckets of sticky resin, trapping many careless insects. We call this fossilized resin amber, and a
few gems contain wonderful records of pollen-eating insects. Amber
from Lebanon offers Cretaceous specimens of early pollen-eating
moths. A jewel from New Jersey estimated to be 80–70 million years
old offers bits of an extinct tropical stingless honeybee named *Trigona
prisca.*

In my opinion, changes in flower fossils of the Cretaceous period
show how interactions between flowers and their insect pollinators
grew more sophisticated and specialized. Let's begin by comparing
the little female flowers on the Koonwarra fossil with the living
bisexual flowers on lizard's tail plants *(Saururus cernuus)* growing in
Louisiana. Fieldwork on this wildflower was completed by Dr.
Leonard Thien at Tulane University and his co-workers at the University of Tennessee, Knoxville, and the U.S.D.A. Forest Service.
They found that the flowers of lizard's tail are so small and simple
that visiting beetles, bees, and wasps and passing breezes all contribute to the movement of pollen from plant to plant. Therefore, it's
probable that the simple, unspecialized flowers of the Koonwarra
vine also depended on a combination of air currents and small insects to set seed.

In contrast, fossils more recent than the Koonwarra specimen have
floral parts that are fused, indicating that the architecture of blossoms changed to limit the entry of animals with different foraging
habits. I'll bet that the evolution of true nectar glands was the ulti-
mate loyalty test. The only sugary reward the earliest flowers could

offer was the jellylike glue oozing from the stigma tips. This was similar to the nutrients dissolved in the watery drops secreted by the naked ovules on a gymnosperm cone.

However, once nectar glands appeared in the flower to offer consistent and generous drinks of sugars and amino acids, insects probably deserted gymnosperm cones for floral cups brimming with true nectar. Gymnosperms still lack the equipment to compete with the sweet rewards in a true flower. It's probable that flower nectar was an important addition to the diet of small climbing mammals, especially early marsupials and tree shrews, that scrambled among tree twigs in the Late Cretaceous.

The Age of Mammals (the Tertiary period, beginning less than 65 million years ago) has seen the rise of flowering plants at the expense of gymnosperms. While the Early Cretaceous period featured a few populations of flowering plants surviving under dense forests of cone-bearing trees, our Tertiary period has witnessed the cone-bearing plants' loss of most tropical and warm temperate zones to flowering trees and shrubs.

However, my scientific co-workers insist that I warn you never to attribute the modern triumph of flowering plants solely to their near monopoly of animal pollinators. Flowering plants also evolved a series of tricks that give them a greater edge when environments are struck by natural disaster over long periods of time. Compared with gymnosperms, flowering plants are usually much more flexible when confronted with hostile conditions.

Flowering plants, for example, have many more growth forms than do gymnosperms, allowing them to flourish in such unusual niches as land without true soil, deep shade, and both freshwater and salt water. Flowering plants also contain cells that move water from roots to stems more quickly and efficiently than do the cells of cone-bearing trees or shrubs. Also recall that fertilization and maturation of seeds proceed much faster inside a flower than on a cone. Flowering plants recolonized land more rapidly than gymnosperms during the Tertiary period after the retreat of glaciers and drought conditions.

Since these adaptations made survival easier, they probably permitted a second wave of flower experiments during our Age of Mammals. Fossils of this period show such exaggerated forms as the flag and keel of the earliest pea blossoms. By 45 million years ago, members of the philodendron family had appeared, with hooded flowering branches capable of trapping gullible flies. Oh, yes, this was also a special time for roses.

A rocky outcrop near Princeton, British Columbia, yielded the fossil remains of *Paleorosa similkameenensis,* also estimated to be 50–45 million years old. This great-grandma of dog roses and American beauties bore a minuscule flower that contained only nineteen stamens and five carpels. A cross section of the blossom revealed the modern arrangement of five sepals (although all five brothers lacked beards) and the fusion of sepals to petals to stamens, forming the perigynous flowers we admire on wild bushes.

I must emphasize that a great number of novel changes have appeared in blossoms during the Age of Mammals. In particular, fossil flowers show an increase in the length of tubes and spurs that contain nectar, indicating that animal mouths have also expanded and elongated. Remember, since this age has encouraged the diversification of warm-blooded animals, almost all bird and bat pollination must date from its onset.

New insects have appeared. In contrast with those ancient pollen-nibbling moths of the Cretaceous period, the oldest fossil butterfly is probably less than 40 million years old. This could help explain the inadequate behavior of certain butterflies as pollen carriers. We all know that the course of young love, though intense, is often marred by clumsiness and acts of selfishness.

In 1879, Charles Darwin wrote a letter to J. D. Hooker, director of the Royal Botanic Gardens, Kew, London, that has since become famous. Frustrated by the absence of solid evidence regarding the earliest history of blossoms, Darwin called the origin of flowering plants "an abominable mystery." He had a right to feel miffed, as the study of fossil plants was in its infancy. We should be grateful to Darwin for keeping interest in the subject alive, largely through his experiments on form and function in living flowers.

As you can see, there are still plenty of unanswered questions concerning both the first flowers and our present wealth of living species. Scientists would love to find fossils dating back further than the Cretaceous period to see when leaves first closed around unfertilized seeds to make bottle-shaped ovaries. Are living flowers with the most primitive structures always pollinated by air currents or small, primitive animals? Since the first bisexual flowers were so tiny, did they cross-pollinate or self-pollinate? Is it possible to chart the evolution of scent glands, floral pigments, and nectar guides? Questions such as these are exciting mysteries we can solve, given time, fresh enthusiasm, and the fostering of new techniques.

Meanwhile, what do you say to a person who insists that evolution is an unexciting affair because the dinosaurs and large land mammals such as mammoths and ground sloths are extinct? Tell this jaded pessimist that we are enjoying the age of the biggest, broadest, longest, and most complex wildflowers. Who would ever trade our roses for a single tyrannosaurus?

adnation. Fusion of different organs in the same flower, as when carpels and stamens unite to form a column.

agamospermy. Formation of embryos in seeds without sexual union between sperm and egg cells.

androecium. The ring or rings of stamens in a flower.

angiosperms. Plants that make seeds inside flowers.

anther. The fertile tip of a stamen, made of lobed sacs that manufacture pollen.

calyx. The ring or rings of sepals in a flower, usually forming the young, protective bud case.

carpels. Female ovule-containing organs that make up the central ring or rings known as the gynoecium.

coalescence. Fusion of organs in the same ring, as when petals form a funnel or bell. Also known as connation.

column. A structure formed when one or more stamens are fused to a carpel or pistil in the same flower (most common in the orchid, milkweed, and trigger plant families).

complete flower. A flower containing four different organs (sepals, petals, stamens, and carpels).

corolla. The ring or rings of petals in a flower.

dioecious. Having either male flowers or female flowers on each plant in the same population.

embryo sac. A variable arrangement of cells inside an unfertilized seed that accepts incoming sperm. Every sac must contain a minimum of one egg cell and two polar cells.

epigynous. Having an inferior (buried) ovary because the ovary has fused to all outer rings of organs.

exine. The outer, heavily sculpted wall of a pollen grain, made of a natural plastic called sporopollenin.

filament. The narrow, sterile stalk of a stamen that supports the anther.

flower. A much reduced branch consisting of one to several rings, spirals, or both rings and spirals of modified leaves in which unfertilized seeds are locked inside bottle-shaped ovaries.

gymnosperms. Plants that make seeds but lack flowers. Gymnosperms bear naked seeds that are exposed to the air before and after they are fertilized by pollen sperm.

gynoecium. The central ring or rings of carpels in a flower.

hypogynous. Having a superior ovary (the carpels are the highest organs in the flower).

imperfect flower. A unisexual flower containing either male organs (stamens) or female organs (carpels).

incomplete flower. A flower containing fewer than four different kinds of organs.

intine. The inner wall of a pollen grain, made of cellulose and its derivatives.

monoecious. Having two different kinds of imperfect flowers (male and female) on each plant in the same population.

nectar. A watery secretion enriched with sugars and other nutrients.

nectar guide. Sharply contrasting colors on flower skin indicating the location of nectar on the flower.

nectary. A gland that secretes nectar.

osmophores. Much enlarged portions of flower skin that produce fragrance.

ovary. The chambered base of a carpel containing one or more unfertilized seeds.

ovule. An unfertilized seed.

perfect flower. A bisexual flower containing both stamens and carpels.

perigynous. Having a superior ovary that is encircled by sepals, petals, and stamens fused together to form a united sleeve or tube. In a perigynous flower, the carpels are never buried under the compound floral sleeve.

petals. Flat, sterile organs, often colored and scented, that make up a flower's corolla.

pistil. A structure formed when all the carpels in a flower fuse together, resembling one giant carpel.

pollen. Living grains made inside anthers. Each pollen grain contains a tube cell connected to one or two sperm cells. These cells are encircled by a tough, double-layered wall.

pollen coat. A layer of fat globules and protein film that clings to the surface of most pollen grains. Often contains pigments and scent molecules that give the grains distinctive colors and scents.

pollinium. A mass of individual pollen grains united to form a lump or sphere visible to the naked eye.

polygamous. Bearing both unisexual and bisexual flowers at the same time.

protandry. Condition in which all stamens in a bisexual flower release pollen and wither before the carpels are mature and receptive.

protogyny. Condition in which all carpels in a bisexual flower receive pollen and wither before the stamens release pollen.

self-incompatibility. Biochemical ability of a carpel to recognize and reject pollen made by the same plant or by plants sharing the same genes.

sepals. Flat, sterile, often leaflike organs that make up the calyx in a flower.

sporopollenin. A natural plastic that makes up the outer wall of a pollen grain. Some biochemists suspect that sporopollenin is made of the same molecules that form vitamin A.

stamens. Male pollen-making organs in a flower that form the ring or rings known as the androecium.

stigma. A carpel's receptive glandular tip that receives and processes incoming pollen.

style. The neck of a carpel, connecting the stigma to the ovary. Pollen tubes grow through the style to reach the ovary.

tapetum. A special layer of cells inside an anther that nourish the pollen grains, construct the grains' outer walls, and often decorate the outer walls with a greasy pollen coat.

tepals. Flattened, sterile structures that form a ring or spiral around the flower, showing characteristics intermediate between those of true petals and true sepals.

Asterisks (*) denote scientific or specialty literature unavailable in most public libraries in North America. Readers are encouraged to use interlibrary loan services or visit libraries maintained by botanical gardens, arboreta, and universities with departments of biology, zoology, and botany.

INTRODUCTION: BEYOND THE FLORIST'S SHOP

Goody, J. *The Culture of Flowers.* Cambridge, England: Cambridge University Press, 1993. An entertaining study of the influence of domesticated flowers on African, European, and Asian societies, describing their uses in art, literature, politics, and religion.

Hollingsworth, B. *Flower Chronicles.* New Brunswick, N.J.: Rutgers University Press, 1958. Hollingsworth concentrates on folklore and how flowers have been used as perfumes, medicines, and food, providing an excellent contrast to Goody's book.

Le Rougetel, H. *A Heritage of Roses.* Owings Mills, Md.: Stemmer House, 1988. Garden roses are pawns of fashion, with bloodlines from plants once native to continental Europe, India, and China.

*Moyal, A. *A Bright and Savage Land.* Ringwood, Victoria, Australia: Penguin Books, 1986. A unique history of Australia concentrating on the lives and accomplishments of scientists and naturalists who came to study its plants and animals.

CHAPTER 1: BROTHERHOODS AND SISTERS' ROOMS

*Eames, A. J. *Morphology of the Angiosperms.* New York: McGraw-Hill, 1961. A book that convinced me to study the evolution of "primitive" and "advanced" flowers. Eames's illustrations of the organs of rare flowers are still used in modern treatments of floral anatomy and morphology.

*Endress, P. K. *Diversity and Evolutionary Biology of Tropical Flowers.* New York: Cambridge University Press, 1994. Endress was one of the first botanists to realize that the scanning electron microscope could be a superior tool in understanding flower development. This book includes some of his best shots, showing how floral organs grow, fold, and unite inside buds.

★Raven, P. H., R. F. Evert, and S. E. Eichhorn. *Biology of Plants.* 6th ed. New York: Freeman, 1999. This influential textbook provides a standard introduction to the study of plant life. Chapters 21 and 22 offer a modern introduction to the anatomy and evolution of flower organs.

CHAPTER 2: LIMITS TO PERFECTION

Meyerowitz, E. M. The genetics of flower development. *Scientific American* (November 1994): 56–65. A scientist offers a popular account of how his early experiments on thale cress altered the order of floral rings.

★Reynolds, J., and J. Tampion. *Double Flowers: A Scientific Study.* New York: Scientific and Academic Editions, 1983. A practical approach to understanding flower mutations for both commercial growers and amateur gardeners. Includes many case studies and an appendix listing species known to double.

Schiebinger, L. The loves of the plants. *Scientific American* (February 1996): 110–115. The author blames botanical terminology on male chauvinism.

★Willson, M. F. *Plant Reproductive Ecology.* New York: Wiley, 1983. How much can a plant afford to "spend" on reproduction? Differences between common and rare forms of sex expression in plants are explained with care.

CHAPTER 3: THE PIG IN THE PIZZA

★Porter, C. L. *Taxonomy of Flowering Plants.* San Francisco: Freeman, 1967. Out of print but well worth the search because it uses simple schematic diagrams to explain the fusion of flower parts.

★Weberling, F. *Morphology of Flowers and Inflorescences.* Cambridge, England: Cambridge University Press, 1989. Weberling concentrates on both the architecture of flowers and the architecture of branches that support the flowers. He's especially interested in how the fusion of flower organs can change flower symmetry.

CHAPTER 4: WHEN TO BLOOM

★Bernier, G., J. M. Kinet, and R. M. Sachs. *The Physiology of Flowering.* Vols

1 and 2. Boca Raton, Fla.: CRC Press, 1981. Photomicrographs show how leafy shoots stretch and are transformed into flowering shoots. The authors compared theories concerning the chemical basis of flowering and were among the first to debunk the anthesin story.

*Salisbury, F. B. *The Biology of Flowering.* Garden City, N.Y.: Natural History Press, 1971. Although many advances have been made since publication of this book, Salisbury still offers the most readable introduction to the subject, emphasizing the role of environmental cues.

Chapter 5: When to Die

Bauer, H., and S. Carlquist. *Japanese Festivals.* Tokyo: Tuttle, 1974. In addition to providing information about where to go and what to see, this book conveys the authors' appreciation of rituals using cereal grains, flowers, and fruit.

*De Barios, V. B. *A Guide to Tequila, Mezcal, and Pulque.* Mexico City: Minutiae Mexicana, 1971. This booklet provides a history of maguey drinks and how the plants have been exploited. It corrects misconceptions about the potency of these beverages and how they are manufactured.

*Primack, R. B. Longevity of individual flowers. In *Annual Review of Ecology and Systematics,* ed. R. F. Johnston, P. W. Frank, and C. D. Michener, 15–38. Palo Alto, Calif.: Annual Reviews, 1985. Here are the results of an exhaustive study using the plants in the greenhouses of Duke University and data based on field studies in South America and New Zealand.

Chapter 6: Of Pollen, Perpetrators, Politics, and Piety

*Hodges, D. *The Pollen Loads of the Honey Bee.* Facsimile ed. London: Bee Research Association and Precision Press, 1974. Hodges wrote for a British audience back in the 1950s, offering readers a mixture of charming facts and color-coded drawings of the pollen of dozens of flower species.

*Iwanami, Y., T. Sasakuma, and Y. Yamada. *Pollen: Illustrations and Scanning Electronmicrographs.* Berlin: Springer-Verlag, 1988. An editor should have caught the spelling and grammatical errors in this book, but the photographs offer a fine introduction to pollen shapes and wall patterns.

★Nilsson, S., and J. Praglowski, eds. *Erdtman's Handbook of Palynology.* 2nd ed. Copenhagen: Munksgaard, 1992. This is the updated grandparent of all pollen texts. The Danish point of view is welcome, considering the many contributions these scientists have made over the past century.

CHAPTER 7: FRUITFUL UNIONS

★Heslop-Harrison, Y., and K. R. Shivanna. The receptive surface of the angiosperm stigma. *Annals of Botany* 41 (1977): 1233–1258. These two scientists were among the first to use the scanning electron microscope to compare wet and dry stigmas of hundreds of species.

★Niklas, K. J. *The Evolutionary Biology of Plants.* Chicago: University of Chicago Press, 1997. This is one of the few recent texts to stress the continuity between living and long extinct plants. Chapter 4 compares the fertilization systems of cones and flowers.

CHAPTER 8: THE PRIMARY ATTRACTANTS

★Arctander, S. *Perfume and Flavor Material of Natural Origins.* Published by the author, Elizabeth, N.J., 1960. Molecular skeletons are explained, and the reader is reminded that a chemical may have very different smells at different concentrations. Many laboratories studying natural compounds still treat this book as an important compendium.

★Dafni, A., R. Menzel, and M. Giurfa, eds. *Insect Vision and Flower Recognition.* Special issue, *Israel Journal of Plant Sciences* (Hebrew University of Jerusalem) (March 1997). Twenty-two scientists contributed to this volume. Uniting the work of entomologists and botanists, it is the most modern treatment of the subject available.

★Lake, M. *Scents and Sensuality: The Essence of Excitement.* London: Futura Publications, 1989. A retired Australian physician examines interrelationships between the chemistry and culture of scent, emphasizing commercial perfumes, wines, and certain foods. The bibliography introduces readers to additional popular sources on fragrance and flavor.

Meeuse, B. J. D. *The Story of Pollination.* New York: Ronald Press, 1961. Two chapters of this book, which was written for a general audience, introduce the manufacture and presentation of flower colors. Meeuse is at his best when explaining the significance of behavioral experiments performed to investigate insect vision early in the twentieth century.

★Vogel, S. *The Role of Scent Glands in Pollination.* New Delhi: Model Press, 1990. This is the English translation of a famous work first published in German in 1963. The author emphasizes flowers in the orchid, milkweed, and philodendron families that have the biggest, most complex glands.

CHAPTER 9: REWARDS

Bernhardt, P. *Natural Affairs: A Botanist Looks at the Attachments between Plants and People.* New York: Villard, 1993. Chapter 7 of this book considers nectar research over four centuries, and chapter 10 examines male bees that collect orchid scents.

★Fahn, A. *Secretory Tissues in Plants.* New York: Academic Press, 1979. Fahn's research dominated the study of plant glands for more than thirty years. If you finish the chapter on nectaries, go on to read about glands that secrete salt, poisons, glue, latex, and digestive enzymes.

Seymour, R. S., and P. S. Schultze-Motel. Thermoregulating lotus flowers. *Nature* 383 (1996): 305. Hard proof that the flowers we love the best are often the ones we understand the least. Includes a graph showing how flower temperature fluctuates over a period of several days.

★Vinson, B. V., G. W. Frankie, and H. J. Williams. Chemical ecology of bees of the genus *Centris* (Hymenoptera: Apidae). *Florida Entomologist* 79 (1996): 109–129. An informative review that explains why and how these bees collect flower oils.

CHAPTER 10: UNLOVED BUT EFFICIENT

★Goldblatt, P., J. C. Manning, and P. Bernhardt. Pollination biology of

Lapeirousia subgenus *Lapeirousia* (Iridaceae) in southern Africa: Floral divergence and adaptation for long-tongued fly pollination. *Annals of the Missouri Botanical Garden* 82 (1995): 517–534. Describes the relationship between painted petals *(Lapeirousia)* and several fly species and explains why these insects are so important to other wildflowers.

★Hawkeswood, T. *Beetles of Australia.* North Ryde, New South Wales, Australia: Angus and Robertson, 1987. Introduces unfamiliar insects family by family, describing their foraging habits and preferred flowers. Includes color photographs of flower beetles in action.

Proctor, M., P. Yeo, and A. Lack. *The Natural History of Pollination.* Portland, Ore.: Timber Press, 1996. This book was written with a British audience in mind. The section on fly pollination shows great depth and understanding.

Young, A. M. *The Chocolate Tree.* Washington, D.C.: Smithsonian Institution Press, 1994. One chapter of this book is devoted exclusively to interactions between cocoa flowers and flies.

CHAPTER 11: PSYCHOANALYSIS AND SERENADES

★Arianoutsou, M., and R. H. Groves, eds. *Plant-Animal Interactions in Mediterranean-Type Ecosystems.* Dordrecht, Netherlands: Kluwer, 1994. Chapter 13 is written by Drs. S. Johnson and W. J. Bond, who explain the unique association between mountain beauty butterflies and South African wildflowers.

Bernhardt, P. *Wily Violets and Underground Orchids.* New York: Morrow, 1989. Chapter 8 treats moth pollination of *Zygogynum* trees, and chapter 16 discusses Charles Darwin's studies of a night-blooming orchid from Madagascar and how his work was finally vindicated a century after his death.

Buchmann, S. L., and G. P. Nabhan. *The Forgotten Pollinators.* Washington, D.C.: Island Press, 1996. The authors contend that wildflower protection must include preservation of the special relationships between plants and animals. Hawkmoth pollination may be endangered around the world.

★Grant, V., and K. A. Grant. *Flower Pollination in the Phlox Family.* New York: Columbia University Press, 1985. This classic work enables readers to compare the pollination of phlox by butterflies and the pollination of gilias by hawkmoths.

Milius, S. How bright is a butterfly? *Science News* 153 (1998): 233–235. Experiments by Martha Weiss and others suggest that some butterflies may learn how to exploit nectar in unfamiliar flowers more rapidly than do bumblebees and honeybees.

Chapter 12: The Faithful and Unfaithful Bee

*McNaughton, I. H., and J. L. Harper. The comparative biology of closely related species living in the same area. I. External breeding-barriers between *Papaver* species. *New Phytologist* 59 (1959): 15–26. Field observations show that bees can discriminate between different poppy species growing in the same meadow. Graphs in this article illustrate how individual insects "changed their minds" while foraging for pollen.

*O'Toole, C., and A. Raw. *Bees of the World*. London: Blandford Press, 1991. This publication can be hard to find outside England, but it's the best popular introduction to bee diversity, their life cycles, and bees' relationships with flowers.

*Roubik, D. W. *Ecology and Natural History of Tropical Bees*. New York: Cambridge University Press, 1989. Chapter 2 of this book concentrates on insects that forage for resins, pollen, nectar, oil, and fragrance on spurges, morning glories, and jungle trees.

Chapter 13: The Squawking Tree

*Ford, H. A., and D. C. Paton, eds. *The Dynamic Partnership: Birds and Plants in Southern Australia*. South Australia: Government Printer, 1986. Fourteen authors discuss the roles of native birds in the evolution of Australian vegetation. Half of the chapters address bird pollination.

*Grant, K. A., and V. Grant. *Hummingbirds and Their Flowers*. New York: Columbia University Press, 1968. A work of natural history that remains sound more than three decades after publication. It describes the ecology of hummingbirds and the wildflowers of the great Southwest and West Coast of the United States.

*Nowak, R. M. *Walker's Bats of the World*. Baltimore, Md.: Johns Hopkins

University Press, 1994. Descriptions and illustrations in this book make it easy for amateurs to understand differences between leaf-nosed bats and flying foxes. Many of the flower bats were photographed with their bristle tongues extended.

CHAPTER 14: *F* IS FOR FAKE (AND FLOWER)
Dressler, R. L. *The Orchids: Natural History and Classification*. Cambridge, Mass.: Harvard University Press, 1981. Chapter 4 provides the best review of pollination by deceit in the orchid family. The reader is warned, though, that Professor Dressler has since changed his mind about classification and evolutionary relationships within this family.

CHAPTER 15: INTO THIN AIR
Knox, R. B. *Pollen and Allergy: Studies in Biology*. Vol. 107. London: Edward Arnold, 1979. It's a pleasure to offer one of my former professor's shorter, popular works written for advanced high school students.
★Niklas, K. J. *Plant Biomechanics: An Engineering Approach to Plant Form and Function*. Chicago: University of Chicago Press, 1992. Chapter 9 of this book compares plants that release pollen, seeds, and fruits into the air.

CHAPTER 16: SELF-MADE MARRIAGES AND VIRGIN BIRTHS
★Richards, A. J. *Plant Breeding Systems*. London: Allen and Unwin, 1986. Recommended as one of the best reviews of the genetics of plant reproduction. Chapters 9 and 11 discuss self-pollination and agamospermy, respectively.
★Richards, A. J., J. Kirschner, J. Stepanek, and K. Marhold, eds. *Apomixis and Taxonomy: Special Features in Biosystematics and Biodiversity*. Vol. 1. Uppsala, Sweden: Opulus Press, 1995. Contributions by twenty-five authors explore seed production without sex in the daisy, rose, and St. John's wort families. Photomicrographs show healthy embryos developing without pollen and how virgin birth alters chromosome numbers.
★Schemske, D. W., M. F. Willson, M. N. Melampy, L. J. Miller, L. Verner, R. M. Schemske, and L. B. Best. Flowering ecology of some spring

woodland herbs. *Ecology* 59 (1978): 351–366. This pioneering paper was among the first to consider the role of self-pollination as a fail-safe mechanism ensuring adequate seed set under stressful conditions. Five common American species of Illinois woodlots are compared.

CHAPTER 17: THE FIRST FLOWERS

*Friis, E. M., W. G. Chaloner, and P. R. Crane, eds. *The Origins of Angiosperms and Their Biological Consequences.* Cambridge, England: Cambridge University Press, 1987. Ten multiauthored chapters chart the origin and spread of flowering plants. Two of these chapters address interpretations of fossil flowers and flower-visiting insects, and three chapters speculate on interactions between plants, dinosaurs, and early mammals.

Grimaldi, D. *Amber: Window to the Past.* New York: Abrams and American Museum of Natural History, 1996. Here is proof that a science book can be informative *and* beautiful. This volume provides a superb introduction to the origins and contents of a popular but increasingly expensive gemstone.

Labandeira, C. How old is the flower and the fly? *Science* 280 (1998): 57–59. The author offers a convincing argument that flowers date back further than the Cretaceous period, based on analyses of the oldest fossils of pollen-eating insects and their petrified dung.

*Stewart, W. N. *Paleobotany and the Evolution of Plants.* Cambridge, England: Cambridge University Press, 1983. This reference work has become dated as a result of important discoveries since its publication, but it is one of the few books to address the origins of plantlike fossils, from the earliest algae to flowering plants such as *Paleorosa*.

Peter Bernhardt was born in Brooklyn, New York, but received his doctoral degree in botany from the University of Melbourne, Australia. He is a professor of biology at Saint Louis University and a research associate of both the Missouri Botanical Garden of St. Louis, Missouri, and the Royal Botanic Gardens of Sydney, Australia. His current research includes the iris family in southern Africa, fruit set in Israeli mandrakes, interactions between Australian bees and bushes, and pollination of wildflowers native to the tallgrass prairies of Kansas. He is the author or coauthor of more than sixty technical articles appearing in such journals as *Annals of the Missouri Botanical Garden, Plant Systematics and Evolution,* and the *American Journal of Botany.* His descriptions of 101 orchid species appear in volume 4 of *Flora of New South Wales.* Dr. Bernhardt has also written two popular books of essays about plant life, *Wily Violets and Underground Orchids* (Morrow, 1989; Vintage, 1990) and *Natural Affairs* (Villard, 1993). Shorter pieces have appeared in *Bats,* the *New York Times,* and the *Nutcote News,* and his column "The Botanical Detective" ran from 1990 to 1996 in the *Sydney Review.* Dr. Bernhardt and his wife, Linda, enjoy shade gardening in Missouri.